TAU BADA

June 6, 2021

Dear Nick,

Our paths may cross.
Nevertheless, journey
verité.

John Lundin

TAU BADA

THE QUEST AND MEMOIR
OF A VULNERABLE MAN

JOHN E. QUINLAN

MCP BOOKS | *MAITLAND*

CONTENTS

Introduction xi

Chapter 1: The Picnic 1

Chapter 2: First Steps 9

Chapter 3: Refuge 17

Chapter 4: Deliberate Practice 27

Chapter 5: Circling Back 33

Chapter 6: New Times, New Thinkings 41

Chapter 7: Metal-Metal-Metal 51

Chapter 8: The Fiasco 59

Chapter 9: Abeyance 69

Chapter 10: Stafford 81

Chapter 11: Misnomers 91

Chapter 12: The Altercation 99

Chapter 13: On the Road 105

Chapter 14: Chagrin 115

Chapter 15: Pigs 123

Chapter 16: Paradoxes 131

Chapter 17: The Christmas Present 139

Chapter 18: Kiara 147

Chapter 19: Lift the Curse 161

Chapter 20: Kweno Mountain 173

Chapter 21: A Dark Wood 181

Chapter 22: Meanderings 185

Chapter 23: Ahuvo 191

Chapter 24: Haus Win Discourse 197

Chapter 25: Awareness Examen 203

Chapter 26: Adjournments and Abjections 209

Chapter 27: Never Say Never 217

Chapter 28: Welcome Back 229

Chapter 29: OK Corrals Extraordinaire 237

Chapter 30: The Girua River 247

Chapter 31: Tattered Tunnels 257

Chapter 32: Bushwhacked 267

Chapter 33: Diminishment 275

Chapter 34: Spiraling 283

Chapter 35: Reaching Home 291

Epilogue: Minturn Crows 305

Acknowledgments 321

FOREWORD

As an editor at the *Detroit Free Press*, I watched with keen interest as my colleague Mitch Albom had his first book published, *Tuesdays with Morrie*. Mitch's book didn't fit neatly into any of the standard categories. It wasn't strictly a memoir, or a biography, or simply a first-person encounter story, or a philosophical/spiritual treatise. But it rang true, as an eventually vast readership discovered.

John Quinlan's first book is similar in its lack of easy categorization—and in its aim at the human core. Mitch wrote of his revelations as a relatively young man. John's came later in life. A brief description of *Tau Bada* would be:

> After an initially successful CEO career, an un-successful marriage, and a deep sense of uneasiness, a roaming John Quinlan encounters the woman who would become his new wife. In a romantic and business partnership with her, John sets out to develop a sustainable livelihood for several thousand rural farmers in a land where many had never seen a tall white American. The Papua New Guinea home of John and Fiona, secluded in a mountain rainforest, becomes a center of both profound joy and constant anxiety. Death is more than a possibility.

As it happens, I had the opportunity to be John's editor for this book. I became immersed in how John gained and wrestled with deep insights into sharply differing human cultures and into himself as he tried to live out a vision of change. What he found applies to all of our lives.

—Alex Cruden

Dear Reader,

Tau Bada is available both in print and as an e-book. The e-book includes more than a dozen un-staged videos of events as they occurred in Colorado and Papua New Guinea. It is available at www.taubada.com.

On that website you can also learn more about John and Fiona Quinlan and what's happening with them these days.

The author in Copper Harbor, Upper Peninsula, Michigan: "Why is it so difficult, then, to be as genuine and trusting of ourselves . . . as with these volcanic cobblestones beneath our feet?"

INTRODUCTION

"When you're on a journey, and the end keeps getting further and further away, then you realize that the real end is the journey."

—Karlfried Graf Dürckheim

I sought refuge from public and personal humiliation following the demise of my publicly traded company in 1985. One of the northernmost points of the United States became my shade tree. Copper Harbor, nestled in the Keweenaw Peninsula of Michigan, afforded seclusion and safety from the societal circumspection of Grosse Pointe affluence and the harsh judgmentalism of the Detroit business and media community.

Jim Rooks, who with his wife Laurel was the proprietor of the Laughing Loon gift shop and naturalist guide company, became my friend. He distinguished himself by fighting logging interests. One early morning on a geological hike/ lecture, he commented that I was the spitting image of his recently deceased brother, John. Our conversation deepened as the morning mist and light rain were lifting off Lake Superior's ancient beach ridges. The sunlight infused layers of red stone with mottled streaks of whites, browns, and pinks. Lichens, mosses, and liverworts glistened. Such a high-energy environment invigorated me. Jim, in his gentle yet effusive way, asked me what was I really doing up here.

Sheepishly I responded and shared my most recent life excursions, including the body blows to my entrepreneurial career. Within an hour, he had encouraged me to view my experiences a little differently, swaying me to look at these occurrences as inner incursions, including my attempt to pen the happenings of my life into journal entries, a habit I'd begun at age ten. He questioned if it was possible to truly write a nonfiction memoir. Jim helped me to realize, without presumption, that God did not give us the gift for such exhaustive self-understanding. God did give us, though, the genius to objectively view the shale and sandstone ledges jutting out into Lake Superior and accept them completely for what they are. Why is it so difficult, then, to be as genuine and trusting of ourselves and authentic with others as with these volcanic cobblestones beneath our feet?

The *Tau Bada* tale I am about to share is not simply an achievement or an outcome, or a recipe for the attainment of goals and self-improvement, or even a romantic happy ending. It is about the quiet transitions to real courage and the soul milieu that connects and binds us as mutual occupants of a shared planet.

Mine was not a typical hero's journey. It was more of an attitude and openness to life. I did not begin with a clear end goal, a mission, or an awareness of just what I hoped to gain or what I was risking the loss of. Things developed, and only in their development did matters become clearer, deeper, riskier, and enormously surprising. I ended up in an all-consuming and near-fatal struggle at the other end of the world—and learned that the struggle was, all the while, within myself.

So in this high and low adventure that spans a social-pinnacle suburb, the American West, and Australia/Papua New Guinea—this nonfiction memoir as true as I can make it—I expose a path toward rock-solid personal authenticity and become knowingly vulnerable. Will you join me?

Before I understood it fully, I was moving along this path, in the form of solo long-distance motorcycling. In the early 1990s I would bike north through Michigan to the Mackinac

Bridge, make a left turn onto Highway 2, and head west toward the Pacific Ocean.

Rain or shine, the *terza rima,* or iambic three-liners, of biking would slowly transcend my thoughts. The daily monotony of such a routine percolated fears harbored in the secret places of my own reservoir. Lulled into an inner dialogue and gaining self-confidence, I felt myself moving into the unknown: the road before me and within me.

I would view the sapphire-blue Straits of Mackinac, the verdant green pastures of Wisconsin, the endless prairies of Minnesota and North Dakota, the ebony-dark forests of South Dakota's Black Hills, the jagged mountain peaks of Alberta, the high desert of New Mexico, or a solitary oak tree in a recently plowed field. Or I might have essential exchanges with helpful gas station attendants, lonely bartenders, itinerant preachers, Native Americans secluded on reservations, plain-speaking farmers, or irreverent cowboys.

This human collage, set against the backdrop of such profound natural beauty, challenged my cultural and social attention-deficit disorder. It permitted me to move into self-reflection and create meaning. As a result, I would feel self-connected, grounded, and more congruent with my inward man and a little more at one with my outward man. For a slow learner, such a change is largely imperceptible.

Filters, including my own blind spots, beliefs, and stereotypes, defined me as I passed one highway marker after another. But the road beckoned this biker to not only name his condition but to inquire, "What condition is your condition in?" So now, what am I going to do with this experience? The easy accessibility to cheap taverns on an open highway with small towns was a welcome respite from these soul-searching rigors.

Yet I continued to gain self-affirmation in these mini-leaps of faith. My courage inched upward to new levels of self-understanding. It was the beginning of a foundation for the journey to places I never would have imagined.

In *The Soul's Code,* James Hillman purports that such a discovery process "requires a patience to run against ego behavior that is non-compliant, disorganized and so easily distracted."

Jumping on numerous wrong horses along my path, it took a long time to realize that I was in a protracted existential crisis. Now, as I write for you, the imaging and reimaging process feels like learning to walk comfortably in the dark without losing my balance, tripping over things, or bumping into furniture.

On a motorcycle, the Canadian crosswinds can slice you in half. A chilling and unforgiving weather front on the Great Plains can afflict you for days. On this particular trip, I was in for a significantly longer ride. I was tempted to head south and bike out of the misery. But in deciding to stay on this unforgiving course, I felt buoyed. Second winds are worth the effort.

Arriving at a tavern in Babb, Montana, near the east entrance of Glacier National Park, I was looking forward to the comfort of a warm cabin. But first, refreshment. The Babb bar was once rumored to be the toughest saloon in America. I was sipping a shot of Jack Daniel's whiskey and a long-neck Budweiser when the mahogany-slatted saloon doors opened and a cowboy rode inside on his horse, stepping up to the bar. The cowboy, leaning over his horse, asked the bartender for a six-pack. I turned around, looked up, and said, "I would like to buy you and your horse a drink." He said, "No thank you." I remarked that we don't see this kind of thing happen in Detroit,

Michigan. "I bet you don't," he responded as he turned and rode out.

A patron informed me that I had just met the "Zen cowboy." My newfound host filled my ear all night long, urging me to spend the evening at this establishment, as this was where the "dry herd" congregated—the widowed, divorced, and older women. The establishment down the road was where the "wet herd" gathered—the younger, single women. I grimaced at the sexism.

This imbiber of whiskey and spouter of advice had a few strands of white hair drooping over a wedged forehead. He had a round, unshaven face and a red nose framed by a small collection of pimples across his upper lip. With one fluttering upper tooth, he stuttered out a Buddhist koan uttered by the Zen cowboy.

He said: "It is what it is. It ain't what it ain't. Never say never. Let it go."

I borrowed the bartender's pen and scribbled this profundity on a bar napkin. It would stick with me during frequent squalls and a few storms over the coming years.

My attempt to regulate libidinous proclivities kept me corralled for the evening and away from the younger stock down the road. But part of my new mantra was "Never say never."

It occurred to me that the Zen cowboy could have spent some useful moments with Eric Hoffer, the longshoreman philosopher and author who connected the abstract and the accessibly useful. I had carried with me a copy of Hoffer's *The True Believer* as I hitchhiked across Europe and the United States in the 1970s. I also carried the "working man's" Bible, a condensed pocket text that included the New Testament and the psalms of the Old Testament. These companions helped me to connect with the humanness of civilization and the spiritual dimensions within us.

As chairman and CEO of a very successful but ultimately failed corporation, then a management consultant differentiating himself through that failure, then working and living with coffee and chilies farmers in a remote province of Papua New Guinea, and now an executive coach, I continue to plant, nurture, and harvest my life, much like the farmers. As Hoffer said, "My writing grows out of my life just as a branch from a tree."

CHAPTER 1

The Picnic

"The false gods of our culture, materialism, hedonism and narcissism, those upon which we have projected our longings for transcendence, only narrow and diminish."

—James Hollis, PhD

My stepdaughter's balloon popped as we were crossing Kercheval Avenue in the Village district of Grosse Pointe, a highly established suburb bordering the east side of Detroit, Michigan. Barely eight years old, she began to cry, maybe from the surprise of the bang or from the loss of one of her favorite-color (yellow) balloons. She didn't know that, just like the balloon, our family had disintegrated as well. The end came not with a bang but with a picnic that would shortly begin in the park near us. The balloons were the last items I had purchased before the early afternoon gathering. It was mid-July 1999.

The picnic was my ex-wife's idea. She thought there should be a proper farewell staged for her friends and acquaintances and my family members before she and her daughter departed for landing places that would range from St. Louis, Missouri, to Palm Beach, Florida, and Geneva, Switzerland. Her final good-bye was a grandstand event.

My despair was well founded after six years. To be sure, I had continually tried to please whoever I wanted to impact by grandstanding myself. With my ex-wife, I encountered someone who was equally egotistical and self-absorbed.

I had met her through a mutual friend at a University of

Michigan football game against Notre Dame on a September afternoon in Ann Arbor. Wolverine tailgate parties were elegant affairs. I loved the opportunity to nibble scrumptious food, taste wine, and sip iced keg beer. This particular party was populated with a number of investment bankers and hedge fund managers from Chicago and Wall Street. I was keen on acquainting myself with new faces. My networking skills were a little rusty.

I had just returned from a cross-country motorcycle trip with a good friend, where most of our time was spent in the panhandle of Idaho. There my mind was refreshed and I was looking for adventure. Idaho's rivers challenged my kayaking skills. Also, I was captivated by hanging out with "Ruby Ridge" militia types in local taverns, drinking beer and eating venison jerky. The experience met my immediate social needs. Now, intellectually starved, I was primed for a serious and engaging relationship. The lone wolf was finally ready, at the age of forty-eight, to tie the knot. I was driven by emptiness. Out of habit and with pure volition, I was determined to fill my heart. Expeditiously, I did just that and piled yet another heap of misplaced and deliberate imaginations on my shoulders. Unfortunately, the knot turned into a noose, and I ended up hanging myself. I had thought such self-inflictions would ultimately convince me to learn from the past. No such luck. I had experienced one failed marriage twenty years earlier that lasted for two years with no children. Afterward, I embarked on a series of monogamous relationships, but that lifestyle had run its course. I was bored. Control has a dark side. I was effective and therefore had little clue what condition my condition was in. I did not realize I had a self within myself. I was sold on the wrapping paper and gave little thought to what was in the box. The gift was an afterthought. For the most part, it was all about packaging and wrappings, in spite of occasional enlightenment.

I was running out of time—at least, I thought so. Where had that idea emanated from? The subliminal influence of social conditioning is a trickster in its own right and assisted in shaping my choices. Also, my impulsive proclivities were masterfully concealed. Conceit demands no less. My career as a management consultant and my academic credentials were well above average. I paid my office rent and staff, made my mortgage payments, and took vacations when and where I wanted. I had a powerboat moored in a condo next to a yacht club I belonged to on the Detroit River. I also had a Grand Cherokee Jeep and a Harley-Davidson motorcycle. My wardrobe was built around lots of faded jeans and well-worn shirts. My vintage 1927 six-bedroom home was a historical landmark (association of fourteen units), furnished with Oriental rugs and antiques, accented with nice artwork. I additionally had a beachfront condo in Boca Raton, Florida. Hmmm . . . was I the sum total of what I owned? It made sense. Possibly, I did measure my self-worth by these amassed acquisitions. Was this pile of possessions, social capital, and professional accomplishments the essence of who I had become? I never thought I would lose any of it.

The Buddhists teach us to let go of the emotional voltage that literally defines who we *think we are.* Letting go of this voltage allows understanding of our true nature. It is hard to do this.

For instance, I was convinced this woman at the tailgate party was the mirrored manifestation of who I was. I was emotionally invested and greatly charged. Once again charting a fresh course, I would not be deterred. I thought she was a perfect match. She had an MBA from the University of Chicago and was a Wall Street banker, a cello player, a gourmet cook, and a French-speaking avant-garde woman who was really not hard to gaze at. Six years later, she was the person who was leaving in a few hours with my stepdaughter. The perfect match was an illusion. I became proficient in building sand castles.

What a contrast from that day in Ann Arbor when she took a fancy to this "Zen biker" and began to pursue me. At the time it was all good, because she seemed to be everything I thought I wanted. Ultimately, we had a full-blown formal wedding at Saint Thomas Church in midtown Manhattan that included a carriage ride to the New York Yacht Club for one hell of a reception—the icing on the cake. My credit card attested to that. "We drag expensive ghosts through memory's unmade bed," muses Paul Hoover in *Theory of Margins*. The Eagles song "Desperado" was playing as we entered the yacht club's dining area. In my mind, later, it was forever renamed "Desperate-o."

The ensuing years were a yo-yo escapade. One moment I was full of hope that I could fix the relationship, and the next I was dejected and ready to abandon what I had created. The complex resulted in an allegory of home-brewed manic-depression disorder. The surrealism of this short-lived marriage was epitomized by the final afternoon's soiree at the waterfront Grosse Pointe City Park. A question posed by James Hollis rings out in my mind: "Does this path enlarge or diminish me?" As a yo-yo goes, I am afraid as I observe myself; I am in a downward suspension. I have shrunk.

My ex-wife's modus operandi was exquisite. She was just like her favorite wine, Opus One (good taste, high price). Her social and political skills were highly polished. She boasted that Jerry Garcia of the Grateful Dead had been a neighbor. Was this a credibility enhancer? Her emotional intelligence and photographic memory were in high gear, albeit without regard for the casualties. Tautly, I glanced at this woman while I grilled cheeseburgers and sipped champagne. Suspicion and mistrust of certain guests heightened my adeptness in overhearing conversations and observing her antics. My senses strained to validate deeply held assumptions and inward secrets that I was the victim, and she was the perpetrator.

A northerly wind cooled the warm, bright day and rustled the tall elm trees and the balloons tied to the picnic tables. The Canadian shoreline was visible under the blue sky. Sailboats paralleled huge freighters. For a moment, I transcended the foolishness and chicanery of the event. Guests seemed content and happy as they imbibed chilled Veuve Clicquot and pecked on appetizers. I felt gutted, much like a fish on a pier, and ashamed, knowing already that this path diminished me. The geography of this shame was more extended and rooted than I realized. Self-abasement was lurking and soon would pay a visit. Obviously, my observations were biased and guarded. Extracting myself from this mess was the beginning to an end. I did not realize what the price of this inward dissolution would fully entail. Besides, many of my guests already knew before I got married that I was doomed. Unfortunately, I was the most polished of the pretenders. That facade tends to intimidate and keep people at bay. Loyalty is valued above truth. This charade farewell picnic was a testament to such deception. I was tired of repeat performances.

The ride to the airport was the final good-bye. My stepdaughter and I were left alone in the terminal, the result of different flights and destinations all focused on her mother's complex machinations. Sitting there, I stared at this beautiful child with her penetrating ice-blue eyes and white-blond hair, certain I would never see her again. As my stepdaughter jumped onto the baggage scale to weigh herself, she showed little comprehension that her flight was a one-way ticket. A few minutes later, she boarded a plane for St. Louis to be with her father. Just like that. Poof. Gone. I haven't seen her since.

I returned to my storied, empty house. The loneliness was pronounced. I missed my stepdaughter. It felt like a knife was plunged into my heart as I stepped into her bedroom, sat on the bed, and smelled her scent on the pillow. Until now, for the most part, suffering had been just a concept. The following morning, I packed my Harley and headed for northern Michigan, where I navigated back roads. Good friends north of Harbor Springs had offered me their home for the weekend. They called this haven "Destiny Bay."

I arrived early that Saturday evening. Surrounded by cedar pines, I sat on the front porch of the splendid 1918 home overlooking Little Traverse Bay. I searched for the city lights of Charlevoix. The shoreline was barely visible. A mist and empty sky accommodated my seclusion. It looked meaningless. Forlorn, I was on the "Tuscan plains." Dante's words from the *Divine Comedy* echoed in my mind: "The woods is so savage, dense/harsh/first thinking about it renews my fear."

I began to cry and vomit simultaneously, which was something new to me, as I was so single-minded. I threw up toxins, but my insatiable need to compete veiled my vulnerability. I was trained to strengthen my capacity to expand my holding tank. Usually, this shrink-wrapped posture is nearly impenetrable. Fear is a powerful conditioner and has little regard for honest conversations with oneself. Fear is the master builder. Until the threshold of pain becomes greater than the fear to change, I remain in a buoyant state. Therefore, the battle to project control has always been the respected pursuit and the end game. Self-seduction is a potion to which I have grown accustomed, and now I experienced the dregs.

The dry heaving began. My body contorted in anticipation of the agony to follow. This became uncontrollable. For the next two days, I threw my being out, expelling the toxins of self-deception and self-importance. It was the beginning of—and longing for—a deep cleansing and deeper healing. I was grieving for my wounded vision of life. I felt like I had been sucker-punched repeatedly. The discernment to figure out what was happening eluded me. I wanted the feeling of failure to just go away. But I recognized the opportunity to get *better at feeling* versus *feeling better*. This was a different way to look at things. I needed to understand what

I was grieving about. As the vomiting subsided, I sat in a rocking chair, wrapped in a blanket, and breathed in self-understanding. There was an absence of condemnation. I exhaled the questionable choices I had made, for better or worse, including the marriage and the self-orchestrated dance that led up to that decision.

In *The Message*, the Bible as translated by Eugene H. Peterson, it says in Jonah 2, "Those who worship false gods, god frauds, walk away from their only true love." It looks like Jonah wrestled and pleaded his case. The result was the scriptural statement, "Then God spoke to the fish, and it vomited up Jonah on the seashore." I wondered if this was evolution at its best. My inclinations were to go beyond the biology of nausea and assume I was capable of evolving into a different person, with a more realistic view of myself.

Mythologist Joseph Campbell expressed in one of his lectures that I must become "transparent to the transcendent." Sounds trite, but I now sense this way of thinking will allow me to explore my belief system. I want to examine how I have constructed the world and unearth wisdom I haven't, as yet, found in myself. This stripping-away process was an alchemy for which I was not completely prepared, yet I sought it with dead seriousness. I had to stop seducing myself, despite how good I was at it. Again, James Hollis empathizes with his readers and encouraged me, through a Holy Grail text, to go "where there is no path, for it is a shameful thing to take the path that someone has trod before." He concludes: "Your journey is your journey, not someone else's. It is never too late to begin anew."

"During the monotonous magic of the ride I was on, I grasped the preciousness of life." (Photo by Paul Quinlan)

CHAPTER 2

First Steps

"The real motorcycle you are studying is the motorcycle called yourself."

—Robert Pirsig
Zen and the Art of Motorcycle Maintenance:
An Inquiry into Values

Upon my return from Destiny Bay, my home readily became my cave, a hiding place. I was flat-out deflated. Jim Harrison, in his novel *The English Major*, says, "Either you can look at the world or stick your head up your ass . . . self pity is a ruinous quality." But ten years would flow by before I read Harrison's wisdom.

Everyone has problems. I was not a grand exception. This self-absorption is a habit I grew very comfortable with and wondered if it was endemic to my generation since I felt so damn comfortable with it. At the end of the day, I was resigned to carrying my own burden by naming and owning my condition. I was lost and disillusioned. I felt like crap. I did own my own shit. Now, what did I really want, and would it be worth getting, and did I have the capability? My choices were to stay stuck, move on, or even regress. I laughed, comprehending the rigor and insistence I had displayed in such dialectical exchanges with innumerable clients and personal relationships over the years. Now, it was my turn. Just merrily become the change you want to be, John. Was I a little too ambitious, as I might have been with others in my life? Nevertheless, I was compelled to act and get out of this dwelling. The recent past was too raw, vivid, and suffocating. With deliberation, I had to do something, and that something demanded I remove myself from Grosse Pointe. Vomiting at Destiny Bay had dehydrated my soul. My being was wrung out. Now it was time to wrap me around my head—or my head around me—to get a new slant on things. I needed a cultural and social enema in order to renew myself. No better way than to mount a motorcycle, get on a highway, and move forward.

With initial trepidation, I began planning for a solo cross-country motorcycle trip to an unknown destination out west, probably no farther than the Rocky Mountains. I secured regional, state, and county road maps and sketched out the path I would travel. This ride would be on back roads—no freeways—whenever possible. My self-confidence increased as I began to study my future, a labyrinth of highways spanning nearly eight states. A seed of hope germinated. An unnamed force was pulling me forward, yet I was conscious of my own willfulness. Depression would mock my mind, convincing me that I was irrational to make this trip. *It's too risky. This is not the way you work out your stuff.* A repartee of such self-talk was accompanied by the fear of the unknown. I was restless as I tried to sleep. What was risky, and what was I fearful of? Was it the untraveled asphalt and concrete roads or the uncharted inward journey? There were no maps for the latter. A bravado bordering on grandiosity helped mask any misgivings in front of family, friends, and clients. I assumed that the sheer act of commitment to this adventure would somehow make everything turn out right. I pondered whether this was plain stupidity or blind faith—or both. At the end of the day, optimism outweighed my depression. The lure of the future was more powerful than the fear of the present.

On an early Friday morning in the first week of August

1999, I left Grosse Pointe, taking the northern route, hugging the Lake Huron shoreline as much as possible to the Mackinac Bridge. Crossing the Straits of Mackinac, I turned due west on Highway 2, following the Lake Michigan shore across the Upper Peninsula. Once I crossed the Wisconsin line, I entered not just a new state but also a new set of laws governing motorcycle riding. I removed my helmet for the remainder of the trip, or so I thought.

I meandered through the forests of Wisconsin, the plains of Minnesota and South Dakota, and into the Black Hills close to the Badlands. My body was in fairly good shape from jogging five miles every other day. Yet the physical demands of steering a 1,200-pound load ten to twelve hours per day are significant. My body adapted, but I was stiff, and my butt was sore. The annual Sturgis bike rally, a motorcycle convention every August in Sturgis, South Dakota, was in progress and, in typical form, in full-blown pandemonium. I biked into the city of Deadwood. My good friend Max had arranged accommodations with his cousin at a cabin not far from the big event in Sturgis. It was down the road from Deadwood and close to the Buffalo Chip campground. Such accommodations are prized. Thousands of bikers drive daily—one hundred miles, one way—to get to this party from more distant towns.

My entry into Deadwood could have been a scene from Sodom and Gomorrah, with thousands of bikers in procession. Engines revving, bikers cruised along to music blaring from the saloons. It was an outrageous and unforgettable salutation.

The leather-clad biking ladies were on their "cafés" (dressed-up motorcycles), with braided hair replete with feathers, jewelry, and beads. They were eye-openers and heart-stoppers. There were scores of them, riding in formation. I was sandwiched between two groups, one to my right and the other on my left. After a week of biking, my testosterone level spiked. This hellacious spectacle was a tonic of sorts. The saloons were packed with patrons spilling out into the streets. Vintage rock-and-roll was blaring. Bob Seger and the Silver Bullet Band wailed away. The Sturgis rally stood in stark contrast to solo biking across the Great Plains, with its scent of sage after a thunderstorm, crosswinds battering me from side to side with stillness and solitude. I was gratified. A week before, the thought of accomplishing this on my own had been daunting. To become my longing was a new habit, one that required study and practice. Riding into the unknown has its rewards.

In one Spearfish saloon, I took a keen interest in a beauty from Duluth, Minnesota. She was a stunner, with long blond hair draped over a braless leather vest. I quickly deduced an absence of panties under her chaps. My, oh my, were my senses alive! All day long, I had pictures taken by gawking bikers while I partied with her. Unfortunately, that once-in-a-lifetime roll of film was lost the next day in the town of Keystone, where I went after viewing Mount Rushmore. I guess the contrast of the stoic granite faces and the sumptuousness of this woman in biking leathers was too hard to bear. Losing the roll of film was meant to happen. The developed pictures would not have fit into the future. I noted this particular occasion, however, because I cannot recall partying that hard, nonstop, for that long, ever since. This was a highway marker in my life's path. Chasing or being chased by beautiful women would become less and less of an identity. Was I now grasping for deeper self-knowledge and/or becoming older and coming to terms with a lower testosterone level? I vacillated on this vexing conundrum.

As my trip continued, I did my fair share of sightseeing to

Devils Tower, more saloons, and Custer City. It was a different *terza rima.* The pandemonium was electrifying for three or four days, until the realization—*I did this already*—began to sink in. The novelty of the Sturgis rally faded. Change is quietly incremental. With a hundred thousand bikers knocking back tequila shots from the belly buttons of pretty bartenders lying on countertops, limitations appear as well. My neck began to stiffen from bending over during the course of a day. Picking up a shot glass, nestled in a belly button, with my teeth was a strenuous preoccupation. It was indeed straining and a cause of sharp discomfort. Fortunately, I was up for the task—someone had to do it.

I broke away early one morning, taking a secluded highway straight down through Nebraska and crossing into Colorado. It rained all day as I made my descent on two-lane switchbacks from the Black Hills into the Front Range of the Rocky Mountains. Buffalo and free-range cattle crossed the roads. Since my bike was, by choice, absent a windshield, I tied a bandanna around my cap to keep it from blowing off and to protect my forehead from the pelting rain. Recalling the pain I'd endured at the saloons by imbibing tequila shots out of those belly buttons offset the discomfort.

Shit happens. I was forced to retrack on the Colorado border due to a bridge washout. A Nebraska state trooper at a gas station took a long look at me as I refueled.

He walked over and asked why I was not wearing my helmet. I sincerely explained that I assumed the state did not have a helmet law. Wrong. I put it on. No ticket was given. Through the rearview mirror I noted the reactions of the state trooper and the gas station attendant as they read the faded slogan on the back of my helmet: "Shit happens." Occasionally, things work all right, even in an all-day rain on the Great Plains on a motorcycle. Attitude adjustments occur at their own pace, ticking on with each mile marker I put behind me.

Still, the unrelenting rain frayed my nerves. The brisk wind chilled me. My body and mind tired with the tedium of staying alert on wet pavement. I tended to grip the handles tighter, causing my fingers and thumbs to cramp. My gloves were saturated, offering little warmth.

The washed-out bridge cost me two and a half hours of additional biking. The gravel roads and even heavier rain were challenging. Fatigue settled in, yet it was rewarding. I felt like I had achieved something by just moving forward. There was a sweet spot in this monotony and predictability. The absence of fear felt good. Contentment somehow crept into me, and before I knew it, I realized beauty was all around me. Today's endeavor became worthwhile.

I checked into an old motel in Limon, Colorado. Across Highway 71 was a tavern and café. They looked as weather-beaten as I felt. A nice fit to end the day.

Sitting on a bar stool and sipping a shot of Jack Daniel's washed down by a cold bottle of beer is an impeccable routine. I cannot think of a better ritual. I felt so good I wanted to embrace the smiling bartender. She owned the place and suggested I have a grilled steak, fries, and a salad. I headed for the Wurlitzer and dropped in four quarters to hear Hank Williams.

The positive effects of this travel were found in the daily routine. Easiness began to percolate within me. I was less condemning of others and myself. The burden of perfectionism was lightening. I was feeling what I actually felt versus what I thought I was supposed to feel. My experience was becoming authentic. This was effective and cheap therapy. I was resonating with the environment, others, and myself.

Meeting gentle and nice folks along the way, interspersed with the solitude, grounded me. I liked this frequency. The circuits were harmoniously oscillating. I thought of the Grosse Pointe picnic, the day marked by polo shirts, designer shorts, costume jewelry, chilled champagne, and kept secrets. Was I premature in minimizing this affair so quickly? Superficiality has already taken its toll on me. I glimpsed myself in the mirror. Yes, I was the same person, yet the scenery had shifted. I was intoxicated and alarmed by the power to spontaneously create my own stimuli. The voltage of this frequency had to do with my being in sync with whatever I happened to be experiencing. Consciously flowing required a rhythm that was unnatural for me. I mused, *Maybe as a white man, I am from an uptight bunch, bleached, in need of vivification.* I ordered another beer. The picnic seemed much more than a month old. William James's "stream of consciousness" kept on ticking, kept on flowing. I kept on riding.

John Updike's *Dogwood Tree* (1962) sums up what I was feeling during the monotonous magic of the ride I was on. I grasped the preciousness of life. Distractions of my own making were set aside to see that the bush was burning. I was stilling down to see the flame. It was there. As Updike wrote:

Blankness is not emptiness; we may skate upon an intense radiance we do not see because we see nothing else. And in fact there is a colour, a quiet but tireless goodness that things at rest, like a brick wall or a small stone, seem to affirm.

"To my right was a pretty woman with blond braids, milky-blue eyes, and a tender and engaging smile that sprang from a soft, beautiful pale face. I liked the strength in her look. A dozen teenage girls surrounded her. The bartender was busy preparing 'mocktails' for her group." This was Fiona.

CHAPTER 3

Refuge

"All human life can be interpreted as a continuous attempt to avoid despair . . . and this attempt is mostly successful."

—Paul Tillich

Quiet, gentle memories of a place called Crested Butte, Colorado, started to infect me, brewing up a hankering to get back there. Pleasant recollections came to mind, not only of the raw beauty of southwest Colorado and the Sawatch Mountains but also of a vibrant and kind woman named Rita, proprietor of the Last Resort Bed and Breakfast. Rita and I had met in January 1990. I was on a skiing trip. We remained friends throughout the years. On numerous occasions, Rita was a bouquet of fresh spring flowers graciously and unselfishly handed to this man of preoccupations. Now, this is pure speculation, but she seemed vivaciously truthful and direct. For whatever reason, however, the plainness of her transparency never appealed to me. I neither comprehended it nor trusted it. Such consistency was an anomaly. It demanded I be consciously engaged with another person. This assumed that people—and particularly a pretty woman—had other dimensions. These highway markers are appearing more rapidly as this journey extends.

The ebb and flow of our relationship had a magical staying power. It was an on-again/off-again mutual crush, but the timing was never right for the consummation I had in mind. Now I was convinced that this was the moment for a serious on-again. I assumed I was being driven by a well-named appetite—getting my rocks off.

Between the open road, Sturgis, and six months of celibacy, I was starving for human bodily contact. I needed some consolation. I greatly desired the scent and touch of a woman. Ideally, my friend Rita would think and feel similarly toward me. The encounter with the woman from Duluth rekindled a sensuous fire that was quenched some time ago. I was hopeful. Man does not live by bread alone. For this biker, Crested Butte was not a spiritual mecca. Yet it had all the makings of just that, from what I had been told previously by Rita, authors, and friends. The fire for which I was really searching, the warmth I really sought, was much more than I realized.

I arrived late in the afternoon, after a full day of extreme cold-weather biking. My hands were contorted from gripping the handles to counter crosswinds that blew me from side to side over many miles of two-lanes. My chaps were stiff from the sleet. All in all, I needed some warmth. I wanted a fire. My mind raced as I anticipated the sweet loving and understanding I was about to possess.

Our eyes locked as we embraced on her front porch, yet suddenly, instinctively, I knew this dance was not going to happen. I flashed back to a temper tantrum I'd had at about age eight with my mother. I was denied a short-term gratification and stomped my feet on the living room floor, screaming at her with all my might. I took control of the impulse now. Crestfallen, I continued to hug Rita, knowing I was going to be denied. I was getting the love and understanding but not on my terms. The craving only intensified. I think Rita suspected. The bulge in my jeans was a giveaway. My chaps were still on.

New boundaries were immediately established. Rita was now engaged to be married. She expressed her desire for solace and needed to hear from me. It was a self-talk that I heard respectfully yet disappointedly. Rita was always a direct person. Without much of a choice, I acquiesced, feeling a sense of indefinable loneliness I had not experienced since crossing the Great Plains. Hopelessness, after all those miles and highway markers, reared its ugly head. I was back at Destiny Bay in northern Michigan, feeling the wounds of past misunderstandings and betrayals. I was powerless and confused. I had no answers. My head was not worth a sack of beans. The highway seemed to be taking me in circles.

The following afternoon, I biked up to the Colorado town of Tin Cup. Western author Louis L'Amour referred to this mountain hamlet in at least one novel. I had visited it years ago with Rita. God, this was difficult. Realizations of past choices surfaced, all of them with built-in consequences, good and bad. Long-ago afternoon picnics with Rita along these same roads made me yearn for her company. Fate was always a tricky concept for me to grasp. As Tillich shares, "Fate is the rule of contingency having no ultimate necessity—identified with a sense of inescapable causal determination."

Wow! I am caught in the crosshairs of a high-power rifle scope. Mindfulness is bearing down. A sense of irrevocability grips me as I feel purposelessness in the moment. I detest my alertness.

God, this was an effort. Surrounded by all of this natural beauty, I felt a despair bordering on meaninglessness that ran bone deep. I had no one to share the day with but myself.

I wasn't prepared for being alone with a flood tide of thoughts. I needed a floodlight, a broad beam, right now. I wanted illumination. I was in a dark room, trying to get to the other side.

Yet the stillness of the open skies, green meadows, and mountain forests was ever so present. The deep scent of pines and wildflowers grounded me in the present. The wind on my face reminded me I was in forward motion on a gravel road. I felt the tires grip the stones and ruts, and, in spite of myself, I was arrested by the wholeness of this instant. The act of riding on, in itself, was self-affirming. I felt compelled to keep going and prevail. My fate was contingent on my choice. It was an act of faith. I did not feel courageous. Illumination escaped me.

I returned to a paved road south of the Taylor Reservoir, parallel to the Taylor River on my right. Looking on chalky-rouge bluffs nestled in the pines, I spotted a familiar, imposing rock jutting into the river rapids. I pulled over and hiked up to the massive promontory, a picnic site I had enjoyed with Rita. My heart was galvanized by the memory. I was frozen in my tracks. I had to lift my rear end off this spot and put it back on my bike. Self-pity was knocking at the door. I prayed for the courage to move on and to find myself, to discover what mattered to me. . .

Five minutes later, I arrived at Harmel's Ranch. Rita had introduced me to this fly-fishing resort as well. Chilled by the mountain air, in leathers and unshaven, I looked and felt road-tested as I swaggered up to the bar for a shot of whiskey. I was at ease and content with this persona.

To my right was a pretty woman with blond braids, milky-blue eyes, and a tender and engaging smile that sprang from a soft, beautiful pale face. I liked the strength in her look. A dozen teenage girls surrounded her. The bartender was busy preparing "mocktails" for her group.

I casually made an introduction: "Your mother must have been a most beautiful person for you to care for all of these girls." It worked. I still could think on my feet. I'd grabbed her attention.

She quickly remarked: "Thank you. My mother recently died. I'm Fiona Delaney, from Papua New Guinea."

My response was automatic: "Papa *what*?" I soon learned that Fiona had three young daughters. They lived in New York City, and she was on her way out of a bad marriage. Humble and precise in manner, Fiona informed me that she'd been married to a diplomat who'd lived on Roosevelt Island, off Manhattan. The location was unremarkable compared to her being born on another island called East New Britain on the other side of the world. Her New Guinea-Australian accent drew me into further conversation. The melodiousness of her voice was a novel sound. My focus on her cadence nearly derailed my original intention, but I plunged ahead anyway. I casually asked if she wanted to go for a motorcycle ride. Her response: "Only if it's a Harley." I quickly assured her it was. I was in luck.

That small exchange marked the beginning of a new chapter in my life. Somewhere on the life continuum where Rita fell and my ex-wife lay, Fiona was now poised. I was in sync with myself. Twenty minutes later, I was cruising by that same Taylor River promontory, grinning, with Fiona's arms wrapped around my waist. We must have looked like any typical motorcycling couple, out for a simple pleasure ride, but, unexpectedly, I noticed tears running down my cheeks. I glanced into my left–hand mirror and saw that she was crying too. I realized we were unexplainably connected, and I felt really good. I didn't understand what was going on as I switch-backed my way up to the Taylor Park Reservoir. It was magic. We were floating together. The sun pierced the ebony-green pines, casting entrancing shadows over the road.

Few words were shared as we climbed off the bike to view the immensity of the reservoir. The remote vista drew me closer to this woman. Wispy clouds were rioted by iridescent yellow and purple hues as the late afternoon sun danced.

Standing on a grassy knoll, we were in the midst of the remains of the past season's wildflowers. It reminded me of the impermanence of life. I held her hand. We were intertwined in the moment. The thought of losing what I felt disturbed me, as I realized this encounter would soon end.

On the ride down, I turned into a meadow along a stream. The wildflowers and pine scent permeated my senses, imprinting the moment for a future memory.

Within thirty minutes, on her cabin porch, I kissed Fiona good-bye and headed back to Crested Butte to have dinner with Rita and then, the following morning, to bike south for the New Mexico state line. Fiona's parting words had been, "Why don't you come back and give these girls a motorcycle ride?" The thought of a dozen teenage girls riding on the back of my Harley did not strike a chord within me.

Rita would prepare a scrumptious breakfast for her guests daily. That next morning, the smell of coffee, pastries, bacon, and eggs drew me out of bed. As guests departed the dining table, she hooked me into one more day of biking, claiming I would see elk by using a private road through another pass. I signed up, looking forward to a farewell dinner that evening. She was available. Her fiancé was an airline pilot and wouldn't be in town that evening. *Here I go again, idealizing. Old habits are hard to break. Never say die. Rita might change her mind,* I thought. If she wants to have a tryst for old times' sake, I certainly would oblige.

I slowly made my way along the washboard road. The tiredness did not pay off; there were no elk. At the end of the road, the adjoining paved highway looked familiar. Left or right? *What the hell?* I turned left. As I viewed the unfolding bend, another valley opened up, and there was Harmel's Ranch Resort.

Suddenly, I decided I wanted to say good-bye to Fiona again. I pulled up to her cabin. But was I here to say good-bye or hello? As one saying goes, "When the heart breaks open, it can hold the whole universe." My double-mindedness would evaporate soon.

I knocked on her cabin door. No one was there. I got on my bike and went to view the reservoir one last time before heading south to New Mexico. Suddenly, I stopped. Back over my left shoulder, Fiona was standing on the bridge, fishing pole in her left hand, wearing denim overalls and staring right at me. She'd heard the rumbling of my Harley. I made a U-turn and headed back. We walked into her cabin. On her bed, I noticed a heart-shaped pillow, surrounded with wildflowers, bearing the hand-stitched words "John loves Fiona." The mocktail girls had made it. I kissed Fiona and did not want to let her go. I recalled a grad school professor who opened up his lectures with a scribbled sentence on a flipchart that read, "There are no accidents."

The afternoon was taken up by obliging a dozen teenagers with motorcycle rides up and down the valley road. The girls were afflicted with Turner syndrome, a hormonal deficiency that stunts physical growth. Their hearts were truly quite the opposite. Fiona, I learned, was the codirector of the Friendship World Foundation, a nonprofit organization formed to help these children. Such commitments were new to me.

It started to rain hard, and the air chilled quickly. I called Rita to cancel dinner. Cabin 22 at Harmel's Ranch was available. The grocery/fly-fishing store supplied me a cold six-pack of beer, potato chips, peanut butter and jelly, bread, peanut M&M's, and a turquoise necklace. I built a fire, and Fiona arrived for dinner.

Our first embrace in the kitchen, after I gave her the necklace, killed my dinner plans. We were up all night. As we were making love, I quietly wept. Again, this was a new highway marker. My vulnerability was illuminated. I felt normal. I began to wonder, early into the morning, how I was going to say good-bye to this woman from Papua New Guinea.

I knew I had to put in a long day of biking just to get close to New Mexico. Unfortunately, my trip had to end at a certain date, as I had planned to meet up with good friends in Santa Fe, ultimately departing for Detroit. We exchanged addresses and phone numbers. The rain continued as I made my way down to Creede, Colorado. As I viewed the mist on the mountains, with emerald green pastures on both sides of the highway, I thought of Fiona. Her accent and voice were lodged in my consciousness. I wanted to hear her again.

I pulled over in a valley north of Creede to take a pee. Remounting my bike, I glanced into the right rearview mirror and discovered I had hickeys on both sides of my neck. My unzipped leather jacket exposed these cannibal brandings. Within one hour, I found a cheap motel with an attached bar and café in South Fork. I mused over the day. I was mesmerized by how the past twenty-four hours contained so much meaning. In the fictional diary of *Tristram Shandy*, the details are so extensive that it takes the author, Laurence Sterne, one year to set down the happenings of a single day. I started my first diary at the age of ten. I don't think it can ever be completed.

At the log cabin tavern, I sipped a shot of Jack Daniel's and a long-neck Bud. A candle under a red cloth shade helped drive out the chill in my bones as I waited for the trout dinner. The jukebox bellowed Eagles songs, followed by a selection of John Prine. I did not want this good-bye to last for long.

Valley View Hot Springs in Colorado was strict about its rules. One stricture was "clothing optional." On his first visit there, John opted for disrobed. Now, a few years later, "I chose to wear my leather vest and cap." Later that day, in a warm infinity pool on the mountain, "my mind melted into a stream of consciousness as I started to think about that woman from Papua New Guinea."

CHAPTER 4

Deliberate Practice

"The question isn't whether it's true or not but whether you want to believe it."

—Elaine Equi, "Art About Fear," in *Ripple Effect*

The rain ceased in early morning, and the sun was bright, shining in a sky of sapphire blue as I approached the New Mexico state line. Briefly stopping in the town of Del Norte, Colorado, I purchased a bottle of tequila and tucked it into one of my saddlebags.

Impulsively, I turned due north on Highway 17 near Alamosa, Colorado. Santa Fe would have to wait a day. I was soon breathing in the unfettered beauty of the San Luis Valley. Again, I felt content. The purity and integrity of the moment was so significant that I hollered out in exuberance. My right hand shot up, and I waved at the magnificence. I was giddy.

This remarkable parcel of real estate is nestled between two mountain ranges. To the west are the low-lying Cochetopa Hills of purple and violet hues, each one a little taller than the one before it. To the east are the Sangre de Cristo Mountains, which are more abrupt and severe. In the foothills sits the Great Sand Dunes National Park. I have experienced a night hike through this park under a moon so full I wore sunglasses to mark the occasion.

My excitement rose as I traveled this familiar, beautiful highway. The high desert sage smelled sweet,

27

freshened by the rain from the night before. I felt exhilarated, and recalled that to the northeast sat the village of Crestone, Colorado, where a Zen center was located. I had biked through this hamlet before but never spotted a monk, only a few waving hippies with illegal smiles.

In August 1994, I biked the same road. One particular day, hail pelted me ferociously. I stopped to shelter my face and hands from the stinging pellets that fell so thickly they were hiding the lane markers. Another biker pulled up on his Honda Gold Wing with his stereo blaring music by the Doors. His dog was on the backseat in cape and sunglasses, glaring at this stranger. The biker (not the dog) invited me to a nearby hot spring. Strenuously yelling over the music, he shouted, "Why don't you take a break, chill out, party, and meet some nice people at a commune reunion?" I took him up on the invitation and have revisited Colorado's Valley View Hot Springs on numerous occasions since.

Now, on this occasion, less than an hour away from the village of Villa Grove, Colorado, close to the hot springs turnoff, I gassed up and bought a sandwich and a bag of peanut M&M's to accompany the tequila that sustained me through the day. I backtracked south toward Moffat, Colorado, and spent another thirty minutes on a gravel road to arrive at the hot springs compound's entrance. The "sundown" rules stipulated that you must depart Valley View by day's end if you weren't registered in a cabin or camping space. There were no vacancies.

Since the area was "clothing optional," I chose to wear my leather vest and cap. I threw my tequila and goodies into a daypack and hiked up a trail through the pinions to the highest pool. Sipping my tequila, I soaked the afternoon away. It is a pastime I still quite enjoy.

The natural pebbled pool was shallow enough to enable me to sprawl out, perching my elbows on the edge to view the setting sun's violet hues on the mountains. The water temperature averaged eighty degrees Fahrenheit, which made it very comfortable as the evening approached. My mind melted into stream-of-consciousness as I started to think about that woman from Papua New Guinea.

As the sun dipped below the horizon, I hiked down to a lower pool to watch the moon rise. Below this pool, three very good-looking women frolicked in a spring, drinking wine and passing around a pipe filled with what appeared to be an illegal substance. One wave from the most attractive of the three brought me to their pool without hesitation. "Clothing optional" made it monstrously difficult not to stare at what was so outright and disarmingly gorgeous.

Within the hour and feeling no pain, I feebly announced I was leaving. The town of Salida, Colorado, just beyond Poncha Pass, was at least one hour away. Gently, I was halted in my exit by a hand on my arm. The fairest of the three whispered into my ear, "You are invited to dine, party, and spend the night in the cabin." Oh my! Indecision gripped this scantily clad biker. With the influx of unsolicited adoration, seduction, and lust,

I felt drawn into an effortless flow. I was satiated with affirmation. The gentler, nobler, and less bearing form of womanizing reminded me I was still sought after. I felt sensually desired. Without explanation, I politely declined. To this day, I am not sure if I was conscious of what I did. But I did do it, somewhat like making the left-hand turn and discovering Harmel's Ranch just around the bend.

I stumbled back to my motorcycle with the help of the moonlight and paused to contemplate my decision. Did I really want to take up the offer, or stay true to an unspoiled picture of the woman from Papua New Guinea?

I chose the latter. I viewed that moonlight climbing up the highway, listening to the subdued roll of my motorcycle echoing off the cliffs. Neil Young's "Harvest Moon" played gently in my mind, returning my thoughts to Fiona. What was going on here? I consciously engaged myself. The reverberations of this self-symphony made me mindful of the power to make choices. I was my own conductor and the author of my journey. The choice to honor the experience with Fiona and embrace another path was possibly a dissimilar beginning for me. I had jettisoned past belongings that gave me no satisfaction. Clouded by past experiences with money, adult toys, and public acclaim, I detected that this highway marker was significant. There was really nothing wrong with what I had been through. It was how I related to all these things that made it toxic. I had become very proficient at feeling better, as opposed to becoming better at feeling. As a card-carrying member of the walking dead, I had little idea how to resign. On top of that, what do I now become a member of?

I sensed a quiet path unfolding that required a consistent faith in things unseen, while simultaneously affirming a new hope to view myself differently within this world. I had to find lodging that night in Salida, and my faith was answered by a roadside cabin and warm bed.

Could it be that simple?

John in his CEO days, in the early 1980s. "Money, it's a gas. Grab that cash with both hands and make a stash," as Pink Floyd sang. (Photo by Elizabeth Gard)

CHAPTER 5

Circling Back

"Few of us have the heart to follow the circle to the end."
—John Updike, *The Music School*

My courage was being tested as I headed back to Grosse Pointe. After a brief visit with a friend in Santa Fe, I left my motorcycle at a Harley-Davidson dealership to be trucked home. The thought of returning to Michigan to face an empty home was akin to visiting a dentist to have a tooth pulled. I fully anticipated loneliness, stirred by being back in familiar surroundings associated with painful memories. The image of my elated stepdaughter rushing to greet me occupied my thoughts as I unlocked the front door.

Entering the kitchen, I went to my phone and pushed the message button. I listened through a parade of telemarketers, friends, family, and clients, all the while hoping to hear a certain voice with an Australian accent. My heart fell with each successive message. Then, presto! The woman from Papua New Guinea emerged: "Hello, this is Fiona from New York City. I do hope you remember me. I would like you to call." I replayed the message and then immediately called. Her voice was reassuring and familiar. It was to be the first of many such phone conversations. I slowly realized what this woman meant to me. It was just a matter of time before I would circle back through my personal chamber of horrors—New York City— after an immeasurably long five years. It's what it would take to reach Fiona.

The flight to New York awoke memories of a different

era. I recalled circling LaGuardia, dressed in a navy three-piece suit, attaché case in hand, and accompanied by my chief financial officer, lawyer, and accountant. We would squeeze into a Yellow Cab and usually find ourselves stuck in traffic in lower Manhattan on our way to the higher floors of the World Trade Center.

For me, this was deal-making time—the early 1980s. In the business world, it was assumed you went to NYC to reach agreements. "Capital is control" was the motto of this hub. Then, as now, the deal-making center of the universe was laced with a colorful cast of characters including investment bankers, commercial bankers, silk-purse lawyers, and big accounting firms. Throw in the public relations experts, rating agencies, DC lobbyists, floor traders, and market makers, and you had one hell of a production.

It's easy to lose your head once you gain membership into this power club. You begin to drink your own Kool-Aid of self-importance, aided by a collective mind-set that results from everyone drinking from the same pitcher. The fees generated by this group effort to "get a deal done" are plentiful and reinforcing. There is also the intangible reward called "privilege" that fills a man up. Self-deception and self-absorption run high.

Innumerable privileges began quite harmlessly at first, but they soon became everyday entitlements and expectations. The Yellow Cab transformed into a limousine. Working lunches and dinners gave way to elaborate feeding and drinking extravaganzas. A martini at Harry's on Wall Street graduated to steak tartare and champagne at the 21 Club. The nibbling and imbibing segued easily to La Cote Basque for dinner, followed by cigars and cognac in the Plaza Hotel's Oak Room. Depending on the energy level of the party, extracurricular activities would extend throughout the evening, from clubbing to "private entertainment" if desired.

I was thoroughly immersed in these pleasures and amazingly kept this pace despite early meetings the following day. I would remind myself there was a higher purpose and meaning to these tasks. In the interest of my stakeholders, someone had to endure this "drudgery." A squash match and steam bath at the New York Athletic Club always reinvigorated me to endure another evening. The bars, restaurants, and clubs would change, yet the carousel was fundamentally the same. Occasionally, an element of sophistication elevated the proceedings with a cocktail party at the Museum of Modern Art, dinner at the Algonquin Hotel, or perhaps a Broadway play. If wives or significant others were flown in, the club scene and related entertainment were discarded.

Now, en route to see Fiona, I saw myself in these images as the plane descended to the runway. The dimness of early evening highlighted my first glimpse of the skyline. Pink Floyd suddenly drilled me with a familiar song: "Money, it's a gas. Grab that cash with both hands and make a stash."

A sardonic grin materialized in my passenger window reflection. Times had changed since those hard-charging days, and I had paid a steep price. Self-importance and the illusion of invincibility eventually ended my reign as chairman and CEO of a publicly traded company. I failed my organization deeply, hurting employees and shareholders alike. Truthfully, I had evolved into an asshole. Many of my friends disappeared as the king's castle collapsed. Such insights were now mortifyingly obvious.

I did not like what I had become, yet I had exercised the same poor judgment in a marriage that ended with that picnic in Grosse Pointe. As the plane landed, my anxiety spiked. I wondered if I was repeating my previous life.

Riding across the 59th Street Bridge, I was feeling unglued. Barely out of my marriage, here I was entering yet another relationship, potentially jumping from one frying pan into another. Stuck in Midtown Manhattan traffic, I glanced at the street signs to see Fifth Avenue and 53rd Street. The bronze doors of marriage epicenter Saint Thomas Church stared at me. The lifeless eyes chilled me. The limestone steps suddenly rippled upward into a cavernous mouth drawing me in to be devoured. With admonition, I refused the invitation. Damn tired of being regurgitated, I was convinced this was the mother lode of all warning signs. Mozart's Requiem rang out, exclaiming, "Remember, merciful Jesus, I am the cause of your journey!"

On that wedding day, I'd had two best men, the foundation for a classic double bind. I recall compressing in a deep knee bend in the vestibule of the church, my back propped up by the wall, as I attempted to utilize a bioenergetic breathing exercise. My first best man thought this was a good sign. His counsel was to go for it and not be alarmed by second thoughts. His words of assurance: "What do you have to lose?" Minutes later, the second best man walked in and thought my posture was a sign that I should walk out of the wedding. *His* words of assurance: "What do you have to lose?"

Now I was again in an emotional bind, feeling twisted into a human knot. It was a familiar place, but this time I did not have a best man for an appeal. I stared at the bronzed doors with determination. A dry gin martini would embolden me, but that would have to wait. The stasis evaporated as I checked into the hotel and called Fiona.

The evening became a mad rush to fill one another up with everything we wanted to know about one another or to disclose everything we wanted to tell one another but never had a chance. With a backdrop of freshly cut flowers, candles, chocolates, cheese, baguettes, and champagne, we made a wonderful picnic. I enjoyed this one. We frolicked all night.

I met Fiona's children in Central Park the following afternoon. The carriage ride was a treat for all of us. The crispness of the autumn air and bright sun emphasized the facial expressions of the three girls. Their Melanesian complexions were heart-stoppers. Fiona's hair wisped in the air. She was a natural woman. I knew I would be together with her and these three girls cementing a relationship that was meant to be. My entry into the world of Fiona and her daughters—three, five, and seven years old—intertwined our lives. Faint echoes from a deep place spiraled upward. Serendipitous notions flooded me as I glanced again at Fiona. The sunlight perfectly highlighted her cheekbones and smile. I sensed something was going on that I could not put my finger on.

The following year, on a motorcycle, I took Fiona back to Harmel's Ranch, back to the cabin, and back to the reservoir. I introduced her to the Creede valley of hickeys, the tavern in South Fork, and, finally, to the Valley View Hot Springs. We viewed San Luis Valley, Colorado, as we relaxed in a pool, sipping tequila. The lower pool was vacant. I smiled. We stayed in a cabin that night at Valley View and munched on M&M's and peanut butter and jelly sandwiches. Gazing into a fire pit, I put my arm around Fiona. I was aware that the steps I was taking were very different from the past. This time I was fully invested and engaged. I realized it made little difference that I was here, yet I was here, and that made all the difference. The highway was blurred, and the markers were becoming indistinguishable. I walked over to the sound of a mountain stream. The moonlight gave me visibility to realize the water was just below my feet. I knelt down and cupped the water to my mouth. I entered into another stream. This stream was always there. This dance would never end. I was flowing. The water was refreshing and delicious.

A year later, I again found myself on an airplane to New York City. This time it was the week following the World Trade Center attack, and Fiona had urged me to come back to console her and her three daughters. They had lost neighbors in the assault.

When I arrived that day, the airport was nearly deserted and there were no taxicab lines. An overpowering stench was the first thing to hit me as I entered the city. Smoke still rose from Ground Zero. Sirens were ever-present, as was the fear I saw in the eyes of people on the street. Truckloads of National Guard troops were being transported to and from Lower Manhattan.

The gloom and doom drew me into melancholy. This was far different from viewing the event and its aftermath on TV.

The following day, we ventured to the World Trade Center site; the Ground Zero term originally referred to where the first atomic bomb hit Hiroshima. The horror of such man-made devastation overwhelmed me. I braced myself in front of Trinity Church with a prayer. We walked over to Battery Park to move away from the god-awful smell and souvenir vendors. T-shirts already had been designed and printed up. The Staten Island Ferry gave us a view of the skyline minus the Twin Towers. Here today; gone today. The incomprehensibility was staggering and battered both my sense of safety and my trust in politicians. Vulnerability replaced invincibility. Things would never be the same for America.

The crowds subsided as we disembarked on the wharf in lower Manhattan. I broke away from Fiona and the girls for an hour, promising to meet them at the bull and bear sculptures on Wall Street. I would have just as soon had it be the Bull and Bear Bar at the Waldorf-Astoria.

I could see my footprints as I walked the deserted streets of the deal-making center of the world. A white ash covered everything. The streets were vacant. I was humming the Australian song "Waltzing Matilda." Such events stir up deeply embedded Armageddon archetypes. The old movie *On the Beach* flashed across my mind. The stock market had just experienced its largest one-week drop in history. Fear had gone viral. That evening, as I viewed Lower Manhattan from Fiona's apartment, I wept. I turned to Fiona. As I looked into those eyes, I knew the times were changing. Heraclitus said, "Nothing is permanent but change."

I went home that time with little desire to return to New York City. Fiona was going home to Australia. Events that I had little control over were suddenly set in motion, things that would redefine and morph me into a person I would find hard to fathom. Again, the impermanence of the reservoir flowers was keenly felt.

Robert Valk, successful businessman, "once mentioned that his family ate dandelions for sustenance during his days of poverty growing up on a farm. . . . Bob gently tapped my hand and said, 'You must give yourself permission to wander into new opportunities.'" Little did John know then that he would deal with such counterparts to Valk as this chief in Papua New Guinea.

CHAPTER 6

New Times, New Thinkings

*"Paradigm shift: A change to anything being described
by a person who likes to use buzzwords; has no real
meaning, but people pretend it does."*

—Urban Dictionary

Robert Valk—unpretentious, private, a man of few
words—tapped my right hand with his firm, sun-spotted, blue-
veined left hand. My eighty-five-year-old friend and I gazed
out at Lake St. Clair and the empty yacht slips of the Grosse
Pointe Club's marina. A pallbearer at the funeral of Henry Ford
(Hank the Deuce) and a significant businessman in his own
right, Bob knew a lot about life and, after a decade, a lot about
me.

Our lunch in early December 2001 proceeded. We
ordered soup, lemon sole, and Chardonnay, and Bob knew my
conundrum was also on the menu. Fiona and her daughters had
moved to Cairns, Australia. Due to a visa technicality, including
spent legal fees, I was unable to keep her and the children in
America. I was trapped in the routines of my life. In my traditional
navy blue jacket, pleated gray trousers, starched white shirt,
club tie, and shined tassel loafers, I was inconspicuous in this
setting and found comfort in being unnoticed. I always felt out
of place at this club. My upbringing was closer to the border
of Detroit. Growing up, I rode my bike into the city and played
with Detroiters. They were distinguished by excessive use of
Brylcreem, profanity, tight blue jeans, and cigarette packs in
rolled-up white T-shirt sleeves. By contrast, we in the Grosse

Pointes sported butch cuts and shorts as we rode around on new Schwinn bicycles. Fistfights abounded and were usually near playgrounds. If we commandeered their baseball diamond, they would come at us with their fists. These were fair fights. The mafia kids in Grosse Pointe Park would do the same, but they used baseball bats and usually won the fights. They were cultivated for aggression and had privilege. The police never seemed to do anything when we complained of their tactics. It appeared their parents had at least as much money as the other Pointers. Their complexion was darker, though. In the early 1960s, that always posed a problem for them, as it did for Greeks and Negroes. My childhood territory included very few Jews. As I recall, their religion and their support of the young Catholic president JFK and the labor movement were real dividers in our community. All in all, these early impressions never left me. In fact, I am thankful for the experience. My life has been enriched. The Grosse Pointe girls were prettier than the Detroit girls, but stuck-up, and they played hard to get. Yet sometimes they compromised with Spin the Bottle, Post Office, and make-out parties. Adopting baseball vernacular, French kissing lay somewhere between first and second base. The thought of a "home run" was largely idealism, evinced by my friend's *Playboy* magazine pilfered from the closet of an impious uncle.

Bob's simple and penetrating wisdom often mesmerized me. He once mentioned that his family ate dandelions for sustenance during his days of poverty, growing up on a farm. While attending the University of Michigan, he played the violin in campus taverns to defray living expenses. Bob was from the school of experience. He valued his poverty as much as his present accomplishments. He visited China to open up new business opportunities. What did he have to prove? I was looking in all the wrong places, and Bob knew it. In a previous bout of my depression, while having lunch with Bob at the exclusive Country Club of Detroit, he tapped me on my hand and whispered, "You know many of these men here?" I looked around the room and nodded. He exclaimed, "They are four-flushers." I was silenced. He then said, "You should be grateful for who you are and realize I would not have lunch with any of them. You are creating your own life, and someone else does not hand it to you. It is a gift given to you from God. It is your task to figure out how to best use it."

I tasted my vichyssoise; Bob gently tapped my hand and said, "You must give yourself permission to wander into new opportunities."

I reached over for a dinner roll as I responded to his gaze with a blank expression. Momentarily losing my concentration and possibly my composure, I suddenly saw Bob Dylan's countenance overlay my friend's face. Dylanesque odes sprang forth from his lips. I quickly regained my senses. The dining room was otherwise empty. Still, I was self-conscious. Bob glanced at me and continued: "Your motorcycle needs a different road. Your trips have outlived their usefulness. Time for a change, John."

The shaved ice around my vichyssoise was melting, leaving my soup tepid.

Troubadour Bob relentlessly stared at me and observed: "You have had one too many mornings on your bike. The times they are a-changing, John. Lay down that weary motorcycle, and get on a new road."

Bob Valk reappeared in a twinkle of an eye. I felt like we had just rolled and smoked a joint together. Our communion ended. The pow-wow was over. I memorialized this lunch in a journal entry. The sketched map of Colorado's Highway 71, including the detour caused by the washed-out bridge shared with Bob, was folded up and put away. My past bravado and heroic tales did little to capture Bob's interest. Old feats were dust in the wind. *What are you doing with yourself and for yourself today? Time to move into your struggle, John. Time to venture on to the razor's edge.* I noted, without shame and little remorse, that the accounting of this past trip did not impress him. Life was still a daring adventure for Bob. It had little to do with context. It had all to do with process. My perspective—the way I looked at things through my lenses—needed revision. The amendment was an inward journey. It might propel me to other places. Who knows?

The first call of inquiry began with the invitation to visit Cairns, Australia, and then to spend Christmas with Fiona and the girls on the island of New Britain in Papua New Guinea. *Okay, where do I even begin to comprehend this invitation,* I thought, *to jump into a Pandora's box halfway around the world?* I shared the news with Bob. I suspected he was privately snickering.

Fiona's absence was clawing away at me. The tortuous rite of missing someone took on a new meaning. I'd never had a long-distance relationship of this magnitude. The yearning gave way to a decision. I gathered maps and included the islands of New Zealand. For years I had dreamed of motorcycling the south island there. I was on a mission.

My port of entry was Sydney, Australia. I flew north to Cairns and met Fiona and the girls at a hotel. Then all of us flew up to Rabaul, New Britain. This fabled harbor and city that became Japan's South Pacific headquarters and bunker for General Yamamoto during World War II was buried by a volcanic eruption in 1994 and rebuilt as Kokopo. On Christmas Eve day I toured with a nephew of Fiona, Francis, around what was once the most beautiful harbor and through the town ruins, still covered in eight feet of ash. Then we climbed the wasted slope of Mount Tavurvur to the volcano's caldera. I stared down into the stillness, wondering if it would ever erupt again. Thirteen years later, it did—spectacularly—yet this time sparing the town.

On this day, though, the betel nut-stained and litter-spewed town repulsed me with its filth. But the Duke of York Islands in the distant Bismarck Sea were spellbinding. Schools of tuna were so thick the water would churn white, and porpoises would glide along the bow of our boat. My first encounter with Papua New Guineans was framed by my Grosse Pointe perspective: a constant threat of theft, skanky body odor, and betel nut spitting. Yet in the villages the country won, hands down, with the biggest smiles and vigorous arm-waving.

After a week of Christmas festivities, Fiona's sister took the girls, permitting us to take an outboard-powered skiff to the island of New Ireland, east of New Britain. Flying fish skipped along the boat as we maneuvered through the island chain. Pieces of cobalt blue coral were washed up on the white-sand shores of uninhabited islands. The boat owner stopped on an atoll. Fiona and I walked around the island to snorkel naked. The island was ours. There were no intruders. The seclusion was profound. Arriving on the black volcanic sand beach of New Ireland was remarkable, as it was unmarked and secluded. Waiting in the jungle under the palms were three men and a woman. A rental truck was gassed up and ready for us to travel the length of the island, south to north, to reach the capital, Kavieng. For two days we meandered up a beatific coral road, viewing the South Pacific as James Michener once described in his travels. We stayed at the Malagan Lodge and would celebrate New Year's Eve in this port to bring in 2002. At the bar, over rum and cigars, we met the individual who would indulge us to start a fishing business. If he'd had a peg leg, I believe he would have been cast in the movie *Treasure Island*. New Ireland is where Fiona's deceased grandmother's traditional land is located. For the first time in my life, I viewed an uninterrupted coastline with no electricity or modern houses. The unspoiled beauty and unsurveyed reefs struck a primitive chord within me. Compared to the fanfare of the Caribbean Islands, New Ireland was primordial. The island is matrilineal; women by tradition own all the land. No wonder the landscape is so clean. I met both the chief and the sorcerer of her cousin's village, Laraibina. Her cousin Cathy, known as the Eel Lady, feeds up to twenty freshwater pet eels daily as well as on moonlit nights. The sensation of a dozen eels swirling around my legs would be hard to replicate. I was immediately inducted into the Mohotirintz clan, which permitted us to be seen together in public (in private, Fiona and I were already sleeping together) and giving me lifelong shelter. Relics of my rebellious teenage years amusingly emerged, but at the same time I concluded that my country should borrow some of these traditions and bring them back to Grosse Pointe, Michigan.

Within two days of the New Year, we returned to Rabaul. Graciously, Fiona's sister suggested that the girls stay with her at their resort, freeing Fiona and me to fly to New Zealand to pick up my leased Harley-Davidson. There was only one Harley available for the whole south island. The bed-and-breakfast where the motorcycle was stored was located in the city of Christchurch. We partied along a canal one evening with the Kiwis. They extended a friendly warmth to us that was disarming, albeit suspicious at first. I was to learn over the next two weeks that it was genuine. Could it be that my Americanism was somewhat skewed toward paranoia and/or distrust of outsiders in general? Certainly, hailing from Detroit had led me to be a little wary of people's motives, given the financial, economic, and corrupt plight of my dear city. Also, the unpopular fallout of the United States' Iraqi invasion exasperated my thin skin. Between Papua New Guinean villagers' smiles and the initial embraces of the Kiwis, a raging retaliatory war felt contradictory.

The morning was bright and sunny. A chill convinced us to put on our leathers, which I had carted all the way from Detroit. The day's destinations were the towns of Greymouth and Westport, northwest of Christchurch. Not more than fifteen minutes outside the city, I filled up the tank at a petrol station. Across the road and up to my right were two road-tested, ponytailed, and bearded bikers with vintage Harley-Davidsons. One of them had a chopper. They extended themselves by offering a swig of Jack Daniel's. My, oh my, God does work in mysterious ways. We gathered down the road and sipped from the bottle of Jack. They rolled a joint and ceremoniously passed it around. With illegal smiles, Fiona and I mounted our bike and followed these two men. For two days, I experienced the most glorious biking in my life, and Fiona had her arms around me the whole time.

Switchbacking our way up Mount Cook (12,218 feet) was memorable. There was little traffic to contend with; I recounted the congestion at Yellowstone National Park. The kaleidoscope of glaciers, valleys, palm-lined beaches, and mountains ignited me to a sensory overload. We ended up traveling for the day with these gentlemen in Queenstown and then proceeded to Paradise Valley, where a substantial fraction of *The Lord of the Rings* was filmed. Fiona and I dismounted and day-hiked into the forest. The stillness and light drew the two of us into an animated and suspended state. The preciousness of this summation was the closest I have been to the Garden. I was elated and touched the moss and put water from a creek to my lips. Fiona, the landscape, and I became one. Such intimacy and knowledge were unfathomable. I was there.

We reconnected with our biking friends for breakfast on the morning of their departure and were in a jovial mood. Without provocation, the one called Nigel inquired, "John, you aren't from Texas, are you?"

I burst out laughing and replied, "You guys know I am from Detroit. Why would you say that?" Smiling, Morris chimed in, "We know that, but you Yanks are all like Texans. They claim to be the biggest state, the biggest economy, and the biggest politicians and have the biggest wallets. Just like Texans, all of you are the biggest!" Looking down at my crotch, I smiled and knew that might not be true. My grandiosity was deeply engrained. I let them grasp this perception. Yet I reminded them again that I was from Detroit. They cautioned me that most people had not visited America and did think we all acted like we were from Texas. Okay. I pushed a plate of untouched scrambled eggs over to them. I needed to think about that stereotype and questioned if I resonated this image. Reading my mind, they assured me that I was not a Texan and was an exception. I am not sure if I believed them.

Within a year, I was approachable to new opportunities besides my extensive vacations and adventures. My true agenda was to find a way to get to Fiona. A fishing prospect ultimately turned into a business venture. Thank you, Bob Valk (or Bob Dylan?). A deep sea replaced asphalt roads, and my motorcycle was now a fishing vessel. The highway markers were not as visible and predictable. Colorado's Highway 71 was a rehearsal for a bigger play. This trans-world adventure began in 2002. Fiona's aunt was living in Singapore at the time and owned a fishing trawler. She encouraged us to enter the lobster and fishing business. We wanted to purchase her boat, but she could not deliver the vessel to Papua New Guinea due to title issues. Still, we were convinced that entering this business made sense, and we felt emotionally compelled to proceed and to secure another vessel. The bearded Aussie fishing skipper from New Ireland reappeared. We entered a maze.

From high in the air, South Sea islands appear soft and serene. Down on the sea, where John was trying to start a fishing business, "crashing waves churned the water white upon the seemingly inhospitable and ancient shore."

CHAPTER 7

Metal-Metal-Metal

"Invulnerability conjures up the idea of a super-human being, unencumbered by the frailties and foibles that make us vulnerable, less than perfect, in need of each other and, therefore, human."

—Jeremy Rifkin

Early on the morning of February 6, 2003, our boat slowly left its mooring in the harbor of Cairns, Australia. Veering to the port side, the diesel-powered barge headed due north, paralleling the northeastern Australian coast. To the right was the Great Barrier Reef. The day was clear and the water calm as we entered the Coral Sea.

Fiona and her three daughters—Mahealani, Kaia, and Jasmine—waved good-bye from the pier. They receded in the distance as the ten-ton, fifteen-meter-long barge chugged out of the harbor on its way to Papua New Guinea. The steel-hull vessel, propelled by two Gardner V6 diesel engines, would have a top speed of eight to ten knots.

Our new fishing company, Ocean Harvest, had recently assumed the title of the boat that I'm calling the *Bent Sound*. The company was located on the far eastern island of New Ireland, part of an archipelago that stretches for a thousand kilometers east of the main island of Papua New Guinea. Relics of World War II, including battleships, submarines, airplanes, and bunkers, are scattered throughout the archipelago's ocean floor and island jungles.

The *Bent Sound*'s crew consisted of one skipper, first and second mates—all Australians—and one deckhand, a Papua New Guinea native I'll call Marvin. I had been hastily introduced to the three Australians over the last two months. They were a crusty, sea-tested group of men with shaved heads, beards, nicotine-stained teeth, beady eyes, and wiry bodies. Marvin was six foot three, ebony black, and weighed upward of 275 pounds. He hailed from Bougainville, an island east of Papua New Guinea (PNG) that's often compared to World War II's infamous Guadalcanal for its bloody battles. I'd met Marvin two years earlier while open-water diving off the island of New Ireland. I found it easier to understand his broken English than the others' northern Queensland slang. I had eaten, slept, crapped, and dived with Marvin and felt safe having him close while adventuring in this part of the world.

A blind determination took root within us. The further we pursued the business strategy, the greater our commitment grew. It was a decision that eventually got us knee deep in muddy water. Our initial haste, fueled by a romantic notion to run a South Pacific fishing business, eclipsed a more rational approach to create a reliable livelihood for Fiona, her family, and, eventually, me. As an Old Testament proverb says, "A fool soon departeth from his money."

Our voyage of 1,100 nautical miles was calculated to take approximately eleven days, averaging a tedious ten knots in the thirty-three-year-old vessel. Hugging the eastern coast, we would turn due east just below Cape York, Australia, and cross the Great Barrier Reef into the open Coral Sea. Coming up toward the southeastern coast of Papua New Guinea, the *Bent Sound* would cross both the Solomon and Bismarck Seas and enter the Pacific Ocean to eventually arrive in the port of Kavieng, New Ireland.

On a map, this adventure looked predictable, assuming fair weather, an absence of mechanical mishaps, and a sober and drug-free captain and crew. Fair weather was crucial; our vessel was designed for rivers and shoreline navigation, not the open sea. Its forward deck surrounded a large mechanized portal where the catch could be dropped down into the hull for freezer storage. If storm waves arrived, we'd sink and be in the company of fish. I looked out over the barge's bow toward the horizon and felt vulnerable. For a city slicker, I put an immense amount of faith in my skipper's judgment. This added to my uneasiness.

Not more than two hours into the trip, the *Bent Sound* was rockin', musically and otherwise. Bundaberg Rum flowed freely, and a gigantic bong brimming with marijuana was ablaze. My misjudgments were coming home to haunt me. Yet again, I ignored my intuition and chose to imbibe the rum and take a turn or two with the bong. Marvin abstained. Thank God.

My rising anxiety turned into paranoia. The rum and weed, combined with the unfamiliarity of the group and the daunting open sea, played mind games with me.

As I gazed into the azure-blue water, a shallow coral-colored surface appeared. We were crossing the Great Barrier Reef, and it was quite a spectacle. I realized I was crossing over one of nearly three thousand reefs spanning 1,600 miles. The distance was as far as from Detroit to Miami Beach. Remembering NASA pictures of the GBR from outer space, I began to feel diminutive. This was a different orientation. It was an inward spectacle. Again, I was moving forward. I was back on the "razor's edge." There are seven wonders of the natural world, yet of the inward world I could not name one. People in general are more interested in public displays than private performances. Yet this display was a visually striking performance. My travel halfway around the world to the Great Barrier Reef made me comprehend that my interior life might be more remarkable and indelible.

We turned off the engines and dropped fishing lines into the water. We were soon rewarded with a catch of coral trout. This white, flakey meat has a taste similar to lobster and the texture of eastern halibut. For dinner, we fried up the fish with onions and potatoes and sipped on iced Australian pale ale. The sun set behind our backs; the horizon turned pink as we enjoyed a fine meal.

A daily ritual soon became routine as duties were assigned. I preferred the graveyard shift, which assured me solitude. The clear nights rewarded me with constellations and shooting stars. I was dancing with eternity. Trade winds cooled the evenings and salted my senses. The drone of the engines imbued me with a familiar *terza rima*. Cloud formations on the horizon, lit by the rising sun, radiated maize yellow, turning to a buttery cream before vanishing as milky wisps.

The skipper informed me we were less than an hour from land, close to the China Strait. My vision played tricks on me. The forms of other vessels and rafts appeared so real but were revealed to be only mirages. The depth of the Coral Sea haunted me as well. I could not comprehend how the *Bent Sound* was one mile above the bottom. I stood on a low metal bench on the bow, trying to spot land. The *Bent Sound*'s gentle bow wake interrupted stream after stream of thick plankton interwoven with palm leaves, coconuts, and debris. I was disturbed by the endless river of strewn garbage and non-degradable refuse. I surmised it would end up on a distant shoreline. How long can we continue such asinine habits? Looking 180 degrees from port to starboard, I saw no land. Then a vague outline darkened the horizon. Eventually, a dark-green peninsula appeared, protruding into the China Strait. The moss-covered land extended to a shore scattered with massive rocks. The crashing waves churned the water white upon the seemingly inhospitable and ancient shore. We veered northeastward and headed into the Solomon Sea. I felt lonely and small.

A week of hard work as a deck hand, combined with the daily boredom of sitting and staring at the open sea, quelled my initial enthusiasm. I was anxious to jump-start the business. I yearned to get to port. I missed Fiona and, for some reason, I felt unsure of the Aussies.

Travel on the *Bent Sound* had its numerous inconveniences. My daily hygiene, which the Aussies called APCs (armpits and crotches), consisted of pouring buckets of seawater over me, followed by a rinse with desalinized water. The constant presence of sharks eliminated swimming as an option.

The lack of bathroom facilities meant taking a pee off the side of the ship and maneuvering one's behind over the railing to take care of other business. I find it curious and humorous that in all of documented history, including novels, autobiographies, and movies, there is little mention of these basic functions. It is one activity that helps establish connectivity, a common touch point for all humankind!

The vessel was headed north into the Solomon Sea when the desalinization equipment failed. Aside from the inconvenience of no showers, the more pressing problem was that we had no drinking water. I immediately began to get thirsty. Images of stranded sailors on rafts and lost parties wandering aimlessly on deserts jumped to mind as I scurried to the pilot house to find out what we were going to do.

The skipper, with his filthy red beard, yellow teeth, and odious breath, murmured the name of an island called Iwa and pointed to it on his computer screen. It was located northwest of the outer Marshall Bennett Islands and east of the Trobriand Islands. This was the dust speck the *Bent Sound* was moving toward. Our estimated arrival time was four hours. He was hoping for a safe harbor to steady the vessel in order to make the repairs, which required a dive beneath the boat.

Chugging through the sea, I sensed nervousness among the Aussies. It occurred to me that they had never ventured out of Australian waters. They were spooked by the prospect of dealing with indigenous people. Stereotyping, racism, and sexism were rampant in northern Queensland, and these good ol' boys were now in what for them were uncharted waters. Their cockiness began to subside.

I saw a dot on the horizon. I hoped it was the island we were in search of, as it loomed larger and larger. As we grew closer, I had a perfect view of a remote South Pacific island. Cliffs rose on both ends, separated by a palm-tree-lined white beach. Crystal turquoise water sparkled in the lagoon we entered. We didn't see inhabitants until we dropped anchor.

Suddenly, scores of natives carrying dugout canoes on their shoulders streamed out of the jungle into the water, chanting loudly in a dialect I hoped Marvin would recognize. The bearded, light-skinned, freckle-faced Aussies turned a shade of white that resembled the color of an enameled refrigerator door. I wondered if any of them crapped in their shorts.

Marvin encouraged the Aussies to calm down while he took charge.

I felt like I was witnessing a repeat performance of the epic movie *Mutiny on the Bounty*, substituting these PNG natives for Tahitians.

Within minutes, the vessel was surrounded. At least two dozen small-masted sea canoes with radiant blue, red, and yellow sails edged toward the *Bent Sound*. They were a colorful spectacle, filled with piles of fruit, coconuts, and reef fish. Women, children, and young men joined in, chanting, laughing, and talking excitedly with one another. Who would have the courage to climb aboard? I could see the eagerness in their faces.

Once they encircled the vessel, they started to pound their fists on the boat in unison, repeatedly yelling, "Metal, metal, metal." The commotion drew dozens of spectators out to the beach from hidden huts.

The first nonnative vessel to be seen in quite some time was a big deal to these people. My crew's enthusiasm and confidence plummeted as the locals started to climb aboard the *Bent Sound*.

Marvin tried in vain to keep them off the ship. The younger men carried bush knives, while the skipper suffused distress. He hastily departed to his berth. I assumed he went to retrieve his revolver. To my relief, I did not see a weapon, but I was assured he had one.

Nevertheless, a genuine warmth and openness surfaced immediately between the crew and island villagers. The gifts of fruit and coconuts put the Aussies at ease, but I sensed they were craving a hit from that bong. Their stoicism was fading, revealed by their softer and smiling faces.

Standing on the deck, a village man with fuzzy orange-blond hair, light-brown face, and gleaming white teeth asked in broken English, "Are we at war? Are we safe?" Another man, from an island requiring three days of paddling, had brought the news of the Afghanistan invasion. I was perplexed. Fear is viral and has few boundaries. From the Potomac River think-tankers in Washington, DC, to a microdot island village in the

Solomon Sea, we are interconnected. I grasped his hand and replied, "Don't be afraid. You are safe." I gauged his reaction. He was relieved. I believe he trusted me.

My digital camera and the skipper's computer screen were firsts for these islanders. Their gleefulness, hilarity, and spontaneity were electric. Fun filled the bow of the *Bent Sound* as the children swarmed around me to watch as I replayed their expressions on my camera.

After making the necessary repairs and adjustments, we departed late that afternoon, heading north for the island of East New Britain, straight across the Solomon Sea. The villagers lined up on the beach shoulder-to-shoulder, waving and chanting good-bye. The island soon became another mercurial dot on the horizon as the sun set and darkness overcame the day.

Cabin lights were switched on, and music began to play. I inserted Van Morrison's *Hymns to the Silence* into the captain's CD player. We filled cups with rum. I climbed up to the roof to gaze at the stars and ponder what I had seen, especially those pounding fists reverberating along with the chant "metal, metal, metal." Far removed in the background of my mind I grasped the exuberance and kindness of the islanders. Provoked by a steel hull next to their canoes hollowed out of palm trunks, their astonished faces, without pretense, gave me an unforgettable lesson about invulnerability. I believe they were vulnerable and more courageous than we were. The Southern Cross was dimly visible at the moment. Yet I knew it would be a guiding light. I slipped into the solitude of the night and reflected on the day's adventure.

CHAPTER 8

The Fiasco

"You are called to the realm of adventure; you are called to new horizons. Each time, there is the same problem—do I dare? And then if you do dare, the dangers are there, and the help also, and the fulfillment or the fiasco. There's always the possibility of a fiasco. But there's also the possibility of bliss."

—Joseph Campbell

I felt a great sense of accomplishment as we dropped anchor in the port town of Kavieng, New Ireland. The vessel idled in aqua-blue water. The main island was three hundred feet west and two smaller islands were less than a quarter mile east. The setting was idyllic. Poignant colors spawned by the first sunrise and sunset were mesmerizing. French Impressionist Gauguin never left Tahiti. Romantic inclinations surged as I flowed into this tempo. Sailboats and catamarans were moored off the inlets. North, at least a mile away, large commercial fishing boats were at rest from pillaging the open sea for tuna. These behemoths were emblems of the unfettered fishing and illegal business practices I would soon grasp. We posted a local who was a brother of Marvin's wife, Lola, as a guard and to keep rascals at bay. Bandits would stalk one's activity and wait for the moment to board an unassuming vessel. With their banana-boat engines turned off, they would float with the current and quietly find a way to steal whatever was removable. It made no difference what the object was.

Everything was utilized and saleable in this remote landscape. My mind was beginning to comprehend the pervasiveness of the theft. Yet I refused to put a label on a culture I barely knew. As I'd grown up in the metropolitan community of Detroit, a bystander might point out that I was too narrow-minded and politically incorrect and could fall prey to stereotyping and bigotry. Such refrains kept my judgmentalism at bay.

Another day drifted by as we waited for Customs to board our vessel and give us clearance to come ashore. Then I checked into the Malagan Lodge and immediately took a long hot shower, exorcising body odor, sea salt, diesel fuel, and fried food. Be gone, Aussie brekkies (breakfasts)! I would not miss the burned sausages, tinned beans, and eggs. Fiona was flying in from East New Britain Island that afternoon. Splashing on aftershave cologne, I envisioned myself as the seasoned sailor returning from the sea, running along the pier into his wife's embrace.

Fiona and I were soon reviewing the execution of the business plan. I had limited capital, precious little time, few assets, and scant knowledge of fishing. By Harvard Business School standards, none of the components for a successful venture was present. Instead, visions and mappings driven by a proactive American mind-set fueled our grandiosity. We assumed, through a memorandum of understanding, that our business was legally sound and, therefore, enforceable. We also assumed an alignment of business ethics and values among all parties that were mutually understood and agreed to. In fact, I even created a set of assumptions to test my conditions. This presumptuous ball of yarn began to unravel as soon as I took that first bong hit while we chugged along the Australian coast. Deeply embedded precepts would erase better business judgment and diminish the courage needed to stop this unfolding odyssey.

Fiona and I were well aware of our vulnerabilities as we entered into the daily operations. We were not fishermen. Period. Our start-up organization's local village representatives and the *Bent Sound*'s skipper were meant to mitigate such danger by simply collecting the fish from a village network. The fish would be filleted, wrapped, and frozen. The load would be brought back to a refrigerated shed for storage and then shipped to the local commercial market. At every step, payment would be immediate. It was a cash-and-carry business. Unfortunately, the cash-and-carry went to the extreme.

We assembled a base team to build a village collection network, utilizing the *Bent Sound* as the mother ship. Three banana boats (open eight-meter skiffs) with 50-horsepower Johnson engines would pick up reef fish, lobster, and *beche de mere* (sea cucumbers) along the northern coast of New Ireland and the island of New Hanover. This initial area encompassed fifty to sixty miles and thirty villages. Legal licenses were acquired, and all the elements needed to run the company were in place, including equipment, office, staff, and buyers for the product. Yours truly financed all of this. Fiona was required to put up additional collateral, as the original catch forecast was too optimistic.

Daily awareness meetings to expand and train the village network demanded we rise at 4:30 a.m. to board a banana boat. I have never worked so hard, even when laboring on a Chrysler assembly line night shift when I was twenty years old.

One particular February morning in 2003, I rose early to join the skipper, first and second mates, and one local crew member. We departed for New Hanover and the more remote island of Tingwon, which required one hour of travel on open sea. The swells were big and intimidating. I kept wondering what would happen if the engine quit on us. Global positioning systems, phones, or radios were not available. We did have an extra fifty-gallon drum of petrol on board to ensure our return by sunset.

The sun rose beyond the low-lying islands. The inlets mirrored the vibrant pinkness of the sunrise. Palm trees majestically lined the beaches, reaching up to gentle emerald mountains. The beauty seeped into me; I felt fluid and soulful. We passed bamboo huts clustered together in one village after another as our banana boat and crew traveled northwest to open sea and Tingwon Island. The calmness of the sleepy villages reminded me that this uninterrupted place was perhaps in the Creator's capable hands and had been for a long time. Who or what would want to perturb something so unmistakably unperturbed?

Within two hours, we sighted Tingwon Island. The sudden ferocity of the surf quickly ended the relaxation of the cruise across open sea. The sound of waves pounding on jagged coral put my senses on high alert, causing me to wonder if we would reach shore alive. Waves washed over the boat. It was a white-knuckler, giving me pause to glimpse within myself, as I had at the Great Barrier Reef. The geography of purpose is infinite. *Why am I doing? What I am doing?* Would meaning crystallize, affording me an inner view of the significance this risk meant to me? We eventually made it to a beach in one piece.

Villagers assisted in carrying our knapsacks to shore and securing our skiff to a palm tree. The unadorned beauty of the setting suddenly overtook me, making me feel alive yet fragile. James Michener remarked that this corner of the South Pacific was the most unspoiled and untouched in its beauty. Tingwon's dark-green landscape contrasted with the indigo ocean, with its snow-colored, foaming surf. For a moment, in a state of awe, the boundaries of space and time were transcended.

I was the main man. The crew member spoke the local dialect and acted as an interpreter. The community bell, a rusted World War II torpedo shell, was suspended between two poles on a rope. If banged with an axe head for five minutes, it told outlying villagers that a meeting was to start. A prayer followed salutations from one of the elders. The chief was emphatic in his opening statement: "We have already seen the Dutch, the Germans, the Australians, and the Japanese. Now you, an American, visit us. What are you going to do to help us? What are you going to do that will be any different?" I was a long way from my Grosse Pointe office and the customary conference table and whiteboard with an associate taking notes, and the assurance that comes from rehearsing the meeting that will, of course, be like previous sessions.

Sitting cross-legged on a palm log, barefoot and wearing cut-offs and a faded Rolling Stones T-shirt, my response was spontaneous, pragmatic, and cautious. I was nervous yet mindful and explained that we would be different. I was there to build a means for the islanders to sell fish and for all of us to make money. I exuded an air of self-confidence and assurance that together we would succeed. The collecting of fish would commence by the next moon (within thirty days). I ended my story and was self-assured. These ruminations were accelerating at a rapid pace. I did not comprehend my myopia.

The return trip was awarded a sunset for a long day "on the road." Our general manager and Marvin's wife, Lola, were waiting on the pier to debrief with the group. Lola had been a friend of Fiona for twenty-five years and had managed a car-rental franchise at the Malagan Lodge before we hired her. Again, we assumed that shared values and the qualities of transparency and honesty were intact. We established the rules of engagement for the Aussie crew: no fooling around with island women, no drinking in public, and no drugs. The first mate's nickname was Ab, short for abnormal. His real name was Norman. The first week on shore, he bedded down a married woman in our office, drank in local pubs, and got townspeople high on marijuana. The island police received a complaint and visited our office. They issued a stiff warning, threatening to instruct Customs officials to search our vessel, if necessary. That truly ended the open marijuana use, although I suspected there was a stash in the engine room. I feared that our skipper was an addict and a liar. Problems yet unforeseen were on the horizon. He played me like a violin by telling me whatever I wanted to hear.

Unfortunately, with the weed gone, the skipper went into withdrawal. Paranoia and aggressiveness crept into this beady-eyed character. Outside my presence, he snarled at the crew and Fiona. These behaviors were commonplace as I departed New Ireland.

Stateside commitments required me to fly back to Australia and then to America to resume my management consulting business. I had to leave Fiona and the team. Fiona subsequently departed for Cairns the next week to see her children.

To this day, I still cannot comprehend how our company literally disappeared within the next thirty days. We soon understood what a cash-and-carry business was. Australian slang describes such amazement, wonder, or disbelief as "fuck me dead, gently dead." By Wall Street standards, this was unremarkable, but for Fiona and me it was remarkable indeed.

Sociopathic sirens with Herculean power drew us into harm's way.

Fiona was forlorn. Speaking to me from Papua New Guinea, she made it clear the company was coming unhinged. On the positive side, we were achieving our initial daily collection goal of one hundred kilos (225 pounds) of reef fish and lobster. Ocean Harvest would be delivering a ton of product per week within the month. Not bad. But the skipper detested the progress. Negativism was increasing. What was going on here? A hidden agenda, perhaps? I wouldn't believe it. I wanted to be right at any cost. Shove that square peg into the round hole. The ingredients of a strong case of cognitive dissonance were brewing within this expert consultant. I could not be wrong.

We concluded that the business was working but not the skipper. It was time to replace him and send him back to Australia, never to return. His attitude was vulgar. Besides, he had broken the legal contract; he had failed to manage the crew. He failed to take control of Norman, the first mate, and hold him accountable. We had an enforceable agreement.

Fiona flew back to Cairns to bring up a replacement. The only people privy to this decision were the office manager, Lola, and her husband, Marvin. The new skipper and Fiona arrived five days later to discover no vessel, no crew, no equipment, no frozen product, no cash, no Marvin, and no Lola.

We later concluded that they had absconded with the *Bent Sound* and paid off Customs officials, believing that through legal maneuvers they could re-register the boat in Australia and resume the fishing business themselves, minus Fiona and me.

Fiona tracked down Lola and Marvin in a posh Port Moresby hotel, paid for by our former skipper, where they were awaiting approval for the *Bent Sound* to successfully leave PNG waters. Police took the culprits to a holding cell. Australian Customs authorities, alerted to the situation, were waiting for our vessel to enter their waters. The scheme had unraveled, and we became the plaintiffs in a three-year lawsuit. Degraded and mortified, Fiona and I were drawn into a protracted legal battle. The defendants seemed to perceive my wife as a black islander in white skin and me as an imposing, dimwit Yankee city slicker. Australian pub jargon, first inspired by the Vietnam conflict and now anti–Iraq War sentiment, was "Yank, Yank, septic tank." I felt culturally disenfranchised by Papua New Guinea and by North Queensland, Australia. Was I being overly sensitive?

The legal proceedings would ultimately render us a settlement at a Supreme Court hearing, with wigs, barristers, hanging judge, solicitors, and all. The real beneficiaries were, of course, the solicitors for both parties, thanks to the intractable and intransigent behavior of the skipper. He never believed we would drag him into court. His beard had grown down to his waist by the time of the hearing, which he attended in combat boots and shorts.

According to *A Dinkum Guide to Oz English*, the Australian slang translation for what happened to two honest victims who'd gotten taken by a cheat was "bunnies who got the rough end of the pineapple by a wrangler who was as slippery as a butcher's penis."

Who looked more foolish in this fiasco? Who reverted more to intransigence and denial, as things did not work out as mapped and planned? I would opine on these questions in the future. I quickly retreated into my consulting practice in America in order to mitigate the financial losses and possibly find solace and advice among other change consultants. I was beginning to understand the maxim to "know what you don't know." It was not such a shameful and vulnerable posture to be in, even though I'd had little practice in such remedies. The Zen cowboy from Montana flashed into my mind as he reached down from his horse to pick up that six-pack of beer: "It is what it is. It ain't what it ain't." By all accounts, this truly was an extraordinary fiasco.

Albion College English professor Dr. John Hart in his library. He introduced freshman John to the concept of the hero's journey, and their friendship became long-lasting. "Hart would compel me to have a good conversation with myself."

CHAPTER 9

Abeyance

"Religion, particularly at the present time, holds a difference between the revelatory communication that we have through scriptures and the revelation we have with our experiences of the natural world. There's a tendency to diminish one in favor of the other. But this is a qualitative difference, not a contradiction."

—Thomas Berry

"Tester" would be a fitting word for the year 2003. On New Year's Eve, late afternoon, I had a grand bowel movement and flushed the year down the toilet. My ex-skipper and my island associates Lola and Marvin were symbolically included in this biological act.

Endings were not as defined and clear-cut for Fiona. The big NBD (nervous breakdown) almost came a-knockin'. Lola's treachery was a gut punch, and Fiona had trouble catching her breath. Betrayal was a bitter pill to swallow. And whether she'd been bitten by mosquitoes in Papua New Guinea or upon her return to Australia, she was infected. A bout of cerebral dengue fever almost sank her. The seriousness of this sickness did not impact me until I returned to Cairns to be with her and the girls for Christmas. Her emaciated body was a manifestation of not only the fever but also her inner forlornness.

She survived; the foundation of Fiona's character is her resilience. What deeply confounded us, though, was an understanding of justice. The concept seemed to be an elusive hope as we tried to piece together the caper and mount a lawsuit. The lawyers were obliging and were convinced, as we thought, that we had a sound legal case.

Planning for 2004 was a murky affair. The financial farce of Ocean Harvest and acquiring the *Bent Sound* cost us dearly. Legal fees were mounting, with more to come. Australia's lawyers also were a cash-and-carry lot, stipulating "no cash, no service." They always seemed to know when the meter needed reloading. It's a very tight-fisted industry, with a touch of smugness, exceeding our wild bunch in America.

I began to reorient and adapt myself to a consulting cycle in America, coaching company owners and CEOs. Helping my clients identify and deal with their problems was surreal. I was frequently distracted as I reflected on my Papua New Guinea experience and its larger meaning. Creating energy was a precious commodity for this pilgrim. The scarcity of it made my own rehabilitation efforts personally challenging. I was deflated.

I soon settled into a ninety-day consulting routine—three months in America—followed by one month in Australia during 2004–2007. Eventually, I managed more time for Australia and Papua New Guinea by working six months at a time in America.

Supporting two households, three young girls, and a lawsuit was a strain. Northwest Airlines (now Delta) and Qantas Airlines profited. Narita Airport outside of Tokyo reminded me of industrial Gary, Indiana. I often was forced to stay overnight, and was shuttled to a hotel after flying out of Cairns, Australia. The average flying time was twenty-three hours. Layovers were another reality that bordered on self-torture.

The Coral Sea fishing caper was fading as I repositioned my life into this consulting humdrum. Strangely, I felt urgings and aches from deep within. I had little control over these affections; in fact, I desired them. Novelist Pat Conroy called it "the pearly ache." I did not want these inward stirrings to subside. I quietly acquiesced to the curiosities of intuition, hope, and faith. These leanings seemed to be natural, and I offered little resistance to them. This reach for knowledge was not to relieve the ache but to encourage me to explore my longings and paths of understanding. It is an act of renewal, as opposed to a restoration. There may have been a redemptive thread in this emotional conundrum, but the well I was digging was far deeper than I reckoned. I sought a new foundation, akin to tinkering with the structure of a building or the course of a river. The word *inward* took on new meaning, helping me to apprehend that this was my path, not a reenactment or a priori. The abruptness of this fiasco and my willfulness to proceed affirmed that I was still curious.

I wrestled with the spiritual dimension of my traveling path. The skirmishes with darkness and light rattled my cage. In hindsight, I was seized by the thought that during our initial sojourn, the *Bent Sound* skipper and crew had only to push me overboard into the Coral Sea. For the skipper, this option would have been far less complicated.

My spiritual-ontological inclinations became more pronounced. I read, meditated, motorcycled, and attended an inner-city church in Detroit. I found solace in the congregation's diversity. The church's mission to serve the homeless struck a chord, encouraging me to get involved.

I was stilled by evenings of solitude, including sipping Earl Grey tea. The poems of Rumi were a gentle reminder that the knowledge I was seeking "is a fountainhead from within you, moving out . . . a tablet one already completed and preserved inside you. A spring overflowing in its spring box. A freshness in the center of the chest. . . . It's fluid, it doesn't move from outside to inside through the conduits of 'plumbing-learning.'" Our proclivities to pedagogy, self-help texts, and a convenient computer application run counter to this thinking.

I meditated on the mysticism of this thirteenth-century poet as I embraced the personal encounters of patriarchs, like Jacob, found in the Old Testament's Pentateuch. I sought a capacious insight from these sources, seeking to gain a deeper and possibly more absolute faith. My educated peers remarked that this mystical inquiry—or, for the most part, mysticism in general—was futile. They claimed that such mystery is unfathomable, and I should let it be. It is what it is. I protested with faith and asserted, like the Sufi Rumi, that I wanted to see God and be seen by God. One may ask, "Well, did you get a good look at God? And did God have a good look at you?" Yes, as the autumn leaves were falling and my fireplace was crackling, a white coal—whiter than all the other embers—seared my thoughts with stillness. I was cooled down and, at the same time, purged of the past and freed of the future. I was there, even if it was but for a moment. I should have taken a digital picture of the event. It escaped me. I did not want this "pearly ache" to subside. I enjoyed a good mystery.

The aches and pains of becoming spiritually disjointed are graphically shared in Jacob's wrestling match with God. The passage helped me to find "the courage to be—a courage to being—itself," as theologian Paul Tillich comments. The King James Version of the Old Testament's translation of Jacob's one-on-one encounter with God encouraged me. I realized that my perfectionist drive to always have my shit together was a fallible process, yet an admirable pursuit.

The wrestling match was an act of courage. I wanted to enter into the mind of God in order to reach a higher consciousness and a consequent new way of being. Like a wrestling match, this can be a dirty, sweaty, and smelly affair; I gained glimpses of my core rot in secret places. Rottenness is somewhat jarring to accept. It is not a denouncement on the nature of men and women or an irreparable condition. Although, in a blaming society, we sure contrive our way out of our own shit and go to great lengths to obscure our inner hubris. Playwright Henrik Ibsen infers we all have our "vital lies" or fatal flaws. Without them, we would sear ourselves with the reality of who we really are: imperfect. This is a wrestling match of a different sort. It evolves and seems to be subtle and dialectic, gently spiraling us to a different perspective. However, inner beauty seems to appear like intruding cracks of light in remote spaces at the same time. The magic of this alchemy is to recognize one is dependent on the other.

Spending more time in Australia, I realized the so-called "culture of death," characterized by materialism, consumerism, technology, and scientific reductionism, was on a par with—possibly above—America and Europe.

An Australian term used in the far north Queensland is "fairy," which is someone who believes in the unseen and metaphysical world. A fairy is a person who does not feel bound by the natural laws of the universe and hence is from Fairyland. For the materialist, the only thing that matters is matter. Seems simple and to the point. Unfortunately, the blind persistence binds the two opposing camps in gridlock. Sadly, we are flitting away our future. Religious and political stripes don't count. As a human race, we are in serious need of resolution to move beyond the horns of this dilemma. As I view the entropy and destruction of the planet Earth, I have similar misgivings about our global family.

An English professor, Dr. John Hart, introduced me to the concept of the hero's journey when I was a freshman in 1965 at Albion College. Loren Eiseley's book *The Immense Journey* was my first required text and was followed by a stream of authors, including Homer, Swift, Conrad, Dreiser, Thoreau, Emerson, Wordsworth, Hesse, Steinbeck, C. S. Lewis, Bunyan, Salinger, and more. All of Dr. Hart's reading assignments were underscored by Eiseley's admonition to seek "a minor sun." The inward journey never ends. As a seeker, one may find truth and wisdom along the way. In fact, the journey is the reward.

In September 2004, I rode my motorcycle to Albion, Michigan, from Grosse Pointe to visit John Hart. Our friendship has grown over the years, and, to paraphrase Ralph Waldo Emerson, "I would walk one hundred miles in a snowstorm to have a good conversation" with a gentleman like John Hart.

We dined at the local Burger King for lunch. He refused to let me pay for his cheeseburger, fries, and Coke and drove us to our get-together. Self-reliance and forward motion were still definite traits, undiminished by his eighty and some years. In the preface to his book *Heroes and Pilgrims*, Professor Hart writes, "Self-achievement never has and never will mean self-reliance on self. Whether man is chained in Plato's cave or is an Odysseus engulfed in the arms of Calypso, the hero needs help, an awareness from without, an impulse from within, a guide or goad that prompts him to act."

As John munched on his burger and fries, he asked: "Have you seen the new clock on campus? It is much like the same clock we always had. The Science Quadrant wanted its clock. The old one in the Humanities Quadrant still works. Now we have two clocks. Some people think one clock tells better time than the other. Oh! It makes little difference to me. Well, there you are."

Professor Hart whispered the last phrase as he fetched a French fry and waited expectantly for me to respond to his coyness. His genteel abruptness in concluding this line of conversation with "Well, there you are" vexed me. He obviously was trying to trick or, rather, inspire me again, as he had more than forty years before, to have an inner dialogue when time permitted. As I recall, those times were infrequent due to fraternity parties, pretty girls, taverns, and sports. Did I fail to mention studies? I always thought I was making good time. But now he knew I would bike home the following fall day along the back roads of southeast Michigan and possibly be more receptive and responsive and make a different type of time. Possibly he assumed I was less distracted at this point in my life and had finally figured out that the path he was talking about was always there. On a motorcycle, I would assuredly move into the present as I focused on the fall foliage. I communed with the season. It reminded me of redemption and a promise of renewal.

John Hart knew I was hooked and he would compel me to have a good conversation with myself. As he wrote in *Heroes and Pilgrims*: "The story of human nature and of human behavior remains universal. History, it has been said, never repeats itself. Man always does. Man does not create the process of change; he, too, is only part of the process of mutability which forces him into endless acts of repetition."

I departed early the next morning. The brightness of the rising sun radiated. My outward and inward senses were expanding to reach out for the territory ahead. Savoring the autumn air, my adrenaline surged as my Harley-Davidson warmed up and rumbled.

Professor Hart adopted the phrase "well, there you are" from author Henry James, brother of psychologist William James. I was now moving into a "stream of consciousness," aided by a winding country road headed east, back to Detroit.

I pondered the Burger King conversation, stymied by John's abruptness with the image of the two clocks. He provoked me. The dualistic posture of the clocks did not fit into my gestalt. The archetype interrupted my fluidity, and I felt disempowered. Annoyance simmered as I biked through Calhoun County with its myriad lakes. I wanted an easier and accommodating path that would shirk self-knowledge. I demanded immediate answers on my terms. Endless acts of repetition had little appeal for me. Entrapped and pained by past box canyons, I wanted expeditious solutions. Give me the crib notes. "There you are."

What is *there*? Where does *there* go? Where is *there* now? What difference does it make whether it is *there* or not *there*? Hmmm . . . what about the thereafter or thereabouts?

I biked into Jackson County, suspending this conversation, but the two clocks emerged as I gazed into the sun. Uh-oh: I needed a surgeon's scalpel, biking into the maze of county roads looping around innumerable lakes. I feared I was going in circles. The concentration required to be conscious of not ending up in a circle was tiring. It would have been far easier to keep unconscious and unaware. To my alarm and realization, becoming lost was an enormously easier task. I was convinced I had passed this road sign already. Occam's razor would be useful. Problems of induction, such as two equally imposing and accurate clocks, demand a heuristic maxim: The simpler theories are easier to understand and are more likely to be correct. Is truth so readily accessible?

My impulse was to reconcile the two clocks. I recalled having been down this road before. The scalpel was skillfully in hand as I slowed down to see a solitary yet gloriously full oak tree in a distant plowed cornfield. It was there. In the moment, a simpler theory grasped me. I did not have to view clocks in opposition. Deep within the machinations of each is contained an integrity and symmetry that accepts one another's otherness. Presto! The binary cut-point segmentation was completed. I felt relieved. I viewed the clocks from a different perspective. Both of them were integral. They needed one another. "What does this insight have to do with anything?" I murmured.

Nevertheless, I was feeling less defiant. The Papua New Guinea island of Tingwon appeared in my mind's eye. Its elders smiled and murmured: "John, you are here. Whether a Dutch, German, or Australian, it does not make a difference. In spirit we are one. As a human being, we are one, yet we are very different from one another. As the elders of this village, we are one, yet our clans are very different. You gave to us who you are. We thank you for that. It is good enough. We recognize our oneness, yet prize our uniqueness."

Whether one clock was theoretic and the other non-theoretic made little difference. The difference was how I would view the clocks. Whether the clocks were standing apart or standing together depended on how and when I chose to view them. Both of the clocks endeavored to tell the correct time. I felt my misplaced anger dissipate, while my sense of trust and forgiveness grew. My inner wounds continued to heal.

Traffic started to increase, and I was soon in Livingston County. I was still traveling east, within forty-five minutes of home in Wayne County.

Bill Plotkin, the author of *Nature and the Human Soul*, clarified what I am trying to express. He, along with mentor Thomas Berry, describes adulthood as having the capacity to appreciate the complementary character of opposites, which he believes are different but harmonious expressions of a single thing.

Berry further affirms that two things rightly understood tend to be complementary rather than contradictory. He evolves this form of eldership perspective and says: "I think of elder hood, on the other hand, as the easing of the tension of opposites in favor of identity or the serenity of fulfillment. That's why we have the expression 'to understand is to forgive.' Elder hood is a time for fulfillment and forgiveness. It is a time for peace."

I assumed John Hart was banking on his former student to begin to understand these things. The trick is that such understanding requires a beginner's mind. Now, how was I to acquire a beginner's mind in my late fifties?

As I continue to morph/transform into another season of my life, I embrace my current condition. I do not know what I know. Yet now a new understanding has emerged: I can recognize wisdom from both the most obvious places, like John Hart, and also an unlikely place, like an oak tree.

I sensed there is much more that I don't see. The self-responsibility of elderhood may transcend past misunderstandings and futile urgings to remedy one clock at the demise of the other. To accept each one in its right is a lofty thought. To do this without succumbing to my most basic psychological needs will be challenging. I like to be liked. Also, I have always desired hassle-free and instant knowledge. This gratification was routine and socially acceptable. After all, the shortest distance between two points is a straight line. It is all about expediency. The alchemy of today's ride was enough inner exploration for one day. I arrived safely back home and slept soundly.

Stafford, right, standing with his wife and the author, was chief of Tabuane, the village where John and Fiona would marry, make their home, and build their business. As a young man, Stafford was the first person to bring coffee seeds—Jamaican Blue Mountain—to his plateau. Now "this wiry old man could see right through me."

CHAPTER 10

Stafford

"Words exist because of meaning. Once you've gotten the meaning, you can forget the words. Where can I find a man who has forgotten words so I can talk with him?"

—Chuang Tzu

My interest in Papua New Guinea waned as I let go of the fishing business fiasco. I had gone cold on the country of Papua New Guinea, and my feelings toward Australian fisherman in particular were even frostier. Not surprisingly, I became judgmental and stereotyped Papua New Guinea and Aussies in general. My egoism abounded. Ironically, at the same time, I felt deprecated as an American by a megalomaniac president conducting two wars simultaneously. I gained little admiration for being a Yankee. This was a throwback to the Vietnam era, where I had felt like a political and social misfit as I traveled abroad. The people, at least in northern Queensland, initially concealed their disdain for Americans. Numerous pubs, barbecues, and drinking bouts with a plethora of Aussies finally brought their opinions and stereotypes to the surface. Incredulously, their tales reached back to World War II, Vietnam, and then to our current messes. Pride, anger, and mistrust surfaced. Why should I be held responsible for other people's acts and behaviors? In their minds, there was no difference. I was taken back to a campfire one long night on the island of Crete in April 1970. While I was sipping ouzo and passing around a bowl of black hashish, a broad-shouldered woman from Sweden harangued me on the Vietnam War. Her nuance distinguished the conversation, as opposed to my Aussie friends. As revolting as the war was, she reminded me, as a human being, that we were in this together. There was an absence of condescension in her aura.

Fiona renewed contact in early 2005 with an eco-activist I'll call Uttera Notok. (For this book, I've changed his name and those of a number of other persons, but they are all real people. Very real.) Uttera had successfully fought with politicians and the mining and logging bigwigs. Fiona and Uttera first met in 1996. She had helped Oro Province in Papua New Guinea gain financing from the United Nations renewable energy program for a hydroelectric power project. Although approval was awarded, the project died when the partnering non-governmental organization in the country did not follow through on all the necessary paperwork and procedures.

Uttera was from the village of Serafuna, located in the Managalas Plateau of Oro Province, which was north of the country's capital, Port Moresby. He was one of two university graduates from this remote area. Uttera urged Fiona to fly into Oro Province and drive up to the Managalas Plateau to witness the plight of thousands of angry coffee farmers who were burning their crops rather than continuing to deal with unscrupulous coffee buyers. Since first planting their coffee in 1963, the farmers had received few benefits, whether under Australian colonial rule or after gaining independence in 1975. Greed is universal and seemingly has no limits.

Warpa Kephale, a schoolmate of Uttera who was living

in the village of Tabuane, about ten hours' walking distance from Serafuna, was the area's other university graduate. Uttera wanted Fiona to meet with Warpa, see the farmers' predicament, and assess the possibility of improving their circumstances.

Starting from her home in Cairns, Fiona took two plane trips to get to the town of Popondetta, followed by a five-hour drive to the plateau and five hours hiking to Tabuane. Her feet cramped from trekking up Kweno Mountain in an all-day rain. Isaac, one of the guides, gave her foot massages to ease the cramps so she could finish the hike. The thought of spending a second night on a bush track in the rain was a strong motivator to get to shelter in Tabuane. She felt alone yet determined to offer help, and her companions made her feel safe and welcomed.

Once she returned to Cairns, Fiona called me, shared her experiences, and asked if I would be interested in seeing the situation firsthand. I had only the sketchiest of imaginations, but that was sufficient to pique my interest. Steeped in my consulting practice in America, I was less than enthusiastic about an unplanned transcontinental journey. Yet somehow, some way, by the third week of June 2005 I found myself crossing the Owen Stanley Range on an early morning thirty-minute flight to Popondetta. I viewed the mountains for the first time.

The mist-shrouded range sprawls from northwest to southeast, practically slicing Papua New Guinea in half. It reaches elevations over thirteen thousand feet. The island's spinal cord is a treacherous, rugged, and unspoiled relic of our planet.

It wasn't until the 1930s, in an even more inaccessible area called the Highlands, that explorers discovered more than a million people hidden in valleys and mountain passes. They lived undisturbed by the outside world.

Fiona forewarned me that the Managalas Plateau was "pretty remote," adding that the last reports of cannibalism were recorded in 1963. I eventually met the first missionary and his wife, who settled the same year. There were villages on the plateau that had never seen a white man.

If it seemed an inconvenience to get to the city of Popondetta, I was even more loath to drive up the Managalas Plateau and beyond to Tabuane.

We hired Jude, the same driver Fiona had used previously. His fifteen-year-old Toyota Land Cruiser was faded red, with a cracked windshield, rusted body, and bald tires. It was the vehicle of choice and the only one available.

Close to the Kweno Pass, the vehicle struggled to climb the rain-swollen road. We lost traction and started to slide sideways in reverse with the mud offering no resistance. The rain continued to pour. Bush grass slapped my face through the broken passenger window. With mist shrouding the road ahead, Jude gunned the engine in vain. The tires spun, burning off what precious little rubber remained on them. The smell of melting tires created a pall of frustration.

A feeling of futility gripped me, unlike any I had experienced. It looked like we were shit-out-of-luck! Under such circumstances, the mind goes blank, and the brain disengages. I suddenly thought of my AAA road emergency service as I took in deep breaths. I was not expecting such exact detail. The map is not the territory.

I peered into the dense bamboo forest as my body leaned

against the passenger door at a forty-five-degree angle. Five or six apparitions suddenly took on human form. Darkness was upon us, but our host villagers knew we were making our way up Kweno Mountain; they heard the strain of the engine long before we bogged down. They were waiting to step out of the bush to help. Surrounding our tired vehicle, these slightly built yet strong men pushed and pulled the vehicle until it was free. They would melt back into the bush and miraculously reappear when their help was required. Three times they assisted, running through the dense bush grass in the rain, anticipating the next bogging.

The terrain leveled off into a clearing where the first homes of Tabuane appeared. Cooking fires were lit; dried rainforest brush crackled. Women, children, and fathers crouched around open pits, embracing warmth in the coolness of a rainy evening. The crisp mountain air reminded me of camping high in the San Juan Mountains of Colorado, just north of New Mexico.

Slowly, people surrounded Fiona, Warpa, and me. Warpa spoke in the village dialect, Barai. We were welcomed with the salutation "Ese." Over and over, they repeated the word, which meant "welcome" and "hello." Ultimately, this village would become our base, where we would build a home, and Fiona and I would marry.

We settled in for the evening. A dinner of yams, rice, and fried bananas was served. Warpa's home was a little more modern than the typical village house. He had a tin roof, wood doors, and plank floors. The kitchen was in a separate and open structure called a *haus win*. The bathroom, called "the pit," consisted of a hole dug in the ground, bamboo walls, and a sago roof but no toilet seat. One had to take aim. Accuracy in all its forms is second nature here, whether throwing a spear to kill a wild pig or using a slingshot to shear off a mango from a tree branch far above one's head.

The following morning, the sun was shining. I was invigorated by a sound sleep. While sitting on a bamboo mat, we were served tea, fruit, and "flour" for breakfast. "Flour" is a term used for fresh biscuits, and it's a treat for village people, as it is expensive to purchase.

Warpa arranged a *toktok*, or open meeting, with the chief and elders. Everyone gathered in the village's meeting place, a bamboo pavilion.

As I arrived, I noticed a pile of sugarcane sticks; another pile—one of shelled coconuts—was stacked on a lodge pole, and several bunches of green betel nuts hung from the roof beams. The betel nut, chewed and then spit out, is a mild form of speed. Many become addicted to the nuts by their mid-teens. By age twenty, most endure side effects, such as decayed and lost teeth and rotting gums.

I was seated at the middle of the pavilion. My body pressed against one of the bamboo railings and my legs were crossed. Before me sat fifty villagers, including the chief, a priest, ten elders, farmers, and significant landowners. Stafford, the chief, was about seventy-five years old. He was dressed in the customary attire of a man of his position, which included feather headdress, necklaces, leather, and beaded wrist, arm, and ankle bands. He wore a checkered brown-and-white tapa cloth sarong.

Shirtless, Stafford was a lean fellow with high cheekbones, a full head of wiry black hair, very few teeth, and red-stained gums. His brown eyes were wide and sunken into a large, furrowed forehead. He had a strong grip and a serious face, absent of wrinkles.

The meeting commenced with a formal Christian prayer. Stafford, sitting in front of me, looked directly into my eyes and asked: "Why are you here?" I was thrown off balance by his straightforward, non-bullshit manner, yet I was engaged. I began to feebly formulate a response. Disadvantaged by a language barrier and having a vague sense of who this man really was, I hoped I would communicate a sense of honesty. He resonated truth. I felt vulnerable and desired congruency with my inner and outer man. I had no prompters, and my interpreters could not read my mind. I felt I was in the presence of a true elder, a man of peace and forgiveness. This wiry old man could see right through me.

I retreated into my thoughts and did not immediately respond as Stafford continued to talk. Through Warpa Kephale's translation, I understood this man was once a young warrior. Stafford was the first person to bring coffee seeds—Jamaican Blue Mountain—to the plateau in 1963. He taught the villagers how to plant their first cash crop. He envisioned a time when his village and the rest of the plateau would receive equitable benefits. They had not yet arrived, despite all of their labor and hopes. The magnitude of Stafford's story jolted me. I heard him clearly and understood his words. His language of long suffering bound us together. To a baby boomer from Grosse Pointe, Michigan, long suffering is a relatively unknown concept. Though I had worked diligently and experienced unmet hopes, I capitulated that hopelessness was a way of life. I was saddened. Again he asked me: "Why are you here?" This time, I responded: "I am here because I want to be here." The simplest explanation is usually the best.

My integrity seemed to be deepening and evolving in the

87

moment. I did not feel compelled to say or promise anything. I went with the flow. That itself was the purpose. Grounded, the top of my head was connected to the soles of my feet. Every cell of my conscious being was awake and aligned to what I chose. I was bridged into Stafford's interior reality— his soul. I was captivated by a visceral sense of transparency, followed by feelings of peace and goodness. I was content and safe among these villagers. This moment was meaningful with no strings attached. I sensed those around me felt the same way. The absence of affectation was a liberty I found agreeable. A significant shift had begun.

I had experienced this sensation before. After losing my company in the mid-1980s, I felt like I was in a fog or a dark room. I went bonefishing in the Florida Keys and spent hours rummaging through secondhand bookstores. One day I picked up a second edition of Truman Capote's *Other Voices, Other Rooms* on Duval Street in Key West. I felt an empathy with Capote. His loneliness and sensitivity came through in his novel's character of Joel. I experienced an "aha" moment as Joel came to terms with himself: "I am me," he whispers. "I am Joel, we are the same people."

Stafford helped guide me to the next chapter of my life that day in the pavilion. We conversed with few words on numerous occasions afterward. He died a few years later. His family visited me shortly after Stafford's *haus cry* (funeral). I gave his wife a picture of her husband standing proudly in his chief's attire. She wept. Pictures were uncommon there . . . just like Stafford.

It has been said, "Teaching consists of creating conditions that help students to find their path." Stafford's simplicity inspired me to seek another path—a more difficult one than I had ever anticipated. Yes, this highway had been a path of self-discovery. But a faint wind, slight whisper, or a distant windmill of faded memories was alerting me that a greater selflessness was required for me to expand myself. I passed another highway marker.

John's coffee venture had early success. It was time for celebration in Tabuane and nearby villages. "The orchestrated villages' sing-sing would be lifted to a new level of energy by a caffeine buzz never before experienced. They would taste and drink their coffee for the first time since planting began in 1963."

CHAPTER 11

Misnomers

"Nothing in this world is harder than speaking the truth, nothing easier than flattery."
—Fyodor Dostoyevsky

Now fully committed to building the coffee business, I joined Fiona for another visit to Tabuane. The cupping results from our coffee exporter in Goroka were favorable. The drying and cleaning quality of the parchment beans improved. The milled green beans to be purchased by the global market were now upgraded to a level of premium small-holder coffee (PSC AX category). Therefore, our gross profit margins increased, putting us in a celebratory mood. Fiona and I gained assurance that the quality practices and village collection system headquartered in Tabuane were paying off. Warpa suggested that a feast and a "sing-sing" were warranted.

In preparation, Fiona instructed the exporter to segregate ten kilos of green beans. She brought the coffee back to Cairns to be roasted and ground and then packed into two five-kilo vacuum-sealed bags. We carried the coffee back to the village of Tabuane. The orchestrated villages' sing-sing would be lifted to a new level of energy by a caffeine buzz never before experienced. They would taste and drink their coffee for the first time since planting began in 1963.

The levitation mission began on an early mid-February morning in Popondetta. Excitedly, we packed up a land cruiser. Warpa, his wife, and neighbors Nupan and his wife accompanied Fiona and me. The air's stifling mugginess soon gave way to the coolness of the mountains as we ascended. Past the village of Banderi, we stopped at a small river to stretch our legs and have a wash. The women hiked down the river to find privacy, as the men walked up the pebbled riverbed to find pools in which to bathe. Warpa and Nupan waited until I advanced far enough for them to disrobe. They preferred to bathe without me. For the first time in my life, I was segregated. I smiled to myself as I recalled how the Wonder Bread bakery in Detroit once prohibited blacks from handling the flour or being involved in the baking function. The white community somehow concocted and/or believed their bread could be contaminated by black hands. Now I felt the shoe was on the other foot. Without further distraction I dropped my trousers and waded into the clear water. I saw the men below me grasp their penises with one hand and plunge into their pool. They glanced toward me. I suspect this was the first time they'd seen a white man's penis. I perceived vulnerability on multiple levels. Symbolism reverberated. Literally, I was letting it all hang out. Then the draping vines, expansive rainforest trees, and butterflies immediately occupied my mind. I was drawn into a cavernous and ancient place. The babbling water falling over the black granite rocks soothed me. My thoughts now wandered to the impending sing-sing. Anticipation rose as I walked back to the vehicle. Refreshed by the mountain stream, we now headed for the Kweno Pass. I tried to recollect the landscape from my previous trip. Familiarity escaped me, making me feel displaced and that I really didn't belong here.

Gratefully, the roads were dry, which was unusual for this time of year. The rainy season typically lasted until early May. Without mishap and with the rivers now passable, we arrived in Tabuane by three in the afternoon. Relatives and friends of Warpa surrounded the vehicle, excited by our presence. Shouts, giggles, and laughter filled the air. It was a friendly and welcoming commotion. The awestruck children whispered to one another, holding their hands to their mouths. Their widened eyes gave up their facades as they viewed Fiona's golden hair and my height.

Circumspective, they studied every move we made and were soon instructed to help carry the luggage to Warpa's home. Kundu drums were playing west of the village. The continuous beats were penetrating my thoughts. The noise lulled me to an uncomfortable place, making me feel hesitant and lonely. I was more at ease with Fiona beside me and instinctively grasped her hand.

Laziness settled me as the late afternoon sun began to descend behind the mountains and a faint crescent moon appeared behind me. The kundu drums continued to drone without interruption. Commands were given to carry a large iron pot over to the haus win next to the dirt clearing where the dancing would commence. A fire pit was constructed by using bush knives to dig a hole. Young men carried dry brush, branches, and twigs to the site. Women carried pots of water on their heads from a spring over two hundred yards away as they exuberantly shouted to one another. Their prideful faces exclaimed their duty as the men ignored them and built the fire. I would brew the magical potion once darkness arrived. Already ablaze were other fire pits bordering the open ground.

Warpa apprised us that the sing-sing also would include the villages of Dea, Ugunumo, and Kweno. Approximately 1,500 adults and children would attend. *Javar mamar*, in Barai language, is the term for good dance, and this rave, or proclaimed "good dance," would last until eight o'clock the next morning. I was beginning to grasp the significance of this gathering, as well as to be provoked by the thought that it had the appearance of a melee.

Donning blue jeans and denim jackets, Fiona and I were ready to join in the festivity. Fiona had the look of a natural woman. Surging with a primordial energy, she was at home and poised to do some serious sing-sing. Her jeans hugged her hips. With braids dropping down on her shoulders, I felt we were stepping into an elegant evening in formal attire. The kundu drums became louder and chants more audible as we left Warpa's home. Crisp mountain air and the evening dusk contrasted with the numerous fire pits. As darkness continued to envelop the gathering, glowing fires became interlocked with the stars. I sensed I was moving into an upward spiral. With permissiveness, I moved into the flow. Sandalwood, eucalyptus, and rainforest brush scented the air as the fires burned and embers cooked evening meals. The nighttime mist and swirling smoke animated the human figures as they moved through this thin lace.

Spotting the iron pot dangling from a tripod over the flaming fire pit, I broke away from the group and joined the circle of men staring at the boiling water. Unnoticed, I slipped a bottle of whiskey out of the knapsack and imbibed. On average, I stood one foot above the men. My height was a dead giveaway that I was an outsider, besides my being a white man. I was quite conscious of these realities and wondered if they were as well or if I was just an oddity worth having a look at but not giving much more thought to. Could such an encounter be that simple and casual? I was not sure if I wanted it to be anything more. This ambiguity gave me comfort. It was what I chose and wanted to believe at the moment.

I also retrieved a Romeo y Julieta cigar, which was encased in a white tin tube. The fire reflecting off the metal was distracting enough to capture six pairs of eyes. Slowly, I unscrewed the cap and moistened the cigar with my tongue. Astonished by this ritual, they now viewed me biting the tip off the cigar and spitting it to the ground. I bent down to pick up an ember twig and lit the cigar. Deliberately, I rolled the tobacco between my thumb and fingers, looking at it with reverence as I inhaled and exhaled this magnificence. Without hesitation I handed the cigar to a diminutive villager standing to my right. He was wearing a maroon beret. His name was Juda Divish. We nodded to one another. He smiled and remarked, "Tau bada, javar mamar." The other men parroted him as they joined in and smoked the cigar as it was passed from one villager to another. Clueless, I enquired of Juda what was being said. In broken English, he set the record straight and said, "You are a big white man, and we are having a good dance." I responded and also set the record straight. "Yes, I am a tall white man, and now I have a name for the coffee you are about to taste. The name of our company will be Java Mama, which means good coffee." He did not know I would drop the letter R off both names as we proceeded with the new name and logo. Future harvests would be sold into Australia, Europe, and the United States, both certified organic and Rainforest Alliance.

Each villager savored the smoke. They toked and repeated "Brus mamar," meaning good tobacco. Approvingly, I smiled and lit a second cigar for myself. I took another swig of whiskey and began cutting open the bags and pouring the ground coffee into the steaming water. Excitedly, they shouted at one another as they assisted me and tended to the fire. Juda assumed control and barked out instructions. I appreciated his help. Chewing and spitting betel nut, they seemed as content as I was sipping my Jack. We were having a good time together.

The moon was pronounced as I walked into the sing-sing milieu, accompanied by Juda. Fiona called over as I gazed at this spectacle. Yams, easily weighing fifteen to twenty pounds, were nestled in the embers. Cooking pots filled with boiling water were soon used for their rice and tea. Peeled and sliced bananas were frying in open pans. Coconuts were cracked and the delicious meat was ready to eat, along with sliced cucumbers and pineapples.

Returning to the coffee pit, I began to scoop out the scalded brew with a handled jar into strainers that would seep into the containers held by a line of women. Within the hour, four villages were sipping brewed coffee. The significance of this moment nearly escaped me as I reveled with them. Stafford truly was the hero. I was an easy target for misplaced adoration. The gullibility I witnessed was as demeaning to them as it was for me. It was an ingredient skillfully manipulated, resulting in a public esteem that was unwarranted. I realized again that for fifty-one years the plateau's residents had never known the fruit of their labor. What did it look, smell, and taste like? How did it bring pleasure to other people? I caught myself in reflection as the pot was nearly drained. Sipping the coffee, I smiled with Juda and was reminded that this moment was pretty damn special.

Yes, it doesn't get much better than this. The stars filled the sky, looking down on an exuberant village setting where yams were eaten, coffee sipped, and the line dancing went into locomotion. Stoked, I felt like I was fifth-row center, gyrating with the Rolling Stones in concert at Ford Field in Detroit. My feet began to move, yet my hips remained stationary. I soon realized this was a different rhythm. Motown now seemed far distant, yet the energy was similar.

Accompanied by Warpa, Juda, and a man named Daut Kephale (Warpa's brother), Fiona and I entered a line dance. Repeatedly, "javar mamar" and "tau bada" were shouted. We volleyed the same salutations and giggled with hilarity.

The name-calling was enmeshed with the individual village chants, songs, and kundu drums. As the evening evolved close to 3 a.m., it was difficult to distinguish one village from another. Fires flickered on the dancers, casting ghostly shadows on the ground. The high-pitched women singing in unison elevated this etherealness. The men droned on in a barely deviating monotone. A typical dance would last for thirty minutes, accompanied by four different choruses from all four villages, each distinguished by a unique cadence. It was a Tower of Babel for me yet completely coherent for them.

Kina shells, feathers, and plumed headdresses were worn by the men and women. The fires illuminated tapa-cloth sarongs and vivid pink and ochre dyes. Women's breasts undulated with the dance. Fiona noted that the teenage pointers (firm breasts) captivated me. Sheepishly, I concurred.

Pitch darkness enveloped the village square as dawn approached. Loneliness started to percolate, removing and sealing me off from what I was experiencing. The brief fusion I'd grasped was departing. I sensed the party was over, and, as usual, I was one of the last to depart. This disassociation was untimely. The alienation was unmistakable. Yet the frenzied tempo's intensity increased. Entranced and feeling lost by this emotional predicament, I looked for Fiona. I circled around the line dancers, vainly searching for her amid the calls of "Tau bada, tau bada, javar mamar, tau bada." Towering over the crowd, I finally spotted Fiona in a line dance. Two steps forward with head up and one step back with head bowed. Three steps forward and two steps back. Four steps forward and three steps back. At each interval, the line stepped to the left and then to the right. Immersed, she belonged. Laughing and embraced by the village women on each side of her, she exacerbated my own dilemma. Fiona's pale skin made it easier to keep her in sight. My height and white skin only invoked more calls of "Tau bada." It did not resonate as it had earlier in the evening. I wondered if it was motivated by derision or adulation or possibly both. How could it, though? They did not know me. I pondered if they would ever know me, the outsider. Was I capable of knowing them? Would they permit me to know them? I was persuaded to be open and willing to trust myself to let them know me.

Fiona and I found one another and moved into another line dance. Sipping coffee spiked with whiskey, I grew into the flow, placing my ponderings to the side to transcend my misgivings as dawn approached.

We walked back to the house. Salutations continued, along with the kundu drums. Tau Bada faded into a deep sleep, yet the name kept on playing.

A sour desperation grew in the beautiful land. Tabuane men were going around with spears, bridge maintenance slacked off, roads washed out, and employee neglect meant a vehicle needed a $7,000 engine replacement from stalling in the river crossing. "Confrontations were simmering. . . . Our village was becoming unsafe . . . the meltdown spurred by mounting financial problems, tribal intrusions, the Tabuane killing and the threats to our safety."

CHAPTER 12

The Altercation

"Big Daddy: *Think of all the lies I got to put up with!*
Pretenses! Ain't that mendacity? Having to pretend
stuff you don't think or feel or have any idea of?"

—Tennessee Williams, *Cat on a Hot Tin Roof*

Gradually, I supported Fiona's entry into the coffee-export business by assisting with planning, onsite visits, and finances. We founded Earth and Spirit Products PNG to take Managalas Plateau Arabica coffee, certified organic and Rainforest Alliance, into the global market.

Unfortunately, my tank was beginning to run on fumes, the result of frequent commuting from Grosse Pointe, Michigan, USA, to Tabuane Village, Oro Province, Papua New Guinea. The ninety-day consulting cycle, preparations to be married, and attending to the needs of three young girls added weight to the load.

Shortly after July 2006, the stress of overcommitment appeared. I started feeling I was in over my head, gulping for air. Circumstances beyond my control nibbled on my self-confidence. I began to waver.

Unexpected and unimaginable events in our new sur-roundings contributed to my unease. A sorcerer in the village of Tabuane was speared and hacked to death in an incident involving members of Warpa Kephale's family. As a result, clan confrontations were simmering. Demands for financial compensation from our organization were made because Warpa was viewed as a partner in the company. The compensation issue remained unresolved. Our village was becoming unsafe. Chickens and pigs were being stolen. I thought of my beleaguered hometown of Detroit and its problems of corruption and scandal. Chickens and pigs seem insignificantly small-scale, but to these villagers they were very serious. I recalled teenagers being shot over a pair of Nike shoes in America.

Around the same time, I confronted members of a corrupt charity organization operating in the area. They were competing as a nonprofit with our company, using European donor funds to rip off farmers with credit promises. Eventually, they paid an even lower price or didn't pay at all. One afternoon, I gathered the NGO members in a circle, with the assistance of an interpreter, and exposed their scheme. Morally, I pointed out, their actions were wrong. They were hurting farmers and their neighbors, and it was their choice to now practice what was right. Also, appealing to a spiritual theme, I said it was their choice to be in light or to remain in darkness. After further discourse, they nodded. I assumed we were in agreement. Again, I was wrong. They had communicated what I wanted to hear. But as a result of the meeting we were subjected to a violent retaliation. The following evening, our coffee facility was ransacked, our employees were chased off with spears, and our coffee bags were almost set afire. Since the Popondetta police were short of funds for a vehicle and fuel, we paid them to come up in our truck to arrest the director of the NGO, who was not at my confrontation. He arrived later in the day, drunk and with a Popondetta woman. As a married man, this was taboo in the plateau. He was roughed up (without our complicity) by the police and jailed. When released on bail, he fled the province but told his associates to rape and sodomize Fiona. The quality of our work life was seriously deteriorating! Vendettas are a way of life in Papua New Guinea. Up to this point, I grasped this tribal practice intellectually, but now I understood it with my heart. Fear percolated in the core of my experience. This tribal practice was invasive, illusive, and damn personal. The NGO's associates were scattered throughout the plateau in numerous villages. The severity and brutality of such imagery diminished my courage. The spiritual and emotional arrows of trying to block out the thought of Fiona's being raped and sodomized inflicted heaviness on my soul.

The coup de grâce was the arrival of a member of the Papua New Guinea Parliament using public money to buy coffee. After two years of spending company funds to keep roads maintained, we now faced an elected public official using his staff to purchase coffee above the prevailing market price to buy votes, rather than fix the roads. The pork barrel knows no boundaries. This fellow would have felt quite at home in Washington, DC.

Paul Tillich once wrote, "Cynically speaking, one could say that it is true to life to be cynical about it." I cynically agreed.

We took a break and returned to see the children in Australia. One afternoon, on a beach north of Cairns, I went into a postadolescent tirade. One would think at the age of sixty I would be beyond such antics. Never say never. The meltdown spurred by mounting financial problems, tribal intrusions, the Tabuane killing, and the threats to our safety erupted into a tantrum. The upheaval came as sure as a hangover followed a drinking binge. To take control, I was compelled to lose my control. Gazing across the expansiveness of the Coral Sea, my fears likewise broadened. Fiona became the source of all of our ills and misfortunes. Shifting into a "me first" mode at her expense, I broke off the marriage engagement. This deeply embedded trait of circling the wagons to protect myself from attacking savages (other people's needs) was a trait I learned during my years as a thriving baby boomer. I masked it with a slickly articulated, well-framed, eloquent paradoxical argument. "I need to break off this arrangement," I said. "Adios. But please give me the same emotional commitment, and be open to me finally figuring out what I want." I wanted to follow the familiar path of least resistance instead of choosing the more difficult route of sticking to it when the going gets rough.

The same week, I received an invitation from friends in Santa Fe, New Mexico, to join a small group that had gained access to view the Anasazi cliff dwellings on a Ute Indian reservation near Cortez, Colorado. The excursion would include five guests and was hosted by a local rancher and led by an Indian guide. We would be the first white people in one hundred years to view this area.

Interestingly, the outfitter who planned this trip was awarded the invitation by the local Ute chief and tribal council. It seems the outfitter had captured a wild stallion that was breeding excessively with the mares of the surrounding ranches. Wild horses had overpopulated this part of the Southwest.

As tough as it was for Fiona and me after our unsettling beach altercation, I felt—and she agreed—that this opportunity was too good to pass up. Fundamentally, Fiona has a greater sense of adventure than I do. She has cycled, hitchhiked, driven, climbed, and sailed more continents than I have. As a kindred spirit, she knew the significance of the cliff-dwellings invitation and encouraged me to depart. With shared enthusiasm, I gave little thought to the skirmish on the beach. I presumed everything was copacetic.

Escaping, John joined friends in the southwestern US where four states meet. The group discovered a young person's skull, arm bones, and a partial jawbone. They quickly agreed that the area would be preserved, and the Hopi Council would be notified to discuss religious reinterment. While in the mountains, guide Ricky Hayes, a historian, cultural anthropologist, and geologist, examined rock shaped and marked by the Hopi centuries ago, turned, and said, quoting the Bible, "John, remember one day is a thousand years, and a thousand years is a day." John had just read a new book, *Spiral Dynamics.* (Bones photo by Ed Barth)

CHAPTER 13

On the Road

*"I like too many things and get all confused and hung
up running from one falling star to another 'til I drop.
This is the night, what it does to you. I had nothing to
offer anybody except my own confusion."*

—Jack Kerouac

It was August 2006, and my forward motion propelled me
to the Four Corners region of Colorado, New Mexico, Arizona,
and Utah. Again, I was on my way—yes—to see ancient ruins,
but I was also in search of something I could not name. This
touchstone of four states converges into an *axis mundi*, where
time and space are suspended and, as the Bible says, "one day
becomes a thousand years and a thousand years one day." Such
transcendence may just happen if one permits it to unfold.

I was on the road. The familiar liberty felt like an old
friend. The tension of the Australian beach subsided. I granted
myself permission to go out and play in the "neighborhood" with
my friends, vowing to my parents to be home by the time the
streetlights came on. In his book, *On the Road*, Jack Kerouac's
alter ego speaks up:

*"Sal, we got to go and never stop going 'til we get
there."*
"Where are we going, man?"
"I don't know, but we gotta go."

For this sixty-year-old, it was obvious I was on the same stage but wearing a different costume. I was wandering into the future to resolve my present predicament. No better place than the Southwest high desert. I was riding on in manic drive—overdrive. My mind was reeling from the temporary and unpleasant endings of the engagement and Papua New Guinea. Simultaneously, however, I was eager for new beginnings and fresh opportunities. There was no need to think beyond what was going on at the moment. Everything between the ending and perceived new beginning would somehow work itself out. I still believed in the tooth fairy.

My friend Richard Martinez assembled the party at a ranch near Cortez, Colorado. We met up with a mechanical engineer, a professor of architecture, a retired entrepreneur, a three-legged dog, and a goat that thought it was a horse. Our adventure involved the exploration of native cliff dwellings, long abandoned, in remote canyon country. The base camp was already set up in a canyon on a choice meadow. We had packhorses, our own mounts, and two wranglers. The party departed in late morning.

Riding horses is similar to relying on a motorcycle. You are a part of the scene, not watching a DVD. The path in front of me and beneath my feet gained clarity. Similar to vertical and lateral views, I still needed to affix them to a destination point, all while maintaining sure footing. Without a clear target/vision, I would be susceptible to getting lost. Falling off a horse—or spilling over on a motorcycle—results from poor short-term focus. This orientation takes practice. Most CEOs whom I have coached over the years have been challenged by the simultaneity of long- and short-term thinking. The cobwebs of the mind and blockages of the soul become dislodged while riding in the high country. My inner pipes began to unclog, ushering in the "beauty road." Its appearance put me at ease. The scent of pines and pinion and the sounds of wind and water immersed me in a panoramic spectacle. I smelled fragrant sage as an afternoon shower played with the sun. Eagles and hawks stared down on the seven white men. Five of them were city slickers. It had been a long time since these canyon walls viewed palefaces in this neck of the woods.

Ravens called out and laughed, knowing what appeared to be was not always so. Their coyness kept me guessing as to what they were trying to tell me. I was perplexed, as I had been in the past, as I tried to interpret my own dreams.

I was distanced from Papua New Guinea, at least by geography. Struggling to find the words to articulate what I was doing on this horse, I reminded myself that I was not gifted to understand such complexities. I needed an interpreter such as Joseph Campbell, who would walk a commoner like me through James Joyce's *Finnegan's Wake* with a skeleton key. Accomplished but didactic writers of my day, such as Vonnegut, Updike, and Pynchon, would intellectually befuddle this business-degreed careerist, forcing me to underline and reread paragraphs frequently. I always had to work at it, much like reading poetry. This prose condition, I assume, is shared by a great number of my nonliterary generation, reinforcing my belief that these inadequacies are normal. What largely escapes the equation is the joy of what most literary writers try to convey. Information is the endgame. The more you regurgitated, the closer you were placed to the head of the table, if you were not already at the top. Personal transformation is not even on the radar. My mind wandered, but I reminded myself that on a horse, nothing has to make sense.

The crows' blackness offered a sharp contrast to the pine greens and the chalk orange and pink rock formations jutting up into a crystal blue sky that revealed itself as the afternoon monsoons moved east. These birds played with me, knowing I was in need of a compass reading, a present understanding.

Such ruminations were overtaxing at the moment. I let go of the reins and allowed the horse to do the work, to move me to today's destination.

The isolation of living in the village of Tabuane had worn on me. The changing language and dialects from one valley to another confounded me. I wanted to communicate with some consistency and confidence that I could understand and, in turn, be understood. Exhausted, I was beginning to realize the degree of squandered conversations throughout my life. Double-talk was a subject that needed further investigation.

We spent the remainder of our first day riding to the base camp. The group dismounted twice to view caves with wall pictographs. Birds, bear, and antelope were engraved into stone eight hundred to one thousand years ago. Familiar archetypes were present, such as the young man warring on a path, moving to a rainbow, and emerging as an elder dancing with the sun. The Mother Earth imagery was also unmistakable, as depicted by the etchings of women symbols. My Jungian aficionados would have had a blast viewing what I was experiencing. They would provoke me to inquire of my own femininity, as the pictographs suggested. These insights emerged in the latter years of my life. This might be a good thing for executives in the C-Suite. Could we use a little more humanizing in our corporate cultures? But what did this have to do with financial performance? A bolt of enlightenment struck me, even though the thunderstorms had passed an hour ago. I vowed to pursue the subject further, with an organizational practitioner and friend residing in Ann Arbor, Michigan.

We arrived to find the camp set up. Tents were pitched. The cook and his girlfriend had the grub wagon organized, with utensils and pans hanging from a rope between two pine trees. The toilet pit was dug fifty yards from the camp, complete with seat, toilet paper, and tarp walls for privacy.

This Arkansas couple had a fiddle and harmonica. Charlotte was a pretty woman with a weathered face, long blond hair, and blue eyes. She wore a denim shirt and tight, faded jeans tucked into rattlesnake boots. Glen was tall and wiry, with a long, dark, drooping mustache and matching ponytail. His face was unshaven and drawn into a permanent grin. It appeared to be a smile incited by cannabis. Immediately, our eyes met, and before I knew it, I was offered (but did not accept) a bowl of weed in their bivouac. But I did share a bottle of Patrón tequila and become a member of the cooking crew. Subsequently, both Glen and Charlotte invited Fiona and me to spend a month with them in the San Juan Mountains north of Charma, New Mexico. They would provide the base camp. These were really nice people, and I believed they would enjoy hanging out in Tabuane.

We gathered around a campfire, sipping coffee and bourbon, after a dinner of fresh venison steaks (that afternoon's road kill), baked potatoes, corn on the cob, garden salad, and apple pie.

The canyon walls reflected a half moon. The night's stillness quieted the group, encouraging us to find warm tents, inflated mattresses, and sleeping bags.

I was experiencing pure luxury compared to the Managalas Plateau. I enjoyed every minute of this treat. The pit with toilet seat was a personal highlight. So was the fresh apple pie and Charlotte. My mind wandered, and Fiona crept into my thoughts. I desired her company.

On Saturday, August 26, we set out on horseback after breakfast, south through Menios Canyon to Soda Canyon, following our guide, a senior member of the Ute tribe. Soon we tied up the horses and began to ascend to Bone Awl site, about one and one-half miles away. It was steep and more suited to experienced hikers. The site was in good condition. It was tree-lined, built into an overhanging cliff big enough to accommodate forty to sixty people. There was evidence of a spring that once served as a water source for crops such as beans, corn, and squash.

From our vantage point, we also viewed the northwest Mesa Verde property, which included the formally named Balcony House and Hemingway House, about one-half mile across the canyon. I was puzzled by the white-man names. Ernest Hemingway? Give me a break. It was foreign thinking. For example, what did the name "Washington Redskins," as an entertainment sports team, have to do with the American Indians? Later on in the afternoon, we spotted the Swedish site about a thousand feet above our trail. We lunched at the base trail and returned to camp late that afternoon. The isolation and utter complexity of these ancient cliff dwellings was breathtaking. Ricky Hayes, age fifty, our head guide, was a historian, cultural anthropologist, and geologist, all rolled into one. He possessed great familiarity with ancient tribal customs.

Late in the day, we viewed potshards—pieces of pottery—in another cave close to our tents. Ricky turned to me, with his long black ponytail swinging over his shoulder, and remarked, "There is no real time here, John. We have been charged to guard these sites along with our brothers in the Grand Canyon, where Havasu Creek is the ancient home of the Hopi. By tradition, nothing is disturbed or moved without permission from the Hopi Council." Ricky looked directly into my eyes, smiled, touched my arm, and said: "John, remember one day is a thousand years, and a thousand years is a day."

As I started down the path, I spotted a potshard. Painted on a baked-white curved piece of clay was a black spiral moving infinitely upward. I took a picture of it and thought of a new text I'd just read called *Spiral Dynamics*, which introduced me to a new way to understand the cultural evolution of the world's civilization. The framework is a theory that affirms the cultural/

social/psychological components of our past. The critical phrase, labeled Value Meme, is our wet gene, contrasted to the well-known dry gene. The lower meme levels are inclusive and are contingent on current life conditions (e.g., politics, economics, and society). In order to evolve, everyone begins at the first (tribal) level. It is our individual and collective choice to move to higher levels of complexity. I am discovering the application in my work to be impactful. It has encouraged me to be less rigid and more open, helping me to put my thinkings and feelings into perspective. Also, this has assisted my clients to understand their filters of egoism and ethnocentricity and the influence they have on decision making.

Shortly after returning and relaxing at camp, a member of our group explored an area for pottery shards about one hundred yards away in the southwest canyon. In a parched riverbed, he discovered a skull, arm bones, and a partial jawbone with two teeth. Ricky estimated the person had been thirteen to fifteen years old and determined that this was a burial site. The area would be preserved, and the Hopi Council would be summoned to discuss plans for a religious reinterment.

Our daily routine of waking up to fresh coffee and breakfast, horseback riding to another canyon, hiking to a summit for lunch, and viewing one ruin after another melded me into the surroundings. I was losing my sense of space and time. Afternoon naps, followed by splendid cowboy meals, drew me into a comfort zone. Prairie songs at night, sipping bourbon from a tin cup, smoking a Cuban cigar, and gazing at the constellations had me moon dancing with the canyon shadows and gentle warm breeze.

Three full days passed. I was letting go of Papua New Guinea and moving into a new flow. Then, presto—the squawking of blackbirds returned me to consciousness and reminded me I had been in Papua New Guinea just two weeks ago. Fiona's presence reemerged. She has always been a primordial touchstone intricately bound to Mother Earth. Rooted in her makeup is a naturalness I cannot define. When I try to legitimize it with a Western mind-set, I further misunderstand it.

The ruins were reappearing. The skull, illuminated by moonlight in its earthen grave, glanced at me. All of this was remarkably connected, I was sure, yet confusion clouded a clear understanding of what was happening. Inward conflicts simmered. I chose disavowal instead and refilled my tin cup as I spotted a chair near the campfire underneath a canopy of stars.

Ricky saw me approaching the chair and smiled quizzically through the blaze of the fire. The fire was large, reminding me of the movie *Dances with Wolves*, where Kevin Costner does his disappearing act and assumes a new name and persona.

I sipped my bourbon, settling comfortably into a lawn chair. With an exuberant yell, Ricky shouted, "Ese, John, ese! Ese, John, ese!"

I about crapped in my pants. "Ricky, could you say that again?" I shouted through the flames.

He replied, clear as a bell, "Ese, John, ese!"

The embers and wind swirled sparks into the darkness, spiraling upward to the stars. I was silent. It seemed that Chief Stafford smiled as I stared into the fire pit. "Ricky, what does it mean?" I asked, already knowing the answer.

"It is a very old word, John," he responded. "It means you are welcome, hello, and good-bye. Most of all, it means you are welcome to be who you are. You are appreciated for being you right now, John."

I retreated to my tent and hauled out my cot to view the stars. The constellations are ever-present. The unseen becomes the seen at night. During the day, the constellations are there. I trust their presence, though I cannot see them. What I'd heard tonight was the spoken word. What was manifested was the unspoken word. Stafford and Ricky were connected, halfway around the world, and I was smack between them. This was one helluva circle dance. The stars beckoned me to fully participate. I danced into a sound sleep.

Leaving base camp the following morning, I accompanied Richard Martinez in his car and we drove to Santa Fe, New Mexico.

As I mentioned, I am a slow learner, but I understood a tad more. Somewhere between the village of Tabuane and the Anasazi ruins of the Ute reservation, the clocks of Albion College became less and less contradictory. They are mutually affirming. Self-transcendence spiraled me to a more expansive and empathic understanding. I liked the comfort I felt. Ricky's Holy Spirit was named Mosahau, the source of wisdom from the fourth world and the ruler of the land from creation. Ricky seems to find solace as well in his great spirit. A New Testament verse proclaims Yahweh to be "the father of spirits." Hm, I like the inclusiveness of that scripture.

The Jews have multiple levels of wisdom. King Solomon, the main author of the Old Testament book of Proverbs, craved it. The highest level of wisdom is *Tushiyah*. It is a sound wisdom that gives one insight beyond the human and toward divine realities, if one desires it enough. To find it, one must be in motion on the road, moving forward. In fact, it is like mining precious ore.

John was feeling compatible with the old outhouse on the property of the Yale Hotel saloon owner. The saloon is a biker hangout about 60 miles north of Detroit. He realized: "I was blind to what I'd done until my relationship with Fiona became unglued." (Photo by Sharron Carney)

CHAPTER 14

Chagrin

"A man's conscience and his judgment is the same thing; and as the judgment, so also the conscience may be erroneous."

—Thomas Hobbes

The return from my visit to the "lost ones" was greeted by a faint smell of autumn in the air, with its promise of bursting colors. The foliage would soon surrender to the winter. Plunging myself into management consulting and executive coaching gave me little time to reflect on the Australian beach altercation. I presumed things would take care of themselves. No need to give it much thought. The practice of aversion would resume its natural course, and I would again find the equilibrium that seemed to elude me. I have always avoided needless suffering from the gratification of pleasure. I have found little redemption in personal hardship but much self-pity. Somewhere on the flight/fight or pleasure/suffering continuum, a place between pleasantness and discomfort would be found and easiness would return.

Autumn motorcycle trips into the Thumb region of Michigan were not connecting for me the way they used to. They seemed empty. There was little pleasure in these forays. In spite of the spectacle of fall colors along the Lake Huron shoreline on Highway 23, culminating in the town of Port Austin, angst began to take hold, accompanied by a low undercurrent of uncertainty. I was feeling unsteady. This is not a good condition to have on a motorcycle.

The distractions of clients, squash matches at the Detroit Athletic Club, social events, and motorcycling kept me oblivious as well as unconscious to the distance in Fiona's voice and the drop-off in phone calls. I was not aware of my own self-absorption, yet I was feeling pain. The absence of serenity was beginning to tilt my balance from happiness to unhappiness.

This particular Saturday afternoon in mid-October, I biked up to Yale, Michigan, to the saloon of the Yale Hotel to see my friend Sharron, the proprietor of the place. Locally, she is a biker, and a number of motorcycle clubs of southeast Michigan hang out at her bar. Poker runs inevitably include her establishment. It would not be unusual to see one hundred motorcycles, mostly Harley-Davidsons, lined up and uniformly parked on Main Street. Images of the Sturgis bike rally in South Dakota would come to my mind. Sharron poured tequila shots, but it would be out of character in the rural Midwest to have them served from belly buttons on her countertop.

Fiona and Sharron met one time. After 9/11, Sharron was saddened to see Fiona leaving America and she offered her home for us to live together and raise the three girls outside of Detroit in a farm setting. It was natural to think of Fiona in today's gathering. I missed her.

Imbibing Jack Daniel's and draft Budweiser, I found the bar was crowded, loud, and full of bikers. The biking ladies circled the pool table while the men sat at tables, drinking pitchers of beer. Cigarette smoke filled the room, along with grease fumes from the open grill. The Wurlitzer jukebox (circa 1960s) was beyond the two pool tables, next to a wall. I inched my way through the ladies and inserted two quarters into the Wurlitzer for two songs: "You've Lost That Loving Feeling" by the Righteous Brothers and "Lyin' Eyes" by the Eagles. Feeling sentimental, I replayed those stalwarts. I blinked, staring into the mirror behind rows of liquor bottles and the peanut racks. A spike was driven into my heart. The remote possibility of losing Fiona entered my self-preoccupation. I was distressed, and a sorrow began to clog my fount. My verve and hope for the future felt lessened.

Slowly, I zipped up my chaps and jacket, hugged Sharron, and then pecked her cheeks. I walked out of the saloon's haze to see long shadows cast on Main Street, as the sun was setting behind the hotel. The evening's ride back to Detroit would be chilly. Dante's *Tuscan Plains* was a-knockin'. Fear began to intrude as I reentered a familiar "dark wood." I was annoyed, but with whom? I thought Fiona was the most likely target. An inner discourse emerged, splitting this biker into two people, moving me into confusion. I collided with my own dissonance. I put on my gloves, preparing myself for at least an hour's ride back to Grosse Pointe. A phone call to Cairns, Australia, would be made tonight. Crap, I wanted to resolve this inner tension and get back to the good old times . . . the "good old rock 'n' roll times" . . . the Bob Seger denial times, where I would so effortlessly party and rationalize my needs.

The theory of double binds was introduced to me in neurolinguistic programming (NLP) at graduate school. An indigenous Tasmanian from Australia counseled me on this technique one evening. He assisted me in identifying and understanding a paradox within me that bound to me a persistent threat of annihilation. The fear of failure has deep roots and is pervasive in the corporate, political, and religious circles. Largely, CEOs/leaders like me have been driven by fear most of our lives. Yet all along, another fear wanted to protect and keep me safe. I identified the healthy fear and labeled it and talked to it. I felt sounder for it. By explicitly choosing the fear that wanted to protect me, I removed myself (my past conditioning) from a double bind and never looked back at the unhealthy fear that was debilitating and derailing me. This exercise demanded transparency and self-disclosure. Ironically, I came to the same conclusion that Thomas Hobbes did when he said, "Suffering makes man think." I gave my counselor a Cat Stevens cassette tape, *Tea for the Tillerman*, as a gift to take back to his native country. Where in the hell was Tasmania? At the time, I thought it was an African state.

The autumn chill on a motorcycle-minus-a-windshield went right into my bones. Smoldering fires from burning leaves filled the air, bringing back the time, long ago, when burning leaves was legal in Detroit. I was in a hurry to get to my phone. This ride contained few pleasantries, and I felt disappointed. Lamenting over such anguish irritated me and compelled me to drive faster.

Double binds are, for the most part, pretty devious. They create very punishing and inescapable dilemmas for both parties. I never anticipated the blowback from the beach altercation and, therefore, I was blind to what I'd done until my relationship with Fiona became unglued. I became fearful I might lose her. This was the right type of fear. The dangerous and incapacitating fear is the one stopping me from confronting my own bullshit and hubris. I was helplessly self-centered. Ultimately, though, I admitted I was wrong. Such surrender freed me from always having to be right. The sheer conscious act of identifying and owning my own imperfections repaired the damage before it was too late. My vulnerability led to humility and an inspired compassion.

Driving into the village of Memphis, I needed to pee. I decided to pull off on a gravel road before the town of Richmond, where I would take Gratiot Avenue to I-94 west back to Detroit. The traffic was heavy due to a Red Wings hockey game. Shit, I was cold, and the thought of eating crow (my words and actions) was unappetizing, as the inner dialogue became more contentious. Back in my halcyon corporate days, a chief operating officer, whom I'd threatened to fire, remarked that he was eating live crow as opposed to dead crow. Eating live crow, he defined, was the act of truly learning from your experience and applying the lessons with immediacy and self-effacement. The learning agility he described was adaptive and not fixed. He demonstrated a mind-set that encouraged personal growth. Eating dead crow was indicative of a fixed mind-set, as evidenced by resistance to change, repetition, and possibly destructive behaviors.

I remember being in an exclusive and fully licensed restaurant and whorehouse in Acapulco, Mexico, in 1981 with a good friend. It was a classic double bind. We had a splendid Christmas dinner—a feast, really. The restaurant and rooms overlooked the bay, high up on the cliff, with a mariachi band, piñatas, and lots of margaritas. The dancers were lined up in a crescent. Jim and I sat in lounge chairs, taking in the view on the ornate veranda. The host asked, "Señor Juan and Jim, out of all these ladies, which one do you want?" Honestly, Jim and I had not decided that we wanted any of the girls. That was a double bind. Now, the double bind I put on Fiona on a remote Australian beach was far more ambiguous and duplicitous than the encounter in Acapulco.

There are lots of these double binds around. You can run into them in family, church, school, science, business, military, government, and do-good organizations like nonprofits. The spiritual ones, similar to my graduate school seminary experience, can truly play with your mind and fuck you up for a long time. Regardless of my academic success (nearly a 4.0

grade point average), I was not thinking at the higher level that the professors and clergy perceived I should have attained.

My anti–Vietnam War sentiments and supportive view on interracial marriage did not sit well with this Minneapolis Christian sect. I was confounded at the age of twenty-four. As a Christian, I thought I was grounded in my beliefs and felt at peace because my inward and outward man was one. My conscience was intact. New Testament scripture rhymed and connected deeply with me. But to little avail.

Disappointingly, professors and clergy twisted and rationalized the simplicity of scripture into a theological Gordian knot, making it unbearable for me to live with my inner tension. I left the institutionalized church for thirty years. Who was the loser? For the most part, have the church or politicians learned anything constructive about personal and institutional power from the past several decades? I am afraid not. The church and Washington are even more politicized, polarized, and intransigent. Our society is a reflection of this animosity.

Communication gets complex and mighty hazy in double binds. The majority of these seducers want it that way. It is hard to tell fact from bullshit. It is when the bullshit turns into Kool-Aid and one enjoys drinking it that things get out of hand.

Weapons of mass destruction, initially justifying a preemptive invasion and occupation, were never found in Iraq. This was a good shit-stirrer conversation over a dinner in Grosse Pointe. I can only imagine a similar fate as Vietnam—a rationalized, apolitical withdrawal somewhere in the future, anchored with incalculable costs and human misery. The double bind our country was put into will never be fully understood as long as both political sides shun honest conversation.

Uh-oh! I needed to catch myself. My bladder was in

need of relief. The tension I put on my biological condition by imbibing that last Budweiser convinced me to visit a Sunoco station toilet, refuel, and purchase a packet of peanut M&M's. I got home and made the call. Fiona sounded faint. We were out of sync. Within ten days, Fiona disclosed that she was seeing another man. The next two months were a sordid eventuality as I ate crow. It was not a tasty meal.

The long ride home, eventually back to Cairns, Australia, took me into a sandpit. The well-defended walls, impeccably built to filter out anything contrary to my self-agenda, kept cascading back down on me. Both Fiona and I had made errors of judgment. But I fell into my own sandpit. I'd dug it. Being proved wrong after taking such a strong position on that beach brought a humiliation as well as an apology, forgiveness, and reconciliation with Fiona. Resolute, we were reengaged. I flew her in for her fiftieth birthday dinner at the Detroit Athletic Club. Occasionally, in the course of the evening, self-resentment percolated as we sipped champagne. I realized I was equivocal for the most part in this elegant setting. We selected an antique diamond ring from DuMouchelle's jewelry store in Grosse Pointe (in the same building where Bob Valk's office was located). As I slipped it on her finger, an old girlfriend (crush) walked into the store. I introduced her to Fiona. I was becoming more conscious and deliberate moving forward.

Christmas 2006 was spent in Cairns. We decided to be married in the village of Tabuane in early February 2007. A second ceremony that included her three daughters and a licensed minister would be performed on a remote aboriginal beach called Wangetti (the meeting place), north of Cairns, two weeks after the ceremony in Tabuane. The koan "Never say never" was enriched with new meaning by this decision.

In keeping with a local wedding tradition, the groom, Tau Bada, is held by two Tabuane men to prevent him from running away before the marriage. John thought of his first marriage ceremony, a posh and formal event in Saint Thomas Church in midtown Manhattan that included a carriage ride to a blowout reception at the New York Yacht Club. "This was different. I was inwardly awake and very much aware of what I was doing." The village celebration happily crossed cultures. The bride made breast friends. "This was absolute fun. It was a blast. We felt loved."

CHAPTER 15

Pigs

"Fact #1: The orgasm of a pig lasts for 30 minutes. Fact #2: Bacon is quite delicious. Conclusion: Bacon's flavor comes from a 30-minute marinade of intense piggy climaxes."

—Matthew Inman

The day before our wedding, we hiked from the village of Tabuane, crossing streams and walking through coffee gardens, to get to our home. The late-afternoon sun was at our backs, casting shadows on the mountaintops overlooking the valley where our house was built.

Blooming orchids, impatiens, and bougainvillea enclosed us. The entrance to our dwelling was a canopy of flowers. Fiona once had an orchid farm. To spend an evening with her and a botanist is to listen to poetry.

I looked over the cliffs down on the river and saw the waterfall and pool to my right. The gardens were manicured and the grass freshly cut with bush knives. They were expecting us.

Daut, our gardener, cook, guard, and friend, instructed the young men and women to remove the luggage and supplies from their heads. I am amazed at the loads they could carry and the balance they possessed. The terrain was challenging. Their eye/hand coordination was impeccable. They chatted, sang hymns and village songs, and laughed as they traversed through the coffee garden on a very narrow path.

I gave them a few kina and thanked them. Fiona, speaking Pidgin, connected much more deeply. The village women prized her. A Singer sewing machine, lugged up to Tabuane from Australia, created a ton of goodwill with a new sewing circle that generated cash for their families.

We were fading from exhaustion. As I extinguished the lanterns and blew out the candles, Daut grabbed my arm and sat me down. Fiona was in the bedroom.

In his broken English and with arm gestures, he gingerly instructed me not to touch Fiona tonight. It would be inappropriate before the wedding ceremony. Besides, everyone would know.

"Daut, how would they know?" I asked.

"They will smell you and Fiona tomorrow, John. That's how they know," he said.

The image of my father quickly appeared. I could see him in the backyard in Grosse Pointe (circa mid-1950), drawing on a cigarette, sipping a Miller High Life beer at nightfall in its fullness. "Johnny, if you make a habit of masturbating, one of two things can happen and possibly both," he said. I was sitting on the porch steps, looking up anxiously, awaiting his pronouncement. "Either your cock will fall off, or you will become mentally ill." Thanks, Dad. I went upstairs, locked the bathroom door, and whacked myself off. Never gave it a second thought. My cock is still working, though the threat of mental illness still plays on my mind to this day.

This time, I obeyed. The tribe had spoken. I knew they had keen senses. I kept my hands off Fiona.

Daut abruptly woke us up at 6:30 a.m. Standing in a half circle in front of our porch were six village men and women dressed in traditional wedding apparel. Every feather, ring, shell necklace, bead, string, belt, and, of course, traditional clothing, such as penis gourds for the men, had a place and purpose. Innumerable paintings on their faces, arms, and chests captivated me. The dyes and pigments, fresh and plucked from their garden at dawn, were to be used to decorate the bride and groom.

Our separation was immediate and lasted until the ceremony. The three men escorted me to a room in my home on one side, and the three women were with Fiona in another room on the other side.

We were washed, dressed, and painted in a ceremony that was dead serious and perfected to the most exact detail. They'd had much practice over the course of twelve thousand to fourteen thousand years.

Within two hours, we were ready to walk to the village. Fiona was escorted to one home, representing her clan, and I to another home, representing another clan. Both of these clans were to be our *tambu* (kin for life), with all rights, privileges, and demands.

My tambu-to-be Ezekiel mentored me the best he could. The other two men spoke better English. I was instructed by this group of elders to be clear on the number of pigs I would be giving away to gain permission to have Fiona become my wife. The normal village ceremony would last for days, with bartering between clans until agreement was reached on the number of pigs, shell money, and yams. I got off cheap in terms of time. Fiona cost me three pigs and compensation for the feast. But the pigs were the clinchers. This was not chump change.

Again, I thought back to Saint Thomas Church in Manhattan. I knew that was not chump change either. But somehow, besides the cultural environment, this was different. I was inwardly awake and very much aware of what I was doing. I deliberately chose to move into the union with this backdrop. Frankly, anything else would have been boring. I was going with the flow, not having any clue what was around the bend. The deep survival skills that are center stage in a media world of extreme experiences give little credence to the survival skills required in a varied social and cultural milieu. I would soon find this out.

The deal was now struck. I got Fiona. The World Trade Center towers loomed into my peripheral vision, the place where fees were given, agreements signed, deals consummated. Off to the New York Athletic Club for a steam and massage, drinks at the Oak Room in the Plaza Hotel at 6 p.m., and a steak and lobster dinner scheduled at Smith & Wollensky to follow.

The sing-sing was in process. Two long lines representing Tabuane, numbering three hundred people, made a walkway across the village to an open-air, tin-roofed church. Leis, orchids, and other flowers were abundant, and palm branches swayed on both sides. The singing of traditional hymns, chants, and new wedding songs for the occasion filled the air.

Once we crossed the entranceway to the church, the villagers' singing and noise stopped at once. Inside, traditional hymns in their language were sung over and over until Fiona and I were in front of Pastor Daniel, with three women on Fiona's left and three men to my right. We all faced the altar.

Pastor Daniel was in traditional Anglican white robes. His hair glistened from the heat and was matted to his head. I immediately thought of James Brown in *The Blues Brothers*. Fiona caught on as well. The place was packed, with guests surrounding the church.

The singing and tambourines died down. Pastor Daniel was dancing to the music, reminding me of Ebenezer Baptist Church in Detroit when I, as a guest, saw the congregation carried away with the Holy Ghost and members, slain in the spirit, falling to the floor. He finally got hold of himself and quieted down.

Again, we were astonished by the resemblance of our pastor to James Brown. He was ready to explode with excitement. . . . "I feel good." Fiona and I looked inconspicuously at one another with our heads bowed, but we were about to burst out laughing. This was absolute fun. It was a blast. We felt loved.

The ceremony was perfunctory in most respects. But Pastor Daniel's opening remarks were quite entertaining. "My friends, as we gather here today to see the first white people ever to be married in our village," he said, "let us not forget that not too long ago, we would not be marrying them; we would be eating them."

The congregation said, "Amen." Fiona and I responded, "Amen."

It felt much more intimate here than at Saint Thomas Church.

We ended the ceremony by holding hands and kissing. The shrieks and laughter were enormous. One does not display such antics in public on Managalas Plateau. It only occurs behind thatched doors.

We emerged through a double line of well-wishers and personal handshakes and "Eses" from most village members. The traditional sing-sing ceremonial dancing and celebration lasted for two hours. Coconuts were sipped from, and we nibbled on bananas and pineapple. I thought of the New York Yacht Club oysters on the half shell and iced champagne. I was having more fun here and didn't have to rent a tuxedo.

It was a long day. The afternoon sun finally fell behind the mountains. Enough ceremony. I was thirsting for a tin cup of Jack Daniel's and fresh roasted pig with lots of yams and fried bananas. But more than that, I was ready to ravish Fiona. She looked so damn sexy in her wedding outfit. Her breasts kept poking out of her beaded top all day long, staring right at me.

We were holding hands as we walked to the coffee-garden path to our home. I glanced up as a military truck pulled up. At least a dozen uniformed men with automatic rifles piled out. The sudden pandemonium, screams, wailing, and sense of fear were overwhelming. These militia "pigs" took over the village. We were stunned—like an avalanche or tsunami stunned. We were ill-prepared for such an event. Survival skills for such a mishap were not a priori.

Within the hour, twelve men were hauled away and immediately imprisoned under suspicion of murdering the sorcerer, the man who, months ago, had been speared and hacked to death on this very dirt landing. The timing was impeccable. I lost my appetite for roasted pig.

Now, sitting on our front porch steps, I was curious to view some of the photos taken during the day. I unsnapped the camera cover and a piece of paper fell out. I remembered I'd given the camera to Warpa Kephale earlier in the day to take wedding pictures. I read the note that had been left inside and was incredibly shocked. It was a suicide letter from our partner Warpa. He knew of the impending arrests but was not sure when they would happen. The majority of men picked up by the police were his brothers, cousins, and tambu. Warpa gave us one helluva wedding gift.

We were alone. Our caretaker, Daut Kephale, was one of the arrested suspects. As Fiona waited on the steps for my return, my walk back to Warpa's house through the coffee garden was very different from this morning. Was this a dream?

Joseph Conrad, in *Heart of Darkness*, cautions with this remark: "It is impossible to convey the life-sensation of any given epoch of one's existence. That which makes its truth, its meaning—its subtle penetrating essence. It is impossible. We live, as well as dream—alone."

"The beauty surrounding me was a paradox"—symbolized by this endemic orchid, *Dendrobium spectabile*, in their front garden, just off the porch. "With such serenity and perfection in view, darkness lay just beyond and all around. It was evil beyond my imagination."

CHAPTER 16

Paradoxes

"We in the West are alienated from ourselves and from nature. We labor under a number of delusions, one of which is that life makes sense; i.e., that we are sane. We persist in this view despite massive evidence to the contrary."

—Edward T. Hall

Cyclones are the deepest of all low-pressure weather systems. Extreme turbulence develops over warm seas near the equator as the sun beats down. The water and air spiral upward quickly, as cool air rushes in to fill the void. This natural phenomenon continues as air is drawn in and then spirals upward with devastating force. Its clockwise circling movement distinguishes the Southern Hemisphere cyclones from the counterclockwise movement in the Northern Hemisphere, where cyclones are called typhoons or hurricanes.

A ripple of instability over the warm Coral Sea brought disaster and personal devastation to the southeastern coast of Papua New Guinea in November 2007. Cyclone Guba was a stubborn weather system that refused to move, dumping torrential rain on the Owen Stanley Range. This storm spanned more than one thousand kilometers and, within one day, dropped more rainfall than a year's precipitation in London. More than 150 villagers were swept away by swollen rivers and mudslides, and more than fifty bridges were demolished.

The people of our Ijivitari District up in the Managalas Plateau endured untold suffering. Their gardens were destroyed. People were hungry and lacked drinking water. Rivers were cluttered with debris, human waste, and corpses.

Fiona and I assisted in fund-raising within the business community of Cairns, Australia, and were involved with plans to move food and water to the plateau. Sadly, but not surprisingly, we had to confront greed and corruption, even in this obvious gesture of goodwill. I was then and am still deeply conflicted over the avarice I have witnessed in Papua New Guinea. It is never-ending. I doubted reconstruction funds would ever reach the Oro Province community.

Managalas Plateau did slowly recover from the devastation of Cyclone Guba. The significant loss of coffee trees meant precious little cash (known locally as *kina*) would be derived from these crops. The lack of available money further exacerbated stealing, lying, and embezzlement among the locals. This behavior was strongly influenced by cultural undercurrents. The *wantok* tribal system was based on the local dialect and exerted considerable control over the life of the individual. Loyalty was expected. The *tambu* tribal system also demanded loyalty to the group, based on bloodlines. When criminal acts were discovered, the standard responses were either profuse denial or avoidance. They would give American crooks a run for their money. Their Hollywood dramatics, as evidenced by pleadings of innocence and histrionics, were impressive. Overlay these antics with devout public prayers from village elders, and I had a powerful sociopathic brew to contend with on a weekly basis. These defensive postures reminded me of my stepdaughters as they entered their teens.

From February to June 2008, I lived in the village of Tabuane, utilizing a management system practiced for two years.

A core team of elders worked and met monthly. They represented top management, overseeing thirty-five villages and the thirty village-agent network that included two thousand farmers.

We scheduled daylong core team meetings. These sessions took place in my home. I served as the facilitator, moving the group through an agenda. Assuming I knew what was going on in the plateau, the meetings were perfunctory, anticipating business as usual.

Living up in Tabuane, I was becoming a member of the community. The Tau Bada (big white man) was being assimilated, though still an outsider. I was viewed as the *out*side big boss, while Warpa Kephale, our partner, was considered the *in*side big boss.

Meetings opened with a prayer. I solicited any subjects, concerns, and worries to discuss. Silence generally prevailed until a stronger person took the lead. Usually, it was Juda Divish, head of the certified organic program. Juda had reading and math skills and had once held a job as a security guard in Port Moresby. Such qualifications placed him far above his peers. He was not born in Tabuane; therefore, his loyalty was to his tambu, located in another village, even though he lived in Tabuane.

During one meeting, Juda, with an assertiveness that surprised me, declared: "You, John Quinlan, must decide the compensation [cash, food, pigs] due to my family for the killing of my brother Francis [accused of being a sorcerer] by Warpa Kephale's family. We expect the company to pay the compensation to our clan."

My intuition went into high gear. I responded: "My position and our company's is that we have no role in the affairs of your clan. You and Warpa Kephale's clan must work out your problems. You will receive no compensation from Java Mama."

Clueless, I had little comprehension of what had gone down in this interaction. Warpa Kephale was reeling from the public humiliation of his family's imprisonment and the loss of his governorship race. So he was of little help. He was mute, a habit I grew to detest, and he typically avoided conflict. He lost further credibility by embezzling eight thousand kina from the company in October 2008. We forgave him, yet we had not received repayment. There was always an implicit threat that as the "big man," Warpa would withdraw his personal support if compensation was not received. His tactics were not much different from the Beltway lobbyists of Washington, DC, working with politicians who represented special-interest groups. We obliged.

Despite Juda's outburst, the simmering unrest between the two clans would remain calm for the rest of 2009, and the company would gain significant momentum as we entered into a dual cash crop year in 2010, with the chilies ready to pick. Our work was beginning to bear fruit. The organization structure and management system were beginning to take hold. Village chiefs and elders supported our cultivation and planting practices, both for coffee and chilies. We were viewed as sent by a good spirit. We were meant to be here to help them. It was obvious. They had more cash in their pockets than anyone could remember having.

For the first time since Papua New Guinea's independence from Australia in 1975, life on Managalas Plateau felt optimistic. The farm gate price for parchment coffee was at an all-time high, pegged at four kina ($1.60 US) per kilo versus sixty toea ($0.25 US) per kilo four years earlier. Chilies were purchased for three kina per kilo. Our initial shipment of bird's-eye chilies in late 2010 marked the first time in twenty-five years that this commodity entered the global market from Papua New Guinea. Signs of prosperity were evident. School fees were being paid and kerosene purchased for lanterns. Rice and canned beef complemented yams, in addition to taro and fried bananas. Tin roofs replaced thatch, and, for the first time, many villagers could afford the six-hour trip to the city of Popondetta via public transit versus walking bush tracks for two days. Many farmers made their first visit to the town.

It was apparent to everyone that the Managalas Plateau had been blessed. All of the villages but one enjoyed these new fortunes. Sickness, untimely deaths, and a rekindling of threats between two clans plagued Tabuane. The chilies yield per tree was 30–50 percent higher in other villages. These factors were ingredients for sorcery and threats against our company. Somehow, Fiona and I were characterized as bringing misfortune to Tabuane.

As 2010 unfolded, the problems of Tabuane became the talk of the plateau. Fear grew, and the curse on Tabuane was prophesied to spread throughout Managalas and destroy livelihoods. Village sorcerers became more vocal and were viewed with a renewed sense of power. They demanded that their advice, warnings, threats, and poisonings be heeded, adding, "This white man company is the root of our problems to come."

Village chiefs, elders, and ministers throughout Managalas reacted and implored Tabuane to host a crusade including all the villages of the plateau. It would be Tabuane's responsibility to plan for this five-day gathering. Tabuane leaders would have to feed and house approximately five hundred people.

Slowly, the village of Tabuane responded. The first order of business was to have a village meeting with Fiona and me. At this point, villagers resisted the crusade. Warpa Kephale would not vocally support it. I was at a loss. Pressure mounted for Fiona and me to publicly support and help pay for the crusade.

We were being drawn into a vortex of confusion. Another cyclone was brewing.

The crusade was named "To Lift the Curse." Plateau-wide churches, including the Anglican, Pentecostal, Adventist, and Catholic faiths, prescribed an exorcism of the Tabuane village, along with surrounding farm plots.

A second meeting in preparation for the crusade included the chief, elders, and farmers. The toktok convened early one morning in the coffee shed, with its metal roof and cement floor. Sitting alone in a semicircle, Fiona and I faced a group numbering approximately fifty people. We were tense and felt unsure of ourselves. My fear was well concealed. I really did not know what to expect.

Immediately following the opening prayer, to our surprise, a handsome young man immediately took charge. Paul Kephale was Warpa Kephale's younger brother and a schoolteacher, returning from Port Moresby. He was vocal and imposing, and he delivered a dire message: "If you do not start treating John and Fiona and this company with respect and thankfulness, you will suffer and lose your blessing. You are a blind and greedy village and should be ashamed of yourselves."

All hell broke loose. The obvious truth of Paul's declaration was revealed and made public. For the first time, this village was reminded how fortunate it was to have us living in Tabuane rather than another village in the Managalas Plateau. Warpa was conspicuously and deliberately absent, but this publicly drew him into a larger conversation. He must offer an olive branch to Juda's clan to bring about reconciliation. Warpa would have to seek forgiveness for the killing of Francis and make compensation. Fiona, for the first time since walking up to Tabuane in 2005, openly wept for its people, warning of dire consequences if villagers refused to admit their wrongdoing. She spoke of future suffering, even predicting more deaths.

The elders were shocked that a white woman should openly share such strong words and were alarmed by the event's significance. They interpreted her statements to mean that more suffering indeed would visit the village unless a crusade was initiated.

Another six months elapsed before the crusade took place. I lived up in Tabuane, working with the farmers in building chilies-drying tunnels, and walking to other villages to encourage the picking and drying of this new cash crop. I would return home early evenings to wash in the pool below the waterfall as the sun sank behind the mountains. Daut prepared dinner over an open pit in the detached kitchen. Fiona was away for an extended period, supervising the build-out of a warehouse, offices, and a solar drying facility in the village of Afore. Strategically, the centralized location of Afore in the Managalas Plateau for the new company headquarters, minus the drama and internal politics of Tabuane, was logical. But sitting alone, night after night, I yearned for her company.

I often sat sipping whiskey from a tin cup, smoking a cigar, and studying the shadows cast by lanterns and candles on the bamboo walls. Fireflies hovered brightly over the gardens flanking our doorway, lighting up the surrounding bush.

But the beauty surrounding me was a paradox. With such serenity and perfection in view, darkness lay just beyond and all around. It was evil beyond my imagination. Over the next two months, Tabuane would agonize over the death of the crusade leader's wife during childbirth, the horror of a village woman hacked and buried alive, and, sadly, the death of the handsome young Paul Kephale from blood poisoning. Fiona had been ever so insightful. More suffering arrived. The curse had to be lifted.

While John, Fiona, and their daughters enjoyed a peaceful, elegant Christmas in Michigan, a call came from Papua New Guinea. Their business associate had taken a company Toyota, against instructions, and had run over two people, killing one of them. That led to a five-thousand-person attack on the company's facilities and vehicles. "The ultimate impact to the company, livelihoods and personal finances would be staggering for the next three years. The social, cultural and psychological damages would be immeasurable."

CHAPTER 17

The Christmas Present

"Murphy's Quantum Law: Anything that can, could have, or will go wrong, is going wrong, all at once."
— Paul Dickson, *The Official Rules*

To fully comprehend the situation around Tabuane in 2009, one must go back a few years. Fiona and I were mentally and physically depleted by the ordeals of 2007 and 2008. Yet we were more optimistic than we ever had been. In spite of the devastating cyclone that impacted the plateau in late 2007 and created havoc most of 2008, we positioned the company for significant results for 2009. We yearned for a reprieve from the unrelenting problem-ridden pace. Budgeting enough funds, we traveled back to Grosse Pointe for a Christmas holiday with our daughters. Assuming we had instituted enough management structure and controls, we determined that we could depart Tabuane operations and the Popondetta facility, leaving them in the trusted hands of our partner, Warpa Kephale, Popondetta supervisor Nicie Dimwita, and security staff.

Our assumption was soon invalidated. Returning from a jacket-and-tie cocktail party on Christmas afternoon, we felt pampered. My neighbor's high-walled, private Victorian mansion with marble floors, Oriental rugs, French furniture, sculptures, and landscape oil paintings, bracketed by a fireplace at each end of his home, provided an elegant setting for holiday festivities. Our daughters enjoyed roaming the rooms and climbing the spiral staircase, looking down on a massive crystal chandelier above the entranceway and foyer. Chilled champagne, shrimp, cheeses, sliced tenderloin, and blintzes filled my senses with pleasure.

A cheery mood prevailed as we walked home as a family. Snow, piled a foot deep along the sidewalk, glistened in the setting sun. The luxury of an impending nap only two blocks away was lulling. Another family dinner was planned for the evening. Our intention was to pack and load up the Jeep the following morning. We would drive north to Destiny Bay to spend a week enjoying my friends and teaching our daughters to snowboard and ski. Then we would cross the Mackinac Bridge and holiday at Copper Harbor in the Keweenaw Peninsula.

Arriving home, I pushed the replay button on my kitchen telephone to retrieve messages. Already, my mind was upstairs, buried in the pillows and bed comforter. My body only had to follow and fall on the mattress for that snooze.

I was yanked out of this mirage by the following message: "John and Fiona, this is Dan Moser in Cairns, Australia. I have bad news to give you on Christmas. I'm afraid it will spoil your day. . . ."

Dan, who had agreed to join our company in mid-January, had received a call earlier that morning (fifteen hours ahead of Eastern Standard Time) from Nicie in Popondetta. On Christmas Eve day, Warpa Kephale had taken our Toyota Land Cruiser against instructions, loaded with his wife, three children, and supplies, to drive up to Tabuane. He encountered a grim situation. He ran over and killed a pedestrian—and then, panicked, he backed up and ran over another person. Fortunately, the second person was alive and at a hospital. Fearing for his life, Warpa drove to the police station, where he was placed in protective custody. Within a half hour, five thousand people rioted and charged our office and warehouse facility. They climbed over the fences, carrying spears, axes, and bush knives. They chased the guards and employees away. Vehicles were smashed, doors and windows bashed in, and inventory and equipment stolen, along with cash and personal valuables. The police arrived with guns and dispersed them, with no arrests. Both clans, representing the pedestrians, threatened to kill Warpa and our employees. Immediate financial compensation was demanded.

As the message ended, I heard Christmas music playing in the living room. Bing Crosby crooned, "The weather outside is frightful . . ." I put the phone down and stepped into the library to talk to Fiona. At the very least, I knew I was about to diminish not only the moment but also her holiday. In fact, the ultimate impact to the company, livelihoods, and personal finances would be staggering for the next three years. The social, cultural, and psychological damages would be immeasurable.

We did not have many options to deal with such aberrations. But these really weren't aberrations. They were the norm. We had learned that the unexpected was to be the expected. Powerlessness gripped me. Where did we even start? I wanted a nap. I wanted to wake up and hope that this was a bad dream, a Christmas prank worthy of Scrooge himself.

My only hope was to persuade Dan Moser—a six foot four, 250-pound ex–Canadian Mounted Police officer—to immediately hop a plane to Popondetta to take control. His work permit and visa were in order, and he agreed to go. That moment deepened my appreciation for Dan's prowess, zest for adventure, and avowed interest in going up to Popondetta, Papua New Guinea. Few white men have expressed such enthusiasm, especially when the chips are down.

Two days later, our new general manager Dan arrived to find Warpa Kephale still in a cell to protect his life. Except for Nicie, our employees refused to come to work. The clans threatened vengeance if they did not receive immediate compensation. Dan had the police visit daily to present the appearance that we were secured and still in business, though there was little daily traffic to buy goods, equipment, or stock feed. The clans frightened the general population. We were under siege. Keep in mind that Fiona and I were calling on a mobile phone that used prepaid minutes to connect to PNG. This created a difficult imposition. The powerlessness of being so remote was sinking in.

The lovely thought of the green woods, white landscape, and brisk, clear air of northern Michigan appealed to me. I yearned for this setting, in contrast to the humidity, heat, and mosquitoes of the bush. My stifled mind needed a dramatically different image. It needed to breathe the crystal air. The MacCready family and Destiny Bay were awaiting our arrival. This distraction would at least alleviate a foreboding feeling that things were going to get worse. Trying to act normal in front of family, friends, and the children was a strain almost beyond comprehension.

During the first week in Detroit, I treated the family to the Broadway play *Wicked* at the Michigan Opera Theatre. Another evening, I surprised them with a Red Wings hockey game at the Joe Louis Arena. In spite of the Wings trouncing the Chicago Blackhawks, 4–0, I was in a trance. Unconsciously, I was substituting bows and arrows, spears, and bush knives for hockey sticks, helmets, and pads. Papua New Guinea seemed to trivialize many of the activities I once enjoyed. Thoughts of vengeance distracted me as I sipped on a Labatt's Blue Ale and viewed the game. Hockey moves quickly up and down the rink. Emotions run higher with fans when they see an unjust body check. The call for a penalty by the referees or desire for an act of revenge by a player spike the air. The correlation is obvious—the dirtier the hooking, blocking, tripping, or checking, the louder the yelling for retribution. Nobel laureate, author, and anthropologist Jared Diamond says the thirst for vengeance "is among the strongest of human emotions. It ranks with love, anger, grief, and fear, about which we talk incessantly. . . . We grow up being taught that such feelings are primitive, something to be ashamed of and to transcend."

Departing for Harbor Springs the following morning temporarily increased my sense of self-worth. At least I competently loaded the Jeep for the drive north. Meanwhile, whatever self-esteem I had returning from Papua New Guinea after one hellish year dissipated as I watched our companies crumble.

New Year's Eve day was turning into evening as we walked into the refuge of my past. Viewing Little Traverse Bay covered with ice and snow calmed me down as I sipped a vodka martini. The girls were excited. While showering and dressing for dinner, I decided to call Dan Moser, our new hero. It had been two days since we'd spoken. I felt like I was calling my doctor for test results on blood work due to an undiagnosed symptom. I assumed the fort was secure and further damage mitigated by Dan's imposing presence. He answered his mobile phone, his voice unusually clear.

To my chagrin, our new general manager had boarded a plane without notice and fled back to Australia. Happy New Year!

Quite aggressively, Dan shared this harrowing experience: "Just a day ago, I was in our office behind the counter. The guards permitted a young woman to enter. She looked straight into my eyes, identifying herself as the sister of the man who was killed and the person chosen to speak for her clan. She said: 'You white man will be killed if you stay in Popondetta.'"

I imagined Dan turned another shade of white, as those Aussies did on the vessel *Bent Sound* a number of years ago on the Solomon Sea. Within twenty-four hours, he was back in the safety of Cairns, Australia. I could not blame him.

Fiona and I put on our New Year's Eve game faces. The table setting was elegant. Kate MacCready cut fresh cedar pine and surrounded the candelabras with scented boughs. Champagne was uncorked, as the first course of a magnificent evening meal unfolded.

Peering between the red candles, I glanced at Fiona. Her disposition was unperturbed. Her resiliency, which I greatly admire, would be further tested soon. The following morning, on a beach walk, Fiona greeted the New Year with a stumble on snow-covered ice and broke her ankle in two places. So much for her skiing holiday. Over the course of February and March 2009, she would hike the bush tracks of Managalas Plateau with a cast on her right foot.

I had begged off on the walk and found a comfortable lounge chair in front of a stone-inlaid fireplace so large you could burn four-foot-long split birch logs. As I nestled into the chair and pulled up a comforter, I reread Jared Diamond's article on vengeance. It was beginning to click. My head was dulled from the champagne the evening before, but I underlined part of a paragraph. Diamond explained that before there were city-states (institutions), Papua New Guinea's method of resolving major disputes either violently or by payment of compensation was the worldwide norm. PNG is not the only place where those traditional methods of dispute resolution still coexist uneasily with the methods of state government—methods such as I witnessed now in Oro Province and what Jared Diamond purports would seem quite familiar to urban gangs in America, as well as Somalis, Afghans, Kenyans, and other people where tribal ties remain strong and state control weak. I was beginning to understand more clearly the deeply embedded need for vengeance and the hostility displayed toward Dan Moser. As Diamond suggests, these reactions are really not so far from our own inclinations as we might like to think.

Wearing a Detroit T-shirt, John enters the remote village of Kiara—
the first white man ever to do so. Moments before stepping through an
opening in the bamboo wall, a village elder, gripping a knife, demands,
"Are you here to hurt, steal, and rob us, or are you here to help and
save us?" On that day, as proprietor of the company that would buy
the villagers' crops at a fair price, John receives the prodigious gift of a
large live pig.

CHAPTER 18

Kiara

"In the deep glens where they lived, all things were older than man and they hummed of mystery."
—Cormac McCarthy

Tabuane soon owned us. Without much fanfare, Fiona and I were socially assimilated and emotionally adopted by the village. The Christmas Eve situation was painfully addressed. Ransoms were paid to stave off retaliation. We had to proceed with a new harvest. Our lack of trust in Warpa was irreparable, but I could not change horses in midstream. We were stuck with him. Now that the marriage ceremony was completed, we took up residence in our new home. A sense of familiarity and acceptance began to take hold. With innocence and the desire to be liked, we fully opened up our hearts. The walks to the village market, bush track hikes, and working with the farmers became routine. Tabuane indeed became our first and only Garden.

The wives of the elders employed by Java Mama would frequently visit early in the morning. Wilma, Penopel, and Ilma carried fresh-baked flour, pineapple, and bananas to our front door. The three women endeared themselves to us with their smiles, giggles, and dancing. Standing on the walkway surrounded by flowers, they sang village songs. The vibrancy of the begonias and orchids contrasted with their checkered sarongs. The images were etched in my mind.

Birdwing butterflies would dance in pairs, flying from one bush to another. Massive spider webs, acting as refractors, split the morning sun's rays into the colors of the rainbow.

Close to mid-July 2009, I realized that nearly two years had passed since our wedding. The plateau was fully aware of our presence. Benefits from a higher farm-gate certified organic and Rainforest Alliance coffee price were now acknowledged and associated with the white couple living in Tabuane.

The weather was dry. Ice-blue skies distinguished the verdant rainforest. Rain was absent for over five weeks, yet the spring-fed waterfall below our home gave us relief from the day's heat.

One day as Fiona and I climbed back up the embankment to our home, the afternoon sun, sinking behind the mountains, as usual cast long shadows on the forest across the river. We had a refreshing wash at the pool below the falls. Large black boulders heated by the sun warmed us as we lay there to dry off.

A group of girls, numbering not more than six, spied on us and eventually had the courage to appear from the kunai grass. They sang and finally line-danced. The oldest, probably thirteen years old, grasped a tambourine and kept the group in unison as their toes gripped the riverbed's stones. Detroit's 1963 Motown hit by Martha and the Vandellas flooded my mind and I hummed the melody of "Heat Wave."

Let the good times roll! I felt connected. Amid the plateau's primeval forest, Tabuane's charity, and Fiona's sensuality, I was transfixed. The bourbon and cigars certainly accented this ambiance. The glass was presently half full. On occasion, it is a condition worth noting when all the crap and problems seem to compel me to view life as a mistake ready to happen. It may have been an elusive sweet spot to find myself ultimately comprehending two polarities and be fully content. Novelist Jim Harrison—God, I think of this guy a lot—commented in one of his earlier books that man is in search of a place somewhere between a palace and a cabin. At this moment, that dichotomy fused with this panorama. I was content.

Daut, busy cooking dinner, glanced up. Our eyes met, and I thought he was ready to shout something out. Instead, he smiled and waved. Darkness quickly descended and we lit the lanterns and candles. Soon all three of us were sitting down to a dinner made up of sliced cucumbers, tomatoes, and chilies with a touch of olive oil, salt, and pepper, plus a roasted village chicken served with jasmine rice and warmed corn tortillas. Fiona uncorked a bottle of Cabernet Sauvignon. Daut prayed. His invocations were straight from the gut. I felt drawn into a two-way conversation between him and his Papa (God). The detail and description were vivid and presented with such humility that I was encouraged in my own faith walk, which at times has been mighty thin and questionable, especially since the shit hit the fan with Warpa Kephale's Christmas Eve accident.

Fiona and Daut ignored me by having a talk in Pidgin. I sipped my wine and then bit into a tortilla stuffed with chicken and rice, doused with Tabasco sauce. I inquired: What was going on?

Like a boy ready to burst out with a tattletale, revealing to Mama that his older sister was surfing the 'net for a porn site, Daut blurted out that we are expected to be in the village of Kiara at noon tomorrow. They want to honor me with a pig.

Dumbfounded, I took another sip of wine and glared at Daut, feeling shanghaied. Few words were spoken. We finished dinner.

The dishes were washed, cigars lit, and two fingers of bourbon poured into tin cups for all three of us. Fiona took a long pull of my cigar. I wondered where she'd learned such mastery. It reminded me of dragging on the remnants of a spliff. Daut squirmed in his seat, and in broken English, he insisted we leave early in the morning. He saved the best for the last by casually remarking that we would be the first white people ever to enter the village. Until that moment, I presumed the missionary Jim Parlier had visited all of the plateau villages in his forty-five years of ministry. I was wrong. Kiara was too remote and inaccessible from his village of Numba.

We brewed and drank coffee and ate baked flour sprinkled with sugar and cinnamon, before departing at 6:30 a.m. on June 13. I wondered what this day's adventure held for Fiona and me. Daypacks were filled with ponchos, repellant, flashlights, hard candy, and water. We hiked through the coffee gardens down the mountainside to the village of Tabuane, where a Toyota cruiser was waiting with our driver, Lucien. Stepping up into the cab, I peered through the windshield into the distance. The unknown mesmerized me as I tried to fathom what mystery this day would reveal.

To get to Kiara, we drove for one hour south, veering slightly west through the villages of Dea, Ugunumo, and Jorura. After parking the vehicle at Jorura, we hiked a bush track around steep ravines. After two hours, we neared Kiara. The Sibium Range was directly south and therefore in front of us. To our west was the Owen Stanley front. Looming behind us, to the northeast, were the Hydrographers Range and Mount Lamington. The track crossed one deep river and two significant creeks and was largely an escarpment. Looking down, I saw deep-forested valleys on either side.

Mid-morning heat from a bright sun, along with stifled

humidity, soaked my T-shirt. I rested under an okari nut tree to gain shade and sipped on bottled water. My mind drifted to other places and other rooms. The antiquity of the landscape and density of the forest pulled me into a long-forgotten cave where I viewed pictographs etched in limestone at the bottom of the Grand Canyon. The stars on that night had drawn me upward into a spiral, a boundless and infinite experience as I lay on the shoreline in a sleeping bag next to the Colorado River. I'd looked at the sheer canyon walls and glimpsed a slice of the sky's expanse. Things were put into perspective for this young CEO of a publicly traded company. I'd breathed the arid air and felt and tasted the river's mist.

Now the scent of musk and decay touched the sinews of my soul. I dug my fingers into moist black soil. My breathing reminded me that, forty years later, I was still connected to the same life force that had embraced me when I was a young man. Such mystery was too profound to understand then and even more profound on this day. The sixty-three-year-old tent called my body had weathered pretty well.

My legs began to stiffen. I stood up and stretched my back.

Surprisingly, three men appeared out of the bush and stepped on to the track. They engaged Juda and Daut in conversation. Juda, the coffee general manager, stepped away and informed us the Member of Parliament was not happy that we were in his neck of the woods, and he resented the intrusion by white people. We were not welcome, and he advised us to depart. What a nice salutation. I gazed into the dense canopy arching over the path leading to Kiara. My reaction, without using the "F" word, was "Screw him." Immediately, Fiona was distracted by the mating cry of the bird of paradise. She scampered up the track with two men, voicing instructions as she disappeared into the forest to video it. This diversion was enough to keep me steady as I began to comprehend the warning that just had been shot across our bow.

As we neared the village of Kiara, a vine net spanned the open space between towering gum trees. Within the webbed labyrinth were flying foxes (fruit bats), cockatoos, and eclectus parrots. Ingeniously snared, these poor creatures would soon be the villagers' dinner. Their plucked feathers would be interwoven into costumes or traded for other goods. I was grateful that Fiona would not permit the men to capture or kill the bird of paradise with their slingshots. Five warriors with chiseled gleaming bodies, dressed in traditional celebratory costumes, greeted us. The village was now visible on a knoll. Directives were given. I was to speak with the chief, elders, and a councilman before the door in a bamboo wall that separated Kiara from us would be opened.

Following tradition, I walked ahead of the group. Fiona and Juda followed and were within speaking distance to assist me with translation. Sweating profusely, I was on edge and tried not to appear nervous. To my right and then quickly to the left, two warriors jumped out from behind the welcome committee, thrusting spears at my feet to signify I was welcome. Highly stimulated, my response was typical: I almost crapped in my pants. Fiona reassured me by saying, "Everything is fine, darling. The closer the spears, the more you are hailed."

A rusted tin plate suspended from a pole dangled in the breeze. An elder, gripping a knife, banged the dish three times and pronounced in Barai dialect: "Are you here to hurt, steal, and rob us, or are you here to help and save us?" Fiona handed me a bottle of water as she started to film my response. Cotton-mouth tied my tongue.

Stammering, I pictured myself as a Washington Beltway politician, imparting a canned cover-your-ass media response. No, I could not go down that slippery road. Another Stafford moment was at hand. I mumbled, "No, I am here not to steal from you, and I may be able to help you. But I cannot save you. Only our God can save you."

Juda translated my response to the man under the tin plate. Whispers and giggles could be heard behind the wall. Numerous eyes, peering through the bamboo slates, unnerved me. I realized that over five hundred people were curious to see what the Tau Bada and his wife looked like. My mind raced as I waited for a rejoinder. This episode was more disconcerting than being grilled by a rating agency on Wall Street, where I would try to convince a panel of financial analysts to give my company a higher grade on a security to raise money.

The old man nodded, the tin pan banged, and the door was pushed open to permit Fiona and me to enter the village. Children sang songs and hymns in harmony to us. Kundu drums, tambourines, and guitars created a feverish backdrop of noise. Villagers placed orchid necklaces around our necks. They tossed flowers and sprinkled water in the air. We stepped forward and followed a line dance of a dozen painted and plumed men and bare-breasted women in grass skirts. With their beads and shells on wrists and ankles rattling a cadence, they summoned us into the village.

Swaying and stepping forward, I was drawn into an immense throng. Fiona was now separated from me as teenage girls rushed up to touch her golden hair. I viewed the distant mountains as the middle path split the village in half. Huts on both sides were landscaped with flowered gardens. Freshly cut palm branches protruding from the ground created a tunnel for the guests to walk through, extending as far as I could see. A fury of screeching villagers shook the palms, stirring the air into a swishing crescendo. I was lost in translation and unprepared for such a gush of raw emotion. The unfettered release of energy, so ecstatic and drumming, numbed my senses. Drawn into a mystical and ancient vortex, I flowed down the pathway to the center of the village, losing recollection of time and space.

Grandparents stood in open windows and waved and shouted. Broad smiles exposed lost teeth and red betel-nut gums peppered the cornucopia of adulations. We stood in front of a palm canopy where two wood chairs and a table were placed. Pineapples, bananas, and coconuts were piled high. Bunches of betel nuts hung from poles.

The Kiara chief and elders gathered in front of the furniture. James, our Java Mama coffee agent, was the host. Gerrod, who personally donated the pig, stood next to the village pastor, who immediately bowed his head and prayed. Introductions were made. I shook hands with each clan chief as I expressed my happiness. Fiona, speaking in Pidgin, explained her national heritage and reminded them she was a "white woman with a black heart." Laughter followed her comments as she endeared herself to the meeting members and village onlookers. Fiona's blond hair, blue eyes, and pale skin, along with her self-confidence, threw them for a loop! The "man in a woman's body" unpinned a social-cultural grenade, tossing it into their world and turning it upside down.

This woman was the one unmistakably responsible for creating cash benefits by buying their coffee in a remote area at a fair price. Prior to this, local men would profiteer with roadside buyers or male expatriates to connive and cheat the farmer. She also paid extra per kilo to reward the farmer for carrying a forty-kilo bag down the mountain to Jorura, for weighing and purchase. We were thanked for compensating the youth and church groups to maintain the roads. Also, they were excited by the news that a new company was to begin distributing chilies seeds for a new cash crop called bird's-eye chilies. This unfolding event was inspirational.

The warrior archetype loomed in my mind as I saw my wife firmly lead and communicate. I was grappling with my own need for affirmation as I saw her effortlessly empathize with deliberation. I felt estranged and of little value, since I had difficulty understanding Pidgin as well as Barai dialect. As a fifth wheel, I remained silent while observing the spectacle. Within moments, a commotion behind us attracted my attention. I turned around and viewed a prodigiously large pig, hanging upside down from a pole, carried by two village men. As the panicked pig squealed, the crowd became silent. Unbeknownst to the crowd, a "red badge of courage" was being pinned on my chest.

The immediate honor, tradition, and solemnity of this rite were not only profound for me but also for everyone present. Yet the deeper self-recognition was unspeakable. I glanced up from the swine at my feet and looked into the faces and examined the eyes of a semicircle of ancient men. "A thousand years is one day" ruminated in my mind as I savored the purpose and meaning in this speck of time. I accepted the pig with gratitude. It was my turn. I'd earned it. Fiona smiled at me. My testosterone spiked. I was tempted to have a chew of betel nut and spit with the best of the men, in lieu of a swig of bourbon. I kept my eye on my pig and gave specific instructions that it be brought to my village the following week. This was one gift I would fully savor at a later date.

Again, pigs had invaded my life. I remembered our wedding in Tabuane and realized how precious Fiona was to me. I gained far more that day than what was given to me today.

Humorously, I knew I still got a bargain. In PNG terms, Fiona was worth immeasurably more than the three pigs I'd bartered away to consummate the marriage. Sheepishly, I grinned as I looked at the food being carried into the gathering by the village women.

Feasting is an art form and is a mark of a good chief. Dozens of pots, trays, and dishes brimming with cooked vegetables accompanied the simmering pork, chicken, and fish cooked for this occasion. Yams had been baked in coconut oil and sprinkled with ginger shavings and diced green onions. The sweet potato's purple, yellow, and rouge hues contrasted with white jasmine rice. White taro served on platters embroidered with orange marigolds, red hibiscus, white and pink bougainvillea flowers, or native purple orchids called *Spathoglottis plicata* entranced me. The display hit me with just as much artistic allure as a Velázquez painting in Madrid's Prado museum or Florence's statue of David did when I was hitchhiking through Europe in my early twenties.

Arranged on a polished bamboo mat were dishes of fried banana, sliced watermelon, diced pineapple, cut-up cucumber, and cubed tomatoes. Trays of rice topped with roasted chicken, pork, and fish astutely sat on the haus win floor. A few men, swaying side to side, waved banana leaves to keep the flies off the delicacies.

I observed prideful women shouting instructions to one another as they carried food atop their heads from their huts. The smoldered fires left a dim haze. The faint smell of dying embers would be ever-present as I stored this moment away.

Wrinkled russet faces, fuzzy white hair, and twinkling eyes were among the clan chiefs' physical features. Respect for the older ones kept the festivity's dignity intact as the food and celebratory joy continued to grow in intensity. James stepped forward and requested the pastor bless the food. The commotion ended as bowed heads and silence prevailed. Within seconds, Fiona and I were handed tin plates, and the feasting procession started, followed by the chiefs, elders, and other guests.

The men layered their food, creating six-inch mounds that covered their bowls and plates. These massive portions consumed by such slight bodies reminded me of a python ingesting a suckling pig. I witnessed the men gulp their food and bulge their stomachs with ferocity. When finished, they rolled up their shirts and scratched their round bellies. After picking their teeth with a handy knife, they bit into a betel nut and spat in contentment, and then they retired to their huts for an afternoon nap. I mused about who had the better deal as I contemplated my eventual return to an electronically tethered and paced life in America.

Usually, endings are uncomfortable for me, as opposed to beginnings. I tried to comprehend the finality of this closure as I gathered my daypack and organized our party to depart. The odds of returning to this village were slim. The odds of these people meeting a white couple like Fiona and me were slimmer. Fate became even more pronounced as I began to understand and become more aware of the mystery of participating in the universe. The deepening of my own character escalated as I valued what was in front of my nose. My participation in this universe is ageless. A tribal chord resonated and hummed within me.

Hiking out of the village, we saw children playing hide-and-seek in the shrubbery and behind hut poles; they giggled and followed us. Abruptly, I turned around, lifted my arms, and growled. Delighted, others joined in the play. And did they play! I fetched the penny candy from my pack and tossed pieces all around. Scrambling for the treats, they screamed with laughter. They tried to impress Fiona and me with their quickness and ability to snatch the most candy.

As we hiked back up the escarpment, the children disappeared, yelling out, "Ese, ese, Tau Bada, ese." A few teenage girls followed us into the bush along the track. Sneakily, they emerged from behind to touch the pale woman with golden hair.

Soon, we viewed the late-afternoon sun on the same valleys. This perspective was completely different from the sun at our backs and the mountains casting dark shadows on the forest. A young man carrying a bush knife appeared on the trail before us. A red bandanna was wrapped around his head. Bare-chested, in shorts, he glistened with sweat as he joyfully repeated, "Hallelujah, brother, hallelujah." Frightened, Fiona bolted back to Juda and Daut. The young man claimed he'd been waiting for us, and it was his desire to escort us through this village area for our safety. I felt at ease and enjoyed his chants and attempts to chat with me. He sang songs from his village, old ones passed on to him from previous generations. Later in the evening, Daut remarked that his stories were of warriors and battles with other villages. I wondered if they were going to make up songs and stories about Fiona and me. Daut assured me they would and, in fact, he reminded me that the first song we heard as we walked into Kiara was about John and Fiona.

My new acquaintance, Andrew, hiked with our party for two hours. He grabbed my hand to help this Grosse Pointer walk over the river via a fallen okari nut tree. Daut did the same for Fiona. Andrew's friendliness and spontaneity would now be associated with "hallelujah" for the rest of my life.

Daut scampered ahead of us once we arrived at Tabuane. Fiona and I entered the descending pathway to the home and saw the lanterns glowing and candles lit. In celebration, we uncorked a bottle of Jacob's Creek Reserve Cabernet Sauvignon. Fiona proposed a toast to the timelessness of Kiara. We sat in the screened porch and watched the fireflies hover in the glens. The moon appeared, revealing the rising mist. I was glad for the day.

The crusade to lift the Tabuane curse: "The chants intermingled with Christian hymns enthralled me. The combined sights, sounds, and smells were unlike anything I had ever experienced. They jolted my soul like a defibrillator as the frenzy increased."

CHAPTER 19

Lift the Curse

"Curses are like processions; they return to the place from which they came."

—Giovanni Ruffini

The return to Papua New Guinea to resume operations in February 2010 continued to be emotionally conflicting, in spite of the Kiara celebration. Warpa Kephale's willfulness (insubordination), which had led to one death and the severe injury of another person, had set off a trip wire of vengeance. Compensation demands increased, as did related expenses to pay for all of the yams, pigs, and vegetables to the family of the deceased. Once we settled one set of demands, another disenfranchised clan member stepped forward, and the cycle repeated. Members of both clans visited Warpa's home, threatening to kill his wife and children. Similar threats were made to our office and warehouse employees. As Warpa became more frightened, he developed a greater reliance on us—an odd way to build trust. Warpa had no money, so we ended up paying off both clans and acquiring release statements regarding harmful acts, statements that were enforceable by the police.

To this day, Warpa has never publicly admitted we saved his life or thanked us for the compensation payments. Our naïveté and penchant to empathize with and help Warpa and others was a deeply embedded altruistic principle that Fiona and I shared. It never crossed my mind that Warpa expected this treatment. But it is now my understanding that a "cargo mind-set" has evolved in the rural indigenous people of Papua New Guinea since colonial times. The presumption assumes the community will wait for goods to drop from the sky, with no effort or reciprocity on their part. America left a big impression during World War II when its forces parachuted supplies and materials in order to build airstrips and arm and feed the soldiers.

During the ensuing months of 2009 and most of 2010, I began to deconstruct my own belief system as I realized the blind were leading the blind. We had become the designated givers while everyone around us played the role of designated taker. The scale would really never balance as I continued to unconditionally extend myself. I increased their dependency by giving more help. Not only were my psychological and spiritual reservoirs being drained, but my financial resources were as well. Debt was piling up in America as I continued to fund mishaps. A personal day of reckoning awaited me. I remembered the opaque interviewer who was a gorilla in Daniel Quinn's book *Ishmael*. The want ad in the personals section read, "Teacher seeks pupil, must have an earnest desire to save the world. Apply in person." This exposé was about givers and takers. Ultimately, the teacher died. I was disturbed by the book's beleaguered ending.

In my attempt to do the right thing the right way, I began to realize I might lose myself in this determination. A shade of my own mortality crept into this inner discourse as I turned sixty-three years old. As this idealist was being depleted, it was hard to let go of youthful self-perceptions. From June 30 through July 4, 2010, I was a bystander—a scribe—caught up in a drama that mixed people, culture, and spirit. Amid uncontrollable forces, I was now in the eye of the hurricane, with a stillness and silence that was unimaginably deafening.

Wednesday, June 30

Prayer and envisioning fortified my energy and psychological will to travel to Popondetta and to the Managalas Plateau without Fiona. She attended to another coffee opportunity in Morobe Province and a request of the government to assist in the organic certification process. This was my first solo. I was on my own without my trusted interpreter and best friend. I felt vulnerable and guarded. I planned to drive to Afore and spend two nights there before moving on to Tabuane, where I would arrive Saturday, July 3, to observe the "Lifting of the Curse" ceremony on Sunday. The distance between Afore and Tabuane is no more than fifty kilometers (less than thirty miles).

Rain swelled the Pongani River. Our driver, Prout, found a cutaway into the bush, crossed the river upstream, and returned to the main road to Afore. I instructed him to stop in the village of Banderi, where a meeting was planned to introduce bird's-eye chilies as a new cash crop to create new livelihoods and generate kina.

Banderi is located on the mountainside facing due east, overlooking the Solomon Sea. This setting is one of the most idyllic in Oro Province. Villagers are treated to a glorious sunrise while having breakfast in their huts. Emerald-green rainforest stretched to the sea's edge. White cockatoos speckled this canopy of trees, piercing the quiet with their squawks.

Welcomed by the village chief, elders, and farmers, I felt at ease. The chilies agent, Arthur, served as host. I was the first white man to visit and teach them to build a livelihood through a new cash crop. The meeting lasted for two and a half hours. We departed in heavy rain. On the road, we encountered a war party of young men with painted faces, armed with axes and bush knives. They were on their way to another village to track down a man responsible for butchering the wife of one of their clan members. Our driver recognized the leader of this pack and deftly received permission to proceed. My window was rolled up as I viewed their bloodshot eyes and angry faces. I had never felt so threatened. Again, vulnerability gripped me. We arrived in Afore early that evening. I had a tin of beans for dinner and slept soundly in our nearly constructed home there. The front facing was not completed, permitting bats and insects to enter. The mosquito netting was a godsend.

Thursday, July 1

Awakened by the sound of thousands of finches, I was treated to a golden sunrise and a clear morning. Millie, our cook, brewed up coffee and made fresh biscuits. I used a toilet pit to discharge my morning duty and then sought the privacy of the surrounding bamboo and reeds to pour buckets of rainwater over my head for a wash. Later on, as I established my morning routine, village children soon hid in the bush, waiting for the white-haired chest to appear. Most mornings, I faced a chorus of gleeful screams and laughs, a far cry from my solitary, glass-encased shower in Grosse Pointe.

On this particular day my driver and I headed back down the road to visit the village of Damara, fifteen miles north of Afore. When I'd passed by this hamlet early the previous evening, villagers shouted, "Ese, John, ese!" and "Tau Bada, Tau Bada!" They were expecting me on this bright and hot morning. I had had three meetings in the village and was working with the chief's son, John Matthew. They had planted twenty-one thousand of our chilies trees, now fully ripened and ready to pick. We had received zero bags due to little follow-through. My instinctual work ethic was of little importance to these people. The absence of productivity perplexed me. As it was, the coffee season would end in two moons and free them up. Unfortunately, by the end of the year, squabbles among the villagers and a shared laziness robbed them of needed cash even to pay for their children's school fees.

My disappointment soon dissipated as the meeting, a team-building session, progressed. I sat in the traditional haus win, sipping and nibbling on a coconut and bananas.

Suddenly and without warning, a bare-chested man with a beard, lifeless eyes, matted hair, and a large bush knife in hand abruptly stood up and charged me, claiming our company, Java Mama, had cheated him out of forty kina ($15 US). Daniel, our coffee village agent, tackled the man. Violently, he swung his field axe, shattering the bamboo floor. Momentarily, the charger was restrained. Yet a brawl quickly ensued and spilled out into the village center. I moved between Daniel and the assailant, both now restrained by the farmers. I dug into the pocket of my trousers, handed the machete-swinger fifty kina and said, "Keep the change." He calmed down, and we regained control of the meeting.

Within fifteen minutes, the hot-tempered farmer was informed that his own family had cheated him. He apologized and gave my money back. Two days later, he delivered a gift of three chickens to my Tabuane home.

Following the meeting, I returned to Afore. Shamefacedly, Daut, the gardener and caretaker from Tabuane, disclosed that our village home had been robbed—again—of food and supplies. I sat down on my front porch and reflected on the day while sipping on a tin cup of bourbon and then lit up a cigar and took a long draw. My head was trying to put itself around the day's events, even as I prepared for my Friday afternoon departure for Tabuane.

Friday, July 2

The rain resumed, prohibiting us from driving up Kweno Mountain en route to Tabuane. As it turned out, the Toyota had run out of petrol earlier in the morning while transporting coffee bags down to the Afore facility. It was not even available. So I waited for petrol to be hiked back up the road so the vehicle could be returned to Afore. Such mishaps and uncertainties were par for the course. When life's circumstances reveal you have little control over day-to-day events, a numbing powerlessness sets in. I found myself asking, *Is incremental change really possible, or is it just an illusion?*

I watched as farmers carried forty-kilo bags of coffee to our shed. Each bag was emptied and examined for quality and then weighed and payment was made. I felt a sense of accomplishment, knowing farmers were receiving the highest cash payment ever for their harvest. I witnessed the excitement and joyful shouts as they realized the extent of their payments. At the same time, I quietly rejoiced in the fact that we were winning the battle against the corrupt Member of Parliament, who was trying to compete and purchase the same harvest for five kina per kilo on credit. His novel approach to buying votes would be a long-term irritant for our company.

The day ended as rain poured on my tin roof with such ferocity that I strained to hear Millie's knock on the door, announcing dinner was prepared. I sat on the porch by the light of a kerosene lantern, eating a delicious dinner of prawns, rice, sliced tomatoes, and cucumbers. A bottle of Australian Shiraz accompanied dinner. Hopefully, we would depart for Tabuane on Saturday.

Saturday, July 3

I received word that the Land Cruiser was ready to go. The rain had ceased. We packed up the vehicle. Prout, Daut, and I would soon be on our way up Kweno Mountain. We sat in the cab, ready to leave. The vehicle would not start this time because of a dead battery, improperly maintained. Just business as usual—what else was new? We push-started the cruiser and were soon on our way up the mountain. The mud was deep. Prout could not let the engine die. We would be screwed if he did.

He did. We were stuck. I secured my daypack, and Daut carried my duffel bag, while Prout remained with the vehicle. The hike up the mountain, including a bush track off the road to circumnavigate the mud, worked to save us time. Nevertheless, it would be four hours before we arrived in Tabuane.

I smiled as I crossed frequent creeks and climbed up and down numerous ravines. My reward for the day would be a crusade dedicated to expunge the evil of this village, inviting admissions, forgiveness, and healing going back to murders twenty years ago. The dark secrets were hidden surrounding the machete murder of Warpa Kephale's father by Juda Divish's father, though the two younger men both continued to work for us. The subsequent killing of Jesu Millipede's brother, the Catholic priest, poisoned two years ago by Francis, Juda Divish's brother, was another riddle. The true story would never be revealed. Secrets would be kept. These events, compounded by the spearing and hacking of Francis in broad daylight by Warpa's brothers, puzzled and confounded me. Warpa claimed his family did the village a favor. Francis had been suspected of being a sorcerer responsible for a number of missing villagers, including children in Tabuane. Another accusation rationalized the vengeance for Francis's killing: The sorcerer was jealous about Warpa's coffee and chilies success. Warpa's consequent increase in power threatened the sorcerer's status.

The vengeance just did not stop—Juda Divish embezzled funds in our Warpa-associated company and ended up in jail the following year. He was the same person who orchestrated the roundup of Warpa's brothers by the police on our wedding day. I doubt that vengeance ever runs its course. Compensation, killings, injuries, and even genocide are counteractive. Memories, the deeper scars, never disappear. The scar tissues collect and are carried forward as the "Mother Culture," so eloquently named by writer Daniel Quinn.

Sunday, July 4

When we arrived early Saturday evening, the village of Tabuane was gathered at a stage built for the crusade. The energy level was high. Priests and preachers were stirring up the crowd. Singing, accompanied by guitars and tambourines, was interspersed with hallelujahs and amens. Tabuane awaited the exorcism that would free it from its curse.

I slept fitfully that Saturday night. Daut slept in my home with a spear. He was spooked, fearing retaliation against his family until the final public ceremony lifted the curse. It was not unusual to be clubbed or speared while wandering outside one's village. In earlier times, the victim, once immobilized, would be hacked up and eaten. Cannibalism no longer existed in this area, but isolated robberies and assaults persisted.

Recalling previous Fourth of July observances, I could not remember a more unique, out-of-body experience than this one.

I climbed the final hill to the village center and viewed the crusade's panorama. The afternoon was hot and humid, the sun unforgiving. Umbrellas and shade trees afforded some protection for the participants but made little difference. The clamor of kundu drums, chants, singing, and evangelism rose to a frenzy. One was easily drawn into a hypnotic flow, swirling like a cyclone and increasing in speed and intensity.

I stood outside the melee, sweating and swatting black flies off my neck and legs. The smells of dog and pig shit and body odor permeated the air. I grew dizzy from the acrid odors and suffocating humidity. I was forced to sit down under a palm tree.

Three men, obviously the crusade leaders, left the stage. They walked directly toward me and spoke to Daut and my guard, Remagus. Warpa Kephale suddenly appeared and translated. The leaders were asking me to be part of the final ceremony. As the "Big Outside Boss" for both chilies and Java Mama, I was instructed to join the center circle. Daut and Remagus grasped my arms firmly and escorted me through a crowd, which numbered some three hundred to five hundred villagers.

I sensed I was losing control as I was pulled into this tide of humanity. Sounds, sights, and smells became blurred and turned into a maze. Arms were extended, and the hands of crusade leaders rested on my shoulders. I was thrust into the center. Warpa Kephale and Juda Divish, their two clan chiefs, and the head Anglican priest drew me into an embrace as our arms intertwined.

Another ring representing Warpa's clan encircled us. Soon a third circle formed, representing Juda's clan. Then an outer circle of several hundred villagers surrounded us. The chants intermingled with Christian hymns enthralled me. The combined sights, sounds, and smells were unlike anything I had ever experienced. They jolted my soul like a defibrillator as the frenzy increased.

The first ring behind me started to move clockwise. The next circle moved counterclockwise. I was chanting within my orbit and repeating "Hallelujah." Songwriter Leonard Cohen would have been gratified.

I gazed up at the hot sun. Was the curse lifting? After thirty minutes, clan members were dropping into prostrate positions and contortions. Wailings and deep grieving poured forth from the deep recesses of these souls. The names of lost ones were called out.

The circling eventually gave way to stillness. The chief of each clan entered the inner ring together. Warpa's clan sought and received forgiveness from Juda's clan chief. Juda's clan chief did the same. Every clan member spoke for reconciliation. Subsequently, the chiefs instructed me to step forward into the center and place one hand on Warpa's chief and the other on Juda's chief. The Anglican priest stepped forward in white robes and raised a spear over his head. Lunging forward, he broke the spear in half over his left leg and then thrust the broken spear above his head. The curse was lifted. Tabuane village erupted into a joyful noise. Relief was visible in the eyes of the elders. The children continued to play. The crowd began to disperse.

Minutes later, I was asked to sit in the village haus win. Rain began to fall, cooling off the late afternoon. Sheltered and sitting cross-legged, I sipped from a coconut and ate fresh pineapple. Dehydrated and tired, I longed for the comfort of my house. Nevertheless, the spectacle proceeded with another gathering of chiefs, elders, and clergymen. Moments later a ceremonial pig was presented by two villagers. Tied to a pole and hanging upside down, it squealed with ferocity. I was numbed as I realized this helpless creature would soon end up in our bellies.

They bludgeoned the pig and drained its blood. With surgical precision, they severed the head and cut up the carcass in preparation for feasting. I looked away and kept having broken conversation with the other guests.

I had had enough drama for one day. Exhausted and feeling drained like the pig, I politely excused myself and walked back to my house in solitude. Daut brought a plate of roasted pork to my home for a late dinner. Diving into the cool pool below my house, I let the waterfall cascade over and cleanse my body and my mind. I did not have the energy to reflect. I did, however, have the strength to place my lips to a tin cup and let the warmth of the whiskey move into my belly. I ruminated on how dissimilar the road less traveled had become and how awesome it was to be a bit player in a larger drama.

The rainy season ruined roads. Village greetings lacked enthusiasm. "I had invested five years of my life coaching in leadership and management development on the Managalas Plateau. Five years of team building. Five years of developing a value chain and supporting an organizational structure comprising 125 square kilometers, thirty villages and 2,300 contracted farmers. . . . Had all of this work and progress been thrown away by one person's desire for personal gain, and was that possibly condoned by the community at large?"

CHAPTER 20

Kweno Mountain

"Oh, where have you been, my blue-eyed son?
Oh, where have you been, my darling young one?
I've stumbled on the side of twelve misty mountains
I've walked and I've crawled on six crooked highways
I've stepped in the middle of seven sad forests
I've been out in front of a dozen dead oceans
I've been ten thousand miles in the mouth of a
graveyard
And . . . it's a hard rain's a-gonna fall."

—Bob Dylan

Fiona and I arrived by plane in Oro Province, Papua New Guinea, at 2:00 p.m. on Thursday, April 28, 2011. As we collected our bags and supplies from a pushcart, I noticed our new general manager, Benjamin, was nowhere to be seen. We found ourselves alone, sitting on our bags in the parking lot, staring at one another. *This is not a good sign*, I thought.

We hitched a ride into the town of Popondetta and soon discovered that no room reservations had been made for us at the hotel. We next moved on to our company office, the headquarters of Java Mama and Chilies Mama. I was anxious to meet with Benjamin's brother, Didymus, whom we employed as the manager of the Popondetta chilies team, but he was away for a family funeral. We haven't seen him since. After six months of full employment, he didn't even leave a notice of resignation. *Uh-oh!* These three events within a two-hour time span were not a good omen. A foreboding feeling crept up on me to the tune of an old Bob Dylan song, "A Hard Rain's A-Gonna Fall."

The next day, Fiona and I had an early breakfast meeting with our partner Warpa Kephale. The first order of business was to decide whether we should immediately seek the arrest of Juda Divish, our general manager for the coffee and chilies business. We had verified through signed witness statements and his own confession statement that Juda had stolen 15,000 kina ($6,500 US) from the company to purchase gold for himself. The money was supposed to pay chilies farmers for produce we had already acquired on the Managalas Plateau. The farmers were upset due to payment delays and unfavorable weather. Tensions were running high. The coffee harvest was delayed by wet weather, and the farmers needed their money. Fiona and I were taking the heat for the payment delay.

The PNG economy is poor. It ranks as one of the most impoverished developing countries, and it is run by one of the most corrupt governments in the world. Suspicions and deceptions are commonplace; unfortunately, they seem to be aimed first at the people who are trying to help the indigenous people the most. Did I say help? That wonderful ideal, dripping with an altruistic coat of do-gooder honey, was becoming tainted by my personal disillusionment.

I slowly realized that my assumptions regarding "helping" were in serious need of revision. Irrespective of life conditions (e.g., social, economic, and political) and cultural and psychological underpinnings, help, as a social currency, is not always understood and/or wanted by its intended recipients. It is presumptuous to assume that in any language or culture, help is desired, and desired enough to establish and maintain trust and mutual commitment to change.

As a result, fairness and equity escape the equation. They seem to get lost in translation and a thwarted conversation. They are not sufficiently defined and understood by the helper or the recipient.

Our waitress that morning, Jenny, refilled the coffee pot. The restaurant table became a conference table. We were the only patrons. She had just informed us that the town was basically under siege by a warring clan of villagers seeking immediate compensation for a roadside robbery, during which one of their members was clubbed and hacked to death. Staying with the morning's agenda, I asked Fiona and Warpa for their opinions on arresting Juda. The clan mind-set surfaced—culturally embedded within the *wantok* (network of friends and family), it was the philosophy of "anything goes as long as everyone benefits." Consensus bordered on conflict-avoidance, and "let's not rock the boat" summed it up. *A little patho-adolescent behavior was understandable,* I thought, *but this guy Juda has crossed the line!* Warpa was more concerned with the political fallout from any action we might take, as it might impact his campaign for governor. He, like most politicians, wanted to be liked by everyone. Fiona backed away, concerned with how we would replace a man of Juda's importance. I was utterly disgusted.

I ruined their morning before the omelets arrived, as

I decided to press charges. The police arrested and jailed Juda the next day while he was unsuspectingly wandering the streets of Popondetta. He remained there for five weeks, until his clan and wantoks scraped together enough cash to bail him out. He was expected to go before the magistrate within six months.

We adjourned the meeting. Steven, the restaurant manager, quickly approached us. One of the warring clan members, a man armed with a bow and arrow, had sought compensation but was shot dead by a policeman in front of our office entrance.

Meanwhile, Warpa chose the path of avoidance and decided not to accompany us to his village, where our business enterprise had begun in 2005. Warpa's health had faltered. His legs had begun to swell due to an undiagnosed problem, and walking required the use of a crutch. His monthly bout of malaria and gout also had reappeared. He was down for the count. Timing is everything. He declined to make the six- to eight-hour drive up to Managalas Plateau and Tabuane. The village would be in an uproar and state of disbelief. Juda was not only the manager of Java Mama and Chilies Mama, but he was also a community leader of Tabuane. Fiona and I were on our own.

The rainy season had not abated. Swollen rivers kept us in Popondetta for a week. By Friday, May 6, the weather broke, and we were able to cross the Pongani River and make our way to Tabuane. There we were to meet with members of thirty villages represented by Java Mama village coffee agents and Chilies Mama village coordinators. We estimated forty to fifty people would attend an all-day meeting on

Saturday.

The trip was rugged. We bogged down three times. The clay surface roads were slippery. Maneuvering through the standing pools of water was an art form. Our driver, Lucien, brought three helpers/pushers to dig out the Toyota whenever mud and ruts immobilized it. The ingenuity and "never give up" attitude they possessed impressed me. Just when I was convinced there was no way we would get the vehicle out of a bog, helpers would free us, even though mud covered their arms, chests, and legs. A good chew of betel nut, and they were reignited for the next bogging-down.

A drizzle started around 5:00 p.m., and the roads became treacherous. Once we began to ascend Kweno Mountain, a heavy mist enshrouded us. We bogged down just outside Sila Village. This delay took an additional thirty minutes. Darkness fell. I was edgy and anxious about our arrival in Tabuane. What type of reception would we receive?

The killings back in Popondetta played on my mind. In Papua New Guinea, once a group becomes agitated, a bloodlust soon envelops the collective psyche, and a surge of violence propels spearing, clubbing, and hacking. The frenzy subsides only when the killing, property damage, and theft are completed. It is a frightening spectacle. The main difference now was the absence of armed police. Fiona and I were scared and felt very alone and vulnerable.

My mind was divided by the unsettling reality of this unfolding event. Half my mind was scarred by the past, provoking me to reminisce. I had invested five years of my life to coaching in leadership and management development on the Managalas Plateau. Five years of team building.

Five years of developing a value chain and supporting an organizational structure comprising 125 square kilometers, thirty villages, and 2,300 contracted farmers credentialed with dual organic and Rainforest Alliance certifications. The previous October, just six months ago, the first container of chilies in twenty-five years was shipped to the global market. Had all of this work and progress been thrown away by one person's desire for personal gain, and was that possibly condoned by the community at large?

The other half of my mind was galvanized by the reality of the present. I felt compelled to confront this culture of stealing and demonstrate the morality of transparency. I was compelled to claim the role of a leader. Warpa was unwilling to confront. The indirectness of my consultant's role was ineffective. I had to exercise and demonstrate power. I could not fail to speak strongly, deliberately, and without compromise. Binary thinking appealed to this Tau Bada from Grosse Pointe, Michigan. No shades of gray. Synthesis was out. A moral line in the sand was drawn. I was mesmerized by fear of the unknown.

A Midwest Ottawa war chief, known by white people in America as Pontiac, had once said: "The heart has two chambers. I believe it because I do know that the heart has two sides. One is love and the other is fear. One creates and the other destroys. Not every person kills, steals, and lies, but every person could. It is how the Great Spirit created us. I do not pretend to understand why; I only know it is so."

Within an eye blink, I moved to my own chamber of love with an immediate yet intuitive decision of action. I did not feel courageous. I felt like crapping in my pants. I was, at that moment, empathetically extending myself by not redirecting the truck back down the Kweno Mountain road. The vehicle veered to the left and missed a significant bog. The headlights erratically fell onto the faces of one hundred villagers. Standing in the dark and mist with the stoicism of granite statues, they had been waiting in silence for Fiona and me to arrive. The rain began to fall harder.

"I prayed for protection and to be surrounded by light."

CHAPTER 21

A Dark Wood

"Midway this way of life we're bound upon
I woke to find myself in a dark wood,
Where the right road was wholly lost and gone."
　　　　　　　　　　—Dante Alighieri, *Divine Comedy*

The mist and rain created a thin membrane, a fine organza playing off the silhouettes standing erect before us. I sat, pondering: *What did I just do? Why am I here? What am I doing with my life?*

I was conscious of unlatching the door lock handle with my left hand, lifting the door handle with my right, and putting my left foot down on the grassy knoll. Simultaneously, I was acutely aware of the innumerable peering eyes cast on me as I stepped out of the truck.

On previous arrivals, shouts of "Ese, ese, ese" would pepper the air. "Welcome, welcome, welcome" would embrace Fiona and me. No such luck this evening. Not a word. No outward movements to shake hands or to assist in unloading our luggage and cargo. The hard rain persisted. My heartbeat quickened. I instructed our driver to appeal to villagers to help carry the bags and supplies on the muddied path to the house. There were no takers. A few youngsters related to Warpa's family were enlisted. After a number of instructions, a snakelike procession made its way into the low-lying hills through the coffee gardens to our home.

My mind was racing. Without moonlight, the rainforest in the darkness felt heavy and seemed to stifle my breathing. We soon passed the place to our left where a sorcerer was bush-knifed though his left eye a year ago. I prayed for protection and to be surrounded by light. Psalm 16:1 resonated within me. David was fleeing the irrational wrath of King Saul. He cried out, "Keep me safe, O God, for in you I take refuge."

The caretaker, Remages, unlocked the door to our home. We lit the kerosene lamps and candles. Bags and cargo were hastily placed in a corner. After thanking the children, Remagus spoke in Pidgin to Fiona, apologizing for what had just happened. He felt ashamed by his village. He got to the point: Remagus and two young men would be posted to stand guard all night. Hidden in the bush and armed with spears, they would encircle our home to protect us.

We made up our bed and were about to retire for the night when Remagus knocked on the screen door. In one hand, he held a spear and in the other a bush knife. He counseled us to keep them next to our bed. A solitary candle burned on a bedside table. The draping mosquito netting reminded me of the veiled mist earlier in the evening. The flickering candle created shadows against the sago ceiling and split bamboo walls. The river babbled loudly, swollen from the day's rain. The hum of crickets and cries of the night birds resonated through the forest.

I gazed at the black spear made out of limbum wood, a sturdy black palm. The blade was old and rust-colored, yet sharp like a razor on both sides, and curved and pointed. In all, it was about six feet in length and capable of killing a wild pig when thrown from as far away as twenty meters (about sixty feet). It was the same type of spear that had crippled another sorcerer in the village three years earlier, before he was hacked to death.

The spears carried by the guards, on the other hand, were tridents, which would enter into the body mass and stay embedded, due to the serrated edge.

Speaking of edges, I was on edge all night long. I remained restless throughout the night, envisioning the walk back into the village the next morning to meet with fifty to sixty villagers. The babbling river played tricks on me. I swear it was speaking to me. Fiona fell asleep. The rain kept falling.

The spear was indeed a dark wood.

John had a grab bag of proven business developmental applications, such as the Patrick Lencioni book on the table with the coffee beans, which he used in other village meetings, as shown on the blackboard. Now, as a crucial session with villagers loomed, would a rational addressing of dysfunction succeed, or was the answer in the heart and dealing with an invulnerability that engenders mistrust?

CHAPTER 22

Meanderings

"We are constitutive of our own experience, which crosses philosophy, theology, literary criticism, and psychology."

—Herbert Fingarette

As darkness lifted, I was encouraged to face the day. My mind raced to the reality of the circumstances and a possible course of action. For a moment, a medical paradigm gripped me. A USB table of "fix it" interventions scrolled in my mind's eye as I gazed at the spear in the corner. The doctor was summoned to originate solutions.

I pondered consultation principles and found comfort in authors and past professors. I suddenly recalled a National Training Laboratories (NTL) human interaction workshop debriefing session, where I was given feedback for the first time on how a group perceived me after ten days, circled by chairs, in a classroom setting. A participant who was HR director for the 5th Army claimed I was a fortress, bulletproof and nearly impenetrable. I was then reminded of the constructive developmental framework of Robert Kegan out of Harvard and used in my executive coaching practice, along with essayist James Hillman on revisioning. Quickly, I drilled my memory with the *Emotional Intelligence* competencies of Daniel Goleman. I wondered about my own motives concerning power from a David McClelland lecture. Instinctively, another mental seizure took hold as I began to assess what were the life conditions and corresponding Value Memes purported by Don Beck and Chris Cowan in *Spiral Dynamics*.

Then, within a split second, a litany of team and leadership models by Patrick Lencioni, Chris Argyris, Warren Bennis, Jim Kouzes, Barry Posner, and Edgar Schein registered in my mind. Could it be possible that my self-confidence and credibility were in serious doubt? Before I knew it, I was consoled as I immersed myself in empathic consciousness and dialectical integrative philosophy. Existentialist Martin Heidegger momentarily consoled me. Marvin Weisbord's culture/values writings dashed to the stage accompanied by Richard Beckhard and, in a flash, MIT's Peter Senge's *The Fifth Discipline* handbook recipes on mindfulness appeared front and center as I put on a T-shirt and shorts and slid my feet into thongs while heading to the pit (earthen toilet) to take care of my morning business.

I recalled my personality theory professor Morley Segal's lecture on depth psychologist Carl Jung. My persona was in for a rigorous testing today. Morley began his first class by dancing, circa 1920s, with a top hat, cape, tuxedo, and cane. He undulated to the song "Me and My Shadow." His body image was silhouetted on the wall behind him. He was driving home an important theme for our own development if we chose to evolve into "master change agents." We had to be willing to access our own unexplored or unknown area of self and learn to dance and befriend our shadows. A number of classmates thought this was out of place and too intrapersonal for a master of science program in organizational development. I disagreed.

I finished my pit business and hiked to the waterfalls for a morning wash. The cockatoos were squawking and gliding from one tree to another over the rainforest-canopied mountains. The sun was bright, with few clouds. Last night's rain brought out the sweetness and freshness of the wild orchids. Fiona was still sleeping soundly. I recalled James Joyce's book *A Portrait of the Artist as a Young Man*. The morning's beauty evoked passages of the author's work. Aesthetically, I was arrested, as Joyce once conveyed, by the wholeness of the moment. I dove into the pool carved out by the falls. A primordial sense passed through me, reminding me that these forests had never been logged or contaminated with chemicals, and never fully explored. I was affirmed by all of the work we had accomplished with the organic and Rainforest Alliance certifications. The coolness of the water and the cadence of the falls refreshed me immeasurably.

It was time to walk to the village of Tabuane, where a gathering was taking place. For a second, I shifted into an "abyss" moment. I was viewing a black hole without a bottom. The image lingered. I thought I'd left it in the pool.

Back at the house, I gingerly sipped on a tin cup of steaming coffee. Our caretaker, Remages, informed us that Warpa Kephale had made contact with Samuel by satellite phone, located in the village of Sila. This was the only phone available in the plateau, and was usually reserved for mission work, unless there was an emergency. He explained to Samuel, in detail, why John Quinlan had made the decision to put Juda into prison. Samuel then walked throughout the village of Tabuane for all to hear this story, including the other twenty-nine village representatives. His loud and forceful declarations, while accompanied by Cecil the village constable, served to ease the tension we had experienced the previous night. At least that was my hope, as I recalled the farmer from the village of Damara charging me with a bush knife.

I walked to the village alone. Contained in my knapsack was the same New Testament I carried around in Europe in 1970. I viewed ruby-red coffee cherries on both sides of the path. The trees glistened from the rainfall. Palm trees swayed, while a bird of paradise serenaded a potential mate, doing an erotic dance and fluffing his feathers.

The "hole" dogged me. I had been in some tough places in twenty-five years of consulting but never this intimidating.

My heart was beating hard and not because of the rugged terrain. Intervention typology and *Spiral Dynamics* principles peppered my thinking. What, where, and how do I begin? The schema and thema were eluding me. I descended an embankment and crossed over a creek, climbing the final hill before the first village huts came into view. Women and children were scrubbing their breakfast pots and pans and having their morning wash, oblivious to my intrusion on their nakedness.

I pondered the writing of mythologist Joseph Campbell in search of the bliss he proclaimed as I approached the crest of the hill, anticipating my first encounter. I began to consciously breathe. I was desperate to transcend this predicament in order to gain a clearer picture. I remained focused on my footing. I was now breathing strenuously. Fear had a grip on me, and I suddenly felt constricted. Paranoia was gaining ground. I was exasperated and wondered if I was walking into a minefield. The fear of the unknown had the upper hand. Unquestionably, I did not know what I did not know. Meta-emotion had my undivided attention.

Obviously I was back into my theory-experience grab bag. My attention moved from my head back to my feet, due to the excessive mud on the track. I recalled Kundalini exercises I had practiced to realize the Hindu concept of chakras, a life force that releases the flow of crucial energy in the human body. *Breathe, John, breathe. Breathe, John, breathe.* The unrelenting anxiety would not abate. Still in search of an explanation, a "reason for which"—a telos—my pace quickened.

Memories of my first talking-stick council in the 1990s in Santa Fe, New Mexico, pierced the rhythm of my breathing. I immediately supplemented this with a Buddha quickie, as prescribed by Surya Das in *Awakening the Buddha Within.* Breathe, John, breathe. Men's movement sages Robert Bly and Sam Keen gently reminded me to affirm myself as a man. *I am John Quinlan. I am John Quinlan.* The repeating of my name sufficiently calmed me as I glimpsed the haus win (meeting place).

Ultimately, gentle waves of metaphysics and quantum field theory sprung up. Einstein espoused, "God does not play dice with the universe." I got it! I looked up and was abruptly confronted by a tattoo-faced, bare-breasted woman with stacked breakfast pots on her head. Smiling and chewing betel nut, she called out, "Ese, John, ese." Her young daughter and son, also chewing betel nut, yelled out, "Ese, ese." I went into a relief state. An inner melting was in process. My heart felt warmed by the greetings.

The woman repeated "Ese, John, ese." I responded in the plural, "Esue, esue." Instantaneously, one villager after another greeted me. Samuel the town crier had done his job.

The haus win was an open pavilion with thatched roof, no walls, and bamboo railings, centered in the middle of Tabuane. The typical village congestion encompassed noises and smells of pigs, dogs, chickens, humans, and smoky cooking fires. All this created the old, familiar cultural-social milieu I had become accustomed to over five years. I figured this toktok would last all day.

Depth psychologist Alfred Adler defined the term *Gemeinschaftsgefuhl* as a social feeling, a community feeling, whereby one senses he or she belongs with others and also has developed an ecological connection with nature (plants, animals, and the crust of the Earth) and the cosmos as a whole. I was beginning to feel this way.

I was regaining a sense of purpose. The hole began to fill up. I felt safer. A gestalt (wholeness) reappeared. I felt okay. My heart started to shift. I moved from the chamber of fear into the chamber of care and empathy. The courage to be open and vulnerable was present. It was natural to connect with the villagers. I wanted all of us to be together. Their word for "together" is *ahuvo*.

"I viewed the semicircle of villagers waiting for me to speak. . . . I did not see spears or axes, only an occasional bush knife."

CHAPTER 23

Ahuvo

"He that hath knowledge spareth his words, and a man of understanding is of a cool spirit."
Proverbs 17:24, The Message

After stepping into the haus win, I sat down on the bamboo floor, fully cognizant of every move I made. It was much like stepping out of the truck the night before. My emotional and spiritual instincts were finely tuned. I was in the present and, in Bob Dylan's phrase, "knockin' on heaven's door" for the wisdom I needed—a cool spirit. The integrity of the moment—the truth as I projected—was of utmost importance to my sense of worth and purpose.

Appraising more than two decades of organization development (OD) consulting and coaching, I recalled occasions of meaningful existential discussions with other practitioners as stark and infrequent. The mutual sharing of meaning-making was practically nonexistent. Frank Friedlander's essay "The Three Values of OD," which I read in my first year of graduate school, at least presented an academic opportunity to discuss this conundrum in a safe harbor. Friedlander's three values—rationalism, pragmatism, and existentialism—gave me an objective perspective and freedom to venture into this obscure and relatively unknown domain labeled existentialism. Over the years, the more pragmatic and rational practitioners predictably would withdraw and/or avoid the subjective-existential realities of their own experiences, keeping them abated and on the periphery. It made this field experientially static and, at times, quite dry. The collegial humanness of the profession was absent for the most part, handily displaced by affectlessness. Therefore, the inner experience was ignored, and the encounter to share the inward journey obscured. Such lost opportunities are silent tragedies that are largely unnoticed. They create a predictable flatland void of vitality.

I longed for such conversation and was disappointed by the lack of transpersonal discourse with others, time after time. My empathic impulse would dry up as quickly as the dew on the morning grass, preventing me from sharing such rare conversation.

Now, I am persuaded, as the author of my own experience, that I have a captive audience—the reader. I have the liberty to unearth this vein of ore and share the treasure with those who choose to listen and comprehend. Consequently, a collage of insights, principles, and truths has converged as the story unfolds. The ahuvo event was an emotional and subjective catharsis I am grateful for. Hell's rats to rationality and objectivity.

I viewed the semicircle of villagers waiting for me to speak. My mind (thoughts) gravitated to Beck's and Cowan's *Spiral Dynamics* framework and my heart (feelings) to the empathic bonding qualities purposed by psychologist Clare Graves: "Damn it all, a person has the right to be who he is." The eloquence and civility presented by Stephen McIntosh in the imagery of Bruce Sanguin's book *The Emerging Church* infused the experience with verve. As I interacted with villagers, Ken Wilber's Vision-Logic further grounded me as I moved into Carl Rogers's unconditional positive-regard framework. An empathic consciousness brought a sense of wholeness that had been absent for this gathering. I was on the mend. The abyss disappeared, and fear evaporated. My personal needs became subordinated to the experience, enabling me to be helpful and more aware of the perspectives of others.

The village coffee representatives and chilies coordinators numbered at least fifty, not including another ten Tabuane clan chiefs and elders. I did not see spears or axes, only an occasional bush knife. The attendees were chewing betel nut and chatting among themselves. Calmness prevailed. My interpreters were Paulus Namaisa from the village of Siribu and John Matthew from the village of Tabuane. I was given a traditional kulau (coconut with the top sheared off) to sip. Betel nut was offered to me, but I did not chew. I let it sit at my feet, along with a hand of fresh bananas. All of these items were precious and symbolized that I was sincerely welcome.

The chief of the village, Ezekiel, made eye contact with me. The clan leader played out his role of an obedient elder by ceremonially opening up the meeting, establishing loyalty for his own clan, then his village, and, ultimately, the plateau in general. He was known as the traditional "big boss."

Without question, I was the outsider. After five years, Tabuane was indeed my "first garden," as articulated by the chief. I was reminded that my loyalty was to my first garden, Tabuane; therefore, benefits, goods, and services began right here.

The tradition was pronounced through our marriage ceremony. Four years earlier, I was brought into Ezekiel's clan. This made us tambu (kin). We were not blood-related, but all the rights, privileges, and expectations were in place as if we were.

Chief Ezekiel nodded to another member from Tabuane to further open the meeting with a Christian prayer. Supportive hallelujahs and amens accompanied and ended the prayer. Their invocations are explicit, reverent, and formal. His authority was pronounced in this supplication. The power was firmly established by the chief in his role and, to a lesser degree, in my company position. Power respects power. It is not flashy. It is what it is. This was not a head trip. It was felt.

I was keenly reminded of being an interloper by the very fact that I did not speak their language and was white. Once the rules were established, the meeting proceeded. I spoke in my native English; one interpreter spoke in common Pidgin and another in Barai dialect. I was literally being filtered, examined, and tacitly approved with each oral exchange.

It was essential that I observe body language and eye contact in order to get a sense that I was connecting. This routine went on for eight hours without a break, except for an occasional pee behind a banana tree.

Present with us, in spirit, were all previous kin/elders who had passed on. Again, the tribal consciousness was alive. These spirits were there to protect. Even though I was engaging in a leadership process and assuming I had already established social capital, it was apparent that I was a stranger and broke tradition by stepping out of order in not seeking consensus before I put Juda in jail. Their faces were blank and, for the most part, expressionless.

The cultural and spiritual wave dance began as I entered into this ahuvo (together) encounter. Functioning from a broad perspective, I was thinking and feeling on my feet. I was self-accessible to the present moment, and it connected me to these villagers. I possessed a steadiness and fluidity as I gained entry into the collective tribal community. Ever so gingerly, I engaged with the individual power-warrior presence that served as the gatekeepers. I demonstrated courage and quickly accrued respect and trust with the elder-chiefs. The shifting from one level of traditions and values to another was a conscious and deliberate act. Being aware of my own filtered perceptions as well as theirs within this context was the key. It is a trick akin to alchemy. Such wizardry cannot be learned in a classroom setting or from case studies.

Speckles of my own modernist values system fermented. Since the 1960s, inclusiveness was second nature to me. I exemplified a rationalistic and democratic yet just dialogue during the course of the gathering. I was centered in an expansive perspective, which afforded me the opportunity to effortlessly flow with this group. The freedom to be creative and self-expressive with considerable ease and little duress seemed quite uncanny, considering the drama that had led up to this event.

The vertical experience of swaying up and down this multilevel cultural and social ladder was drawing me into a unique consciousness. I was aware of being part of the experience and, at the same time, objectively "making meaning" at a rapid pace that alarmed me. I spiraled up into a mystical-transcendent posture that connected me to these villagers. I was ahuvo (together) with them and aware that I was viewing an experience that exceeded the meeting itself. I was part of a bigger play and a larger stage, acting out my role with purpose and effectiveness. The self-affirmation received from this experience was rewarding. It felt undeserved, as it was effortless. The day felt complete.

I felt the powerful urge to yell out halfway around the world to my mentor and friend Bruce Gibb in Ann Arbor, Michigan, and say, "This is incredible! Thank you." His commentary in a book review of Jeremy Rifkin's *The Empathic Civilization* provoked me to read the entire text. Gibb's reference to Martin Hoffman's definition of empathy describes precisely what happened in this ahuvo moment:

"A total response to the plight of another person, sparked by a deep emotional sharing of that person's state and accompanied by a cognitive assessment of the other's present condition and followed by an affective and engaged response to attend to the needs and help ameliorate their suffering."

The long, sometimes tense meeting ended not with a trip to the bar, as is usual in the US, but with betel nuts for a good chew, kulaus for a drink, and a buffet that produced smiling faces. People circled back to their traditional values. Would the day have any lasting effect?

CHAPTER 24

Haus Win Discourse

Through the assistance of two interpreters, note-taking, and journal entries, I have reconstructed the toktok that took place in Tabuane on Saturday, May 7, 2011.

John: I would like to thank you for being here today. The words "truthfulness" and "openness" are important for us to understand together. Without these, our talk today will not be a good talk. What do these words mean to you?

Note: The norm setting and use of metaphors served as my reference point for this meeting. The first thirty minutes were utilized in this introductory exchange. I was slow, deliberate, and precise. The interpreters appeared to be effective.

Group: What do they mean to you, John?

John: Truthfulness is being willing to share what you feel and think and believe what is right and what is wrong. Openness is being willing to listen and respect the other individual saying it to you.

Group: We understand what these words mean, but these are difficult things to do with each other. We do not do this very often in public. It is not comfortable.

Note: An hour of lively discussion unfolded in this subliminal and inclusive introduction. Consensual communication was reinforced as everyone stood and spoke in turn.

John: I think it is important to tell you the truth about Juda Divish—how his actions hurt this company, you, and the farmers. Do you want to hear this truth and be open to hear what I will say?

Group: Yes, John, we want to hear the truth. We are very upset. Where is our money? Where is our compensation? Where are the payments for the farmers?

Note: Thirty minutes transpired for safety, survival, and gratification themes to emerge. Cash is scarce. This is survival instinct in an unvarnished response.

John: Java Mama believes in honesty. We do not cheat, rob, or steal. We are an honest company. Truthfulness is like one of your house poles. The pole supports your home. Without it, your house will fall. Is this true?

Group: It is like a strong pole. Yes, without honesty the company will fall like our house.

Note: Fifteen minutes of consensus-building took place. The analogy of the pole was helpful for them to grasp this value labeled honesty.

John: Juda made me angry and sad. He stole fifteen thousand kina. This money was for your compensation and payment to your chilies farmers. He stole the money to buy gold for himself. We know who did this with him. We got a confession statement from him as well as witness statements. I had him arrested, and he is in a cell in Popondetta. He will appear before a magistrate and will be put in prison. Do you have any questions? Do you understand now what happened? Do you agree the company did the right thing?

Group: (*Silence. A shaking of heads and then multiple conversations among the members.*)

Note: Another twenty minutes passed, giving them the opportunity to be open in public with one another. I retreated as I viewed these interactions. This was a unique fishbowl to observe.

The tribal clan's "ethnocentricity" was pronounced and was a critical juncture of the session. The wantok (we) vs. the company's welfare (they) was front and center. The contrast of values and behaviors of the host community versus the outside institutional value system was marked.

John: Who wants to speak? Please share your truth, your opinion, and let's be open and respectful of one another.

Group: I am very angry. We are angry. He did the wrong thing. The farmers need to know what happened. Juda should be ashamed. Now we know the truth. John and Fiona did not hurt us. When are payments going to be made to the farmers? When do we get our compensation? Who is the new boss?

Note: This communal venting process lasted thirty minutes. The responses were thematic. As the meeting progressed, the safety and trust increased, permitting commitments to future actions to evolve.

John: Are we in agreement that this action toward Juda's wrongdoing was the right thing to do?

Group: Yes, it was the right thing to do. I agree. We agree. He did the wrong thing. He was stupid.

Note: Every member spoke. The yelling, venting, warnings, and affirmations lasted for an hour. The meeting was animated and reverberated with persuasive gestures. Strong confrontation followed by immediate resolution was characteristic. It was a satisfaction sought by all of the participants. This social process was dignifying. I observed a solemn peer respect. Individual voices were heard with solemnity. They facilitated their own meeting. It was a normative process that afforded everyone the chance to be heard, with or without eloquence. No one was made to look or feel foolish.

John: Now, I will share with you what we are going to do, starting Monday.

Note: I went to the blackboard and sketched out a new organizational chart (defined hierarchy) including monthly meeting procedures and a clear compensation schedule. This authoritative posture, along with a business orientation, was another building block for greater productivity and results. The exercise took thirty minutes.

John: I would like now to have a talk on a new boss. I have chosen John Matthew. Would you support John Matthew as your new general manager?

Group: We want John Matthew to be our new general manager.

Note: The group was lively, relieved, and exhilarated by the decision. This was pleasing for John Matthew, a diligent and honest member of the plateau team for five years. The democratic attributes of harmony, inclusion, and equity were apparent during the thirty minutes.

John Matthew deftly took over the meeting, fully charged yet humble. He shared his core beliefs, with emphasis on honesty and truth, along with his commitment to his new role, the community, and the farmers. This participative and authoritative discussion, along with a business orientation, lasted another fifteen minutes.

John: I would like you now to tell me why truthfulness and openness are important for yourself and our company. Would you make a public commitment to be truthful with John Matthew, his team, and one another?

Note: Again, each member took a turn by standing up and voicing opinions.

John Matthew stood before the group and participated in the exchange.

The demonstration of his formal power was a significant moment. It was critical for John Matthew to be recognized in his position and affirmed with his new responsibilities. He was being honored. This affirmation process consumed an additional thirty minutes.

John: I thank you for your time today. I will be back in two moons. Ezekiel, would you please end the meeting? I am finished.

Note: The chief thanked everyone and chose the same member to close the meeting with a prayer. The proceedings concluded with "eses" to one another. The group voiced satisfaction for the meeting. Handshakes commenced, indicating their support for one another. They appeared to feel safe and subsumed within this collection of clans from thirty-five villages that made up our company.

The meeting circled back to the traditional values system, bridging/linking to a familiar "touching stone." Members would soon transition into robust oral exchanges, interrupted by betel nut chewing and dinner (*kaikai*).

"Feeling relieved and more secure than I had during the past week, I felt a wave of exhaustion sweep over me. My shoulders drooped. The little bravado left was used to get me back home."

CHAPTER 25

Awareness Examen

"Who lives outside, dreams; who looks inside, awakes."

—Carl Jung

The men broke up into smaller conclaves, having a chew of betel nut under the palm trees. I see their survival instinct in action as they look up to the top of each tree to see if any coconuts are ripe and ready to fall on their heads. When they do drop, if you are not awake, you will suffer.

Today, I sensed for a moment that, together, most of us were awake during the meeting. I hoped our muscles and soul sinew were engaged, retaining our resolve into tomorrow, our future.

The present is a powerful time frame and point of reference for tribal systems. Moving into the future with an expectation for a quantifiable (capability) and/or qualified (attitude) improvement is usually diminished by role ambivalence. Our management and farmers were not convinced they were suited for the regimen and discipline of a full-time job. A sense of urgency required by the economic-driven global market was absent. Competitiveness suffered from being a day late and a dollar short. I wondered if they would ever be fully included in this postmodern world.

They are unaware. So long as immediate biological needs are met, it is sufficient. A "flight back to health" will soon emanate in most of these men. Tribal bonding will overtake both business responsibilities and rational problem solving.

Kaikai was obediently served by the village women. The smells
and tastes of freshly cooked yams, taro, rice, and fried banana
would soon lessen the day's ahuvo experience. My profession
is akin to the tediousness of brick-laying—one at a time.

Salvadoran priest Oscar Romero said, "God is the judge
of all social systems." I played a part in a bigger play. That
was good enough. As a business builder and change agent, I
engaged with this community for what I believed to be its best
interest. I wanted community members to be equipped to create
a better livelihood. This was what they desired when Fiona
first entered the plateau. They would benefit and so would our
company, Java Mama. We assumed all of us together were
on the same page. I chose and wanted to believe there was
a sense of destiny in this effort. As difficult as it was, I was
prepared to view myself as one individual who was involved
in a significant undertaking, which was much larger than the
voice or contribution of one or two individuals. To participate
in the universe is to create meaning. It is the bigger play. Again,
that was good enough.

After gathering my pens and notepads into a daypack, I
was soon on the same path passing by the brook where women
and children had bathed and washed their pots this morning.

I was fully immersed in today's episode. Feeling relieved
and more secure than I had during the past week, I felt a wave
of exhaustion sweep over me. My shoulders drooped. The little
bravado I had left was used to get me back home.

Darkness enveloped me. My cap flashlight served as a
solitary light on the bush track as I reentered the rainforest and
coffee gardens. The solitude lulled me into reflection. Self-
examination surged within me now that this storm had passed.
The rising moon was resting on the mountains to my right as
a shredded purple haze mingled with the horizon and forest

canopy. The air was lighter than on the previous night; I felt lighter as well, letting go of the demands of the day. Aliveness abounded. I moved into a quiet, meditative zone where meaning was waiting just around the bend.

As I stepped carefully along the bush track, reactions began to crystallize. Regaining my composure was fortifying as I mulled over my lost composure on the same path earlier this morning. The inner yin/yang and push/pull of this dialectical process were fuel, a creative tension present for my own emergence. I was walking on the razor's edge. The tension was the self-affirmation motivating me to evolve myself and move to the higher level of the personal transcendence I had experienced. It would have been impossible to ascend yesterday's mountain and eventually participate at the haus win today without these mini-leaps of faith. I drew sustenance from these deliberate actions that generated the courage to keep moving forward.

The purposeful movements of calling out, meditating, and praying as I meandered in the early morning were essential. I had asked for courage and wisdom to walk down that path and step into the haus win. The courage was to extend myself for others. It was a calculated risk, offset by the faith I possessed at that very moment. I initiated the power to act, an urge sustained by what I call my God. This resulted in an empowerment or resurrection that enabled me to step into the experience that I now was examining. This also was a deliberate act that required the courage and stamina to proceed, for better or worse. It was a process of inquiry, and I might be surprised in the findings. Excavation for ore is tough work. But it pays off if you stay at it and fully participate in it. All in all, it is transformative. One learns to learn. It never ends if you choose to view it this way. More than likely you change along the way.

As writer Robert Kegan explains, "Meaning making

is not that a person makes meaning, as much as the activity of being a person is the activity of meaning making, thus no feeling, no experience, no thought, no perception, because we are the meaning-making context." What a beautiful way to view myself. This is a gift. It is a journey. I like this concept. Now it was up to me to do something with today. "Experience is not what happens to you," Aldous Huxley said. "It's what you do with what happens to you." Okay, now I would organize what I just had experienced. This is learning at a baseline and, for the effort, may make me wiser. It made sense. Kegan cautions, "Human being is the composing of meaning, including, of course, the occasional inability to compose meaning, which we often experience as the loss of our own composure." Now, I certainly grasped such losses and realized that to lose is to learn.

Turning onto the walkway to our home, I saw the candles flickering behind the screened windows. The kerosene lanterns hanging on the living room walls created a pale ambience that invited me in from the coolness of the early evening. Fiona was waiting for my arrival. She poured whiskey into a tin cup and handed it to me. We shared the events of the day. Remages was preparing dinner over a fire in the kitchen. I viewed the flames as they licked the pans and cast shadows on the banana trees. Fireflies moved right to left, attracted by the warmth of the river below. The moon became clearer and brighter.

A dinner of prawns, rice, and greens was served in candlelight. Fiona uncorked a nice Australian Shiraz. When she retired to bed, I sat in silence. The urge to compose, to unravel the day, was clawing at me. I was sleepy. For the time being, I was content to let myself move into the inexpressible. Heinrich Zimmer commented, "The best things can't be told—they are transcendent." Yes, I was dog-tired, yet the urge to express the inexpressible was compelling. I would delay it until the new day appeared. To re-create, to make meaning, to learn how to know is a life force that permits me to generate a new vision and serve as a framework for purpose. It was the highway on which I rode.

Guards were not posted. The spear remained in the corner. As I slipped under the mosquito netting, I pulled up the comforter and nestled into the right position. Silver moonlight slipped through the ceiling. A full moon was only days away.

"I am chilling out in a garage built in the 1930s behind our Queensland home in Edge Hill, a northern suburb of Cairns, Australia. This wolf den, reconstructed by Fiona, is my private lodge and offers me respite... Abstract Aboriginal oil paintings... assist in grounding me and soothing my soul." John is desperate for wisdom and hope. "My poise is breaking and being leveled. My confidence in Papua New Guinea is in further decline: it is below ground." *Artwork by Linda Mayers.*

CHAPTER 26

Adjournments and Abjections

"To exist is to change, to change is to be mature, to mature is to go on creating oneself endlessly."
—Henri Bergson

Today is September 10, 2011. Ten years ago tomorrow, the World Trade Center towers in New York City were attacked and leveled. As I recall, I was circling back then, thirsting outwardly as I am today but feeling less than courageous. In a place of stasis, I'm not sure if my life is shrinking or expanding. My mind is made up. I refuse to mature, and I will stop this work in progress. Composure is doomed.

Fuming, I declare an adjournment to halt this forward motion. Be damned, Lord Tennyson. I decline to accept your dictum that change is the great certainty. This recalcitrant self is in a state of arrest in his personal development and will defer such activities and commitments to a future time. He will choose resumption, and to hell with the consequences of his choice.

Coincidentally, the cause for such an effect was abjection. I had humbly rejected myself. The cultural realisms of Papua New Guinea had disallowed the Tau Bada.

This state of abjection, drifting and being cast off, existed somewhere on the conceptual continuum of object and subject without a point of reference. I was in for another cliff viewing, an unsolicited request to gaze into an abyss. Crap! Dante's "Tuscan plains" were knocking on the door. A great maternal archetype loomed below the surface as I struggled for safety and well-being. Likened to the rings of the ficus tree, viewed through the screen door, yielding to the pull of the sun, I craved self-understanding and comprehension. I needed wisdom. The positive impact of the ahuvo event was fading quickly. The spike of self-confidence had dissipated.

Due to recent adversities in Papua New Guinea, my poise was breaking and being leveled. My confidence in Papua New Guinea was in further decline; it was below ground. A Jacob's wrestling match was brewing. It was time to choose. Should I move into omission, to self-embrace and self-love, and, therefore, withdraw? Or should I move into commission and continue to participate and be concerned for others? Courage was required for either choice. It was lacking, however, and I was stuck.

Nevertheless, I was chilling out in a garage, built in the 1930s behind our Queensland home in Edge Hill, a northern suburb of Cairns, Australia. This wolf den, reconstructed by Fiona, was my private lodge and offered me respite. The bamboo walls, abstract Aboriginal oil paintings, terra-cotta floor, ceiling fan, and reclining chair assisted in grounding me and soothing my soul. The paintings orbited me back to the ancient cliff dwellings and caves of the Anasazi Indians.

An easterly breeze from the Coral Sea moved fresh air through the screen door and windows. The scent of blooming plants emanated aromatherapy without charge. Insight was beckoning. I asked for it. She was outside the door. The Old Testament prophet Jeremiah says, "Stand at the crossroads and look, and ask for the ancient paths, where the good way lies; and walk in it, and find rest for your souls" (Jeremiah 6:1 NRSV). *I am alone. I ask for wisdom. Fill me up.*

Fiona was in Morobe Province, northwest of Oro Province on the Solomon Sea. Accessibility was difficult, demanding two days of flights just from Popondetta to arrive in the village of Wasu. This mountainous region reminded her of southwest

Colorado, close to Purgatory, outside the town of Durango. She was starting up a new coffee operation as a result of troublesome events in Oro Province. I had not seen her for six weeks.

The past two weeks had been a reconnecting time with two of my stepdaughters, Kaia, who was seventeen, and Mahealani, who was fourteen. Jasmine, now nineteen, was attending the University of Queensland in Brisbane, nine hundred miles south of Cairns on the east coast.

The daily routine of driving, cooking, grocery shopping, and housekeeping had been a healthy distraction from the incessant onslaught of problems and challenges of Papua New Guinea. Lawlessness had increased in the city of Popondetta, raising serious concerns. Our facility had been robbed twice in the last year, once with a bush knife to the throat of our general manager.

It was a glorious day—not more than eighty degrees, with sun, clouds, and a strong southeasterly wind blowing up from New Zealand. God, this was a big and awesome part of our planet. Between the landmasses of Papua New Guinea, Australia, and New Zealand and the ocean expanses, events are put into perspective.

An occasional earthquake, tsunami, cyclone, or erupting volcano levels our field of experiences and establishes new proportions. Empathy threads and subliminally interweaves all of us into an integral tapestry. I sensed how fragile and fearfully and wonderfully made we are as human beings. In such a natural and thunderous backdrop, the contrast put things into a fresh stance.

So far, 2011 had turned out to be horrific. I was overwhelmed and felt insignificant. Silver linings as of this date had not emerged. The Managalas Plateau coffee harvest suffered its worst contraction in history. Farmers had 80 percent fewer bags due to an extended rainy season, the aftereffect of

2007 Cyclone Guba, severe pruning of trees, climate change—one guess was as good as the other. Regardless, it was a ball-buster punishment for the farmers and Java Mama.

Worse was the uncovering of another embezzlement involving Java Mama coffee agents. Double-accounting of bags and the cheating of farmers by our own employees acting as middlemen again surfaced. Another four coffee agents were confronted. As a result, further police procedures were under way. Cultural change was excruciatingly incremental in the Managalas Plateau. Timing was everything. Personal bankruptcy reared its ugly head. Without sufficient bank financing and/or outside capital infusion, we were in harm's way. In December 2010, we had borrowed an additional $125,000 to purchase coffee and chilies by pledging our Edge Hill home with a second mortgage to secure capital from USA note holders (friends). My Grosse Pointe, Michigan, home had been pledged for an equity loan in 2006 to purchase coffee.

The banking community of Papua New Guinea, Australia, and the United States turned a deaf ear to these rural endeavors. The scorecard for admission into such an exclusive club was reinforced by massive schemes such as the $16 billion (US) Exxon Mobil Corp. project in the Highlands district. Easy funding was made available for this behemoth. Why did they deserve $3 billion in financing through US export/import banks? How about peeling off a million and sending it our way? Nevertheless, our immediate response was to continue to support the farmers to ameliorate their plight, as well as to eke out a livelihood. The escalation of commitment was on the rise! Being isolated from my own city of Detroit, where economic suffering had been severe for more than a decade, I found it profound to care so intensely for these villagers. The interconnectedness was unmistakable. The Buddha said, "Participate with joy in the sorrows of the world."

However, the transcendental unity in which I was immersed was now extinguished by the simple fact that I was mentally exhausted by the drama of the ahuvo event and subsequent adversities. I am pressed to recall being so low on fuel in my own tank. I believe it was fumes that kept me moving forward. Adapting to chaos will drain you. My contracting the flu three times and dysentery two times in six months attested to this exhaustive condition.

Viewing the palm trees as they reached up to a spotless blue sky, with clouds disappearing over the hills of the Daintree mountains, I sojourned inwardly, feeling like crap. Kaia had deposited her cold with me three days ago. Self-pity was a-knockin'. It appeared my head was slowly making its way up my ass again. I was spiraling into a bout of self-rejection and self-invalidation, and I was spawning a spiritual flu. The diagnosis: a loss of purpose and, therefore, meaning.

I was crying like the "motherless child" in Van Morrison's album *Poetic Champions*, picturing myself with puckered lips as my mother drew me closer to her tit for a drop of expectant gratification. Abruptly, I sat up in my recliner. The upper branches of the palm trees housed no ravens. Black birds and bats were not in view, but the tricksters were more than present. These companions were accompanying me to an unforeseen reality.

An inner voice murmured, *"John, what condition is your condition in?"* Responding, I focused on moving my thoughts from the subjective (reactive feelings concerning Papua New Guinea, lawlessness, poor harvest, and embezzlement) to the objective (immediate life conditions and long-term social-cultural realities). In order to accomplish this feat of naming my condition, I stepped outside of myself.

Now, grasping a different outlook, I viewed the field of vision before me quite differently, realizing that it had been contaminated and distorted by previous Kool-Aid drinking (past conditioning). Slurping on old paradigms, traditional beliefs, and embedded values, I was hard-pressed to grab my right arm (impulse), as did Peter Sellers in *Dr. Strangelove*, and constrain it with my left arm. Otherwise, this unregulated appendage would have choked the living crap out of me. Standing up, I ambled to the wall and gazed at my reflection in the embroidered seashell mirror. Within a split second, I gained control over the impulse (right arm) to deprecate myself with an unforgiving self-perfection. I chose to embrace a feeling of self-forgiveness and self-acceptance. Unrealistic expectations for a rural third-world community were not malicious but amiss. I accepted being wrong and consciously repositioned my inner compass and integrity through this dispute. I was not going to yield until I changed my self-perception. By reflecting inwardly, feelings of self-confidence and competency surfaced. The mirror images of past experiences, personal strengths, and vulnerabilities grounded and renewed my commitment to proceed with PNG endeavors. Today's soulful reckoning was sufficient. I looked away from the mirror, affected by this discourse and feeling healthier and reasonably content. The tinkering of my self-concept (filters), abetted by the tricksters outside the shed, was the necessary remedy to stem this miserable spiritual flu.

Life adjustments are required when traveling on the highway. The spark plugs on a motorcycle demand calibrations in higher mountain altitudes. Without such adaptations, the bike cannot operate effectively and may cease moving forward.

It is worth the effort. The journey is not arrested. The courage of Socrates confronting the tribunal as he was sentenced to death was eloquently expressed in the *Apology* and is inscribed in Athens. I viewed this marker as a backpacker in 1970. The ancient inscription says, "No wasted journey."

Soon after "the Picnic"—that casual-elegant marital breakup in Grosse Pointe—I purchased an illuminating personal critique by psychologist Albert Ellis. This survival handbook was timely and gave me instructions on maneuvering techniques for the inner journey. I was fortunate; I'd already assumed "there are no accidents." Also, as corroborated by the "There you are" exchange at Burger King with Professor John Hart, self-responsibility is a chore. To understand one's obligation for one's choices and, even more disarming, the consequences to follow may result in a "chicken bone lodged in one's throat" encounter. It could be a real choker.

Ellis concludes: "Like practically all humans faced with adversity, I have a real choice of how to feel and act at any point. I might not like it, but I can deal with it and ameliorate it, and it is not catastrophic and awful if I can't change it."

Ellis cites Alfred Korzybski: "No one *is* her or his behavior. People wrongly think and follow the *is* of identity. Humans frequently act inhumanely. But no human is sub-human. Or super-human. I am still a bit puzzled when so many of my quite intelligent clients have trouble fully seeing this."

Peeping over my shoulder as I looked at the reclining chair, I imagined a footpath on the tiled floor—the footsteps of past choices and the effects that followed. I surged inwardly with a self-affirming liberty that I'd just made another choice. Another footprint extended the path. The highway behind me lengthened—the road traveled. An immediate synchronicity emboldened me as I viewed "the unseen." The endless re-creations comprising the footpath hinged on an unshakeable faith that would enable me to continue on the journey. Richard Bach said, "You are always free to change your mind and choose a different future, or a different past." I hoped it would become easier. Does patience have a reward?

A miracle walks in: Usha and Mahesh Patel. "He was present to assess me and further inquire about Java Mama's mission. He wanted to help farmers. Mahesh was all about business and sustainable profits. He was brisk and to the point. His demeanor absorbed me." Patel saw an abundance of harvested coffee beans and chilies and a highly efficient passive solar dryer.

CHAPTER 27

Never Say Never

"Mythology begins where madness starts."
—Joseph Campbell

Momentarily resuscitated through a respite of adjournment and abjection, the courage to proceed rose to such a supportable level that I convinced myself to board a plane to Port Moresby to rendezvous with Fiona. My intent was to address present calamities and preempt further financial misfortunes by micromanaging and dictating every cash transaction. I wanted to mercifully end the misery of 2011.

The stealing and embezzlement was a virus we could not contain. Shrinking coffee revenue, the results of a terrible harvest, could not keep pace with the viral ingenuity spawned by this cultural and social backdrop. Thriving with impunity, this corruption appeared to have no boundaries. Jeez, we had all the ingredients for a blockbuster nadir swan song for a hell-in-a-handbasket year.

The discipline of calculus was largely ignored, delegated, or, worse, avoided in my life. This continued long after calculators were mass-produced. I always believed that if I worked hard enough, in the end I would win. This self-assurance seemed to work. Invariably there was ample money left over to at least reward/compensate my subsistence needs. The guys who wore white hats—the good guys—would win.

I was wrong. I now realized there is an altruistic bent to this thinking that borders on delusion. The world does not owe me a living. George Bernard Shaw said, "The golden rule is that there are no golden rules."

I was becoming more calculating and less trusting by the day. A mere credit card represented my last source of liquidity. An unused cash line would afford me the funds to return to America for Christmas and pay my bills for six months. Along the way I would consider restarting my consulting practice to stave off imminent bankruptcy. Fiona and the girls would remain in Australia until I was financially stable. The whole set of circumstances was bizarre and uncanny as I imagined myself circling back to America to a closed consulting practice, circa 2009. I felt defeated. I reminded myself of the "wolf den" and named the feeling for what it was: a feeling.

Ironically, the sensation of defeat became an impetus for me to refuse to acknowledge this life circumstance or reality. I would not let this feeling define me and was determined to move toward what I wanted even though I was incapable of defining what that actually was. Karlfried Graf Dürckheim said, "And the end keeps getting further and further away, then you realize that the real end is the journey." For the first time, the nebulousness of this koan perplexed me, and I was tiring of the journey.

Seeking instant enlightenment, I was soon illuminated by the past. Max, my motorcycling friend, was with me years ago in an obscure tavern in an obscure town in an obscure county in the great northern plains of America. Sipping on a shot of whiskey and chasing it down with a long-neck Budweiser, he asked me, "Why does a dog lick his balls?"

I put the shot glass down on the counter and gazed at him, dumbfounded, with no response.

"Because he can," confided Max. It made perfect sense. I was going back to Papua New Guinea because I could.

Such divine-inspired engagements come surprisingly from the strangest places and least-expected people. I never considered Max to be a theologian or philosopher. But I was reminded of Viktor Frankl in his book *Man's Search for Meaning*. He says, "Between stimulus and response, there is a space. In that space is our power to choose our response. In our response lies our growth and freedom."

As I exited Customs in Port Moresby, my eyes scanned the cornucopia of Papua New Guineans and expatriates hurriedly and loudly getting to their destinations. The familiar smells and odors, along with the humidity, immediately grounded me into the present. After six weeks, I was looking forward to embracing my wife. No such luck. Fiona was not to be found, due to a flight delay out of Lae.

Later on in the afternoon, we met up in the hotel room. Fiona, in the heated exchange of embraces, kisses, and past Harmel's Ranch antics, gently reminded me of a meeting within the hour with an Indian friend and businessman, Mahesh Patel. I wanted room service. She prevailed. I showered and made myself presentable. Fiona had a pleasant grin on her face as I splashed on her favorite cologne. Her smile had a prescience I had seen before. I didn't recall the last time, though.

As I was imbibing a glass of sparkling wine and nibbling on hors d'oeuvres in the executive lounge, Mahesh Patel arrived. His friendship with Fiona spanned twenty-five years. He was present to assess me and further inquire about Java Mama's mission. He wanted to help farmers.

Mahesh was all about business and sustainable profits. He was brisk and to the point. His demeanor absorbed me. The man's taut face, shaved head, bronze skin, and penetrating brown eyes were imposing. He was focused and confident, and I sensed his strength. His manner of urgency was a refreshing contrast to the listlessness of Papua New Guinea. He'd done his homework by viewing our website and plowing through company literature. Mahesh was captured by our five-year achievements in the rural community, and, in particular, he was captivated with raising the farm-gate price fivefold within three years. Mahesh knew that we knew how challenging it was to create sustainable agricultural livelihoods. He commented that the Facebook videos had impacted him greatly. I believed he'd met the right people at the right time to get involved. In other words, he wanted to get his hands soiled and fingernails broken.

Just six weeks previous, Fiona was being entertained at the Royal Papua Yacht Club in downtown Port Moresby. This icon was a throwback to the elitist colonial days of the British monarchy. Now it was an expat haven comprising well-to-dos, business types, professionals, and fortune seekers. Mahesh "happened" to run into Fiona and inquired what she was doing. He requested a follow-up e-mail. These nodal events moved with a consistency and speed I would not have thought possible. In fact, such unfolding disclosures were exceptional.

Within two weeks of our hotel encounter, Mahesh committed to fly up from his home in Sydney, Australia, with his wife, Usha, and eighteen-year-old son, Ajay. They desired to tour the bush to visit villages we had been working with for the past six years. I was caught off guard by such a deliberate decision. An image surfaced of being caught in the middle of a turbulent river. I was helplessly racing toward the edge of a waterfall. I glanced at the embankment and spotted a man hurling a lifeline with an attached harness with such perfect accuracy that it bordered on the miraculous. How could this be? Miracles didn't exist in today's thinking. In that, I was incorrect.

Mr. Patel was chairman of a publicly traded company called the City Pharmacy Ltd. Group. He'd started his first pharmacy with his wife twenty-five years ago. He expanded it into a sizable chain, including supermarket and hardware businesses to complement his pharmacy network. He was a logistics genius. Now it was his desire to give back. I got the clear impression after my first blink that he was dead serious about karma and understood the resolve fate played in his life. This man was very astute. Subsequently, I was motivated to reread Huston Smith's acclaimed text *The World's Religions* to refresh my comprehension of Hinduism. America might be in for a run with a disciplined athlete called India, whom we assumed we understood and might have underestimated. India could very well turn out to be the early bird that gets the worm in the Asian global market.

Mahesh and his family arrived in late October on an afternoon plane from Port Moresby. I was thankful for his flight delay. Our twelve-year-old Toyota broke down on the highway en route to pick them up. Another vintage Land Cruiser from the Popondetta yard came to the rescue. As the plane landed, we arrived just in time. The appearance of normalcy was presented neatly, concealing the usual chaos that ruled the day. Sweat profusely dripped off our foreheads, but we never associated it with our anxiety. We prayed incessantly, *Please, God, no more mishaps today.* Introductions were made. Luggage was loaded into the repaired vehicle. Everything appeared to be normal.

All of us were now secure in one vehicle. The driver confidently made his way southeast toward the Managalas Plateau. Not more than thirty minutes after turning off from Oro Bay, the radiator exploded, with steam and water gushing onto the hood and windshield. Mahesh and I were in the front seat, conversing. He was interested in my commitment and whether I had an exit strategy for departing the company. Smiling, I thought, *I wish I had one at the moment.*

By now, I assumed this businessman had deduced our company was struggling and was questioning if he and his family were ever to arrive in Afore. The vehicle again was repaired. If he'd only known the truth—that this was the second time within two hours. All of us donated our supplies of bottled water to refill the mended radiator. The question of whether I had an exit strategy loomed in my mind. The term was alien to my thinking. Rationality had escaped me for three consecutive years. Being knee-deep in muddy water can do that.

The afternoon's weather was disarmingly beautiful. The breeze coming off the Solomon Sea rustled the palms and kunai grass, creating a fluidity that nudged one into the present. The blueness of the sea contrasted with the green shoreline, enhanced by a strong equatorial sun. The physical scenery mesmerized Mahesh and his family. This particular portion of the drive was an escarpment so breathtaking it would rival the coastal spectacle of Big Sur, California, absent the traffic.

Nature is powerful. The magic of this untouched ancient land was drawing Mahesh into a sacredness called creation. We drove up the mountain, crossing rivers and viewing remote villages, where people began waving and calling out "Ese" (welcome). Recognizing me, many of the villagers shouted, "Tau Bada!" We stopped and an employee named Isaac pulled out a slingshot and severed the stems of fresh mango off a tree. Usha and Fiona enjoyed the fruit as it was gathered up, peeled, and sliced with a bush knife. Eventually, the men joined in the treat.

Damara Village was located just below the plateau. It was there, not long ago, that I was charged with a bush knife at an awareness session. Today was friendlier. We examined freshly picked ginger weighing up to three kilos (6.6 pounds) apiece. We purchased five rhizomes to demonstrate to Mahesh its abundance and the potential utility of our solar drying facility. Our vision was to increase plantings, collect, scrape, wash, slice, dry, and bag this commodity, delivering this pungent spice to the global market with organic and Rainforest Alliance certifications. This would be the third cash crop, fully complementing the farmers with a twelve-month livelihood. We prepared small bags and gave them to Usha to take back to Sydney, Australia. They enjoyed ginger tea. What a novel way to taste-test a promising cash crop! I was stoked. Papua New Guinea, with all of its ginger, had never exported this commodity, yet to grow this quality ginger commercially would be like a duck taking to water.

As we wound our way up to the plateau, the sun was beginning to drop over the mountains. The goldenness of the late afternoon indulged the verdant landscape. The group was drawn into sensuality where all sense of time and space evaporated. They were captured in the moment. Such incredible unspoiled beauty can do that to you. All of a sudden, the vehicle surged onto the savannah. A landing to our right afforded us an elevated view of the valley. A few kilometers down the road, this family would be the first houseguests to visit our new home.

We were greeted by a sing-sing, and then we walked through a tunnel of palms and orchids. Coconuts, mango, and pineapples were shared with the visitors. Father Daniel's starched white robe reflected the late afternoon sun as he sprinkled dedication holy water on the doors of the new coffee and chilies warehouse.

Plateau-wide coffee and chilies agents gave introductions and speeches. Individually, taking turns, they described their roles, families, and commitment to the company. For the first time in five years, an outsider saw the results of our business planning and execution.

We traveled back to Popondetta the following day in order to drive and hike to the village of Kendetta in the Sagua area. One hour southeast of the city, this village included 150 chilies farmers planting 180,000 new trees. I wanted a start-up example of this magnitude to propel Mahesh to support the company.

The final day was spent traveling to Martyrs High School, an hour's drive toward the Kokoda Track. Historically, this school bridges to Britain's colonial rule. A member of the royal family actually attended this iconic institution. The sealed road evinced the Queen's visit many years ago. For her to see today's financial plight would be a sad occasion. Staff members, including faculty, were waiting for our arrival. The school auditorium was filled with between one hundred fifty and two hundred students from grades nine through twelve. In a six-month period, the students and staff had cleared ten hectares (twenty acres) and planted eighty thousand trees.

Mahesh and his wife and son spoke to the student body.

Such an occasion was a unique experience. For the students to see a husband and wife responsible for the pharmacy was an eye-opener. PNG women played traditional gardening and cooking roles, not business. To hear family members from India explain the value of hard work and self-discipline in order to obtain benefits was a strong theme. On previous visits, I'd had significant self-responsibility discussions with the students. The endemic problems of poverty and stealing invariably appeared. Admissions of laziness were expressed to one another. They, without public shame, pinpointed their own parents as being lazy. Wow! Usually, the kids are the guilty party. Raising three teenagers, I could testify to this. For some reason, I didn't completely buy into the students' reaction. Could it be that laziness was really the hopelessness of discouraged parents living with and resigned to the corruption of their own government?

I exuded a touch of playfulness when I took the stage. As mentioned, after twelve field trips they were familiar with the Tau Bada from Detroit, Michigan, USA. They knew of Michael Jackson, Stevie Wonder, and the soul music of the American black man. Motown was a new name I introduced them to, as well as the African-American street handshake. I would select a lone student amid raising hands. The participant would then come up to the stage. The student would practice the art of a "black man handshake," including the proper slang to accompany this social feat. Repeating my instructions, they would say, "Hey, man! What's happening? Are you cool today?" A high-five then would follow, soon becoming a grasping of hands in a power motif, transforming into a gentleman's handshake. This sliding led to a clasping of fingers back to individual fists. The gentle punching of clenched hands was the finale. The incited students would burst out laughing. They were fast learners. No one was offended. An affectionate connecting took place. Numerous hands were raised and names were recorded when I organized the students to pick, dry, and bag chilies so they could earn money, learn a new livelihood, and teach others when they returned to their villages. Students were dismissed for classes. The staff hiked with us to the chilies garden. To gape at eighty thousand ripening chilies trees, spreading over ten hectares bounded by thick green bush, was a beautiful sight. My heart leaped as the sunrays infused this red canopy. I was encouraged that benefits would soon result to help assist this cash-strapped institution, as well as our own company. The Patel family was awestruck. The global buyer McCormick Spices was also impressed with the recent purchase of one container (eight thousand kilos) of Managalas Plateau chilies last month. With an additional six schools and eight new villages, we numbered a million new chilies trees and a thousand new farmers. We were nearing the time to build drying tunnels and to begin picking to fulfill commitments to our buyers. Everything seemed to be falling into place.

Returning to Popondetta, we looked forward to hot showers. The Discomfort Inn (visit the blog site Discomfort Inn Popondetta, Papua New Guinea) greeted us with a plethora of cockroaches. The air-conditioning functioned, as did the running water. This was extraordinary in itself, but to have the TV picking up reception—a threesome—was a wonder! The irrationality of being charged 400 kina ($174) per night stung. This was a varnished version of the black market for the expatriates.

Renewed by a tepid shower, Fiona and I grabbed a bottle of tequila, a bag of peanuts, and a box of cheddar crackers and headed to the Patels' room. I uncorked the bottle and poured the agave over cracked ice and lime wedges. The warmth of this juice trickled down my throat into my belly. I felt comfortable and connected and assumed the Patels felt the same, once the tequila did its magic. We all smiled. I thought of the exploding radiator.

The Patel family obviously had words before we arrived.

Mahesh, propped up by a pillow with his back against the headboard, was enjoying having his feet massaged by Usha. I was jealous. He sipped his drink and, with a staccato of point-blank words, remarked, "Our family and my company want to help. What can we do?"

Grace is a difficult proposition for me, as it is alarmingly unconditional and unmerited. It is a contrast to my achievement orientation. I felt like I had received a pardon or was visited by a white knight. Later on in our room, Fiona claimed she was not surprised by the offer of help.

With the speed of a bullet, Mahesh commandeered his executive team, lawyers, accountants, and two banks to facilitate a bridge loan to fund the remainder of the 2011 season. He also set up a one-million-kina trade financing facility, guaranteed by the City Pharmacy Ltd. Group, to purchase coffee and chilies for 2012 and 2013. Bingo! Few people and companies would do this in a third-world country's tribal rural community. PNG banks wouldn't even service their own rural agricultural industry because it was too risky. Truly, for Fiona and me, this was indeed a miracle.

In a public interview in 2008, John Polkinghorne, a noted quantum physicist and now an ordained Anglican priest, explained that science isn't set up to talk about such rare events as miracles. They are one-off happenings. So it is a theological problem and more of a question of divine consistency. He commented, "God is not condemned never to do anything different, but when God does something different it must be in a consonant, fitting in relationship to things God has done before."

In this interview, Polkinghorne shared that "there seems to be a question of appropriateness. If you take the scriptural record of things seriously, miracles seem to be associated with what you might call nodal events. Therefore, exceptional times call for exceptional forms of divine self-disclosure."

Drawn into this man's tempo and in a moment of reflection, I caught myself. I was mounted on a motorcycle, crossing the Great Plains of America. In all directions, wheat fields stretched out as far as I could see. This was the "beauty road," attested to by our own Native Americans. I'd just left South Dakota, riding over a bridge into Wyoming, peering down on the Missouri River. I entered the Standing Rock Indian Reservation. On a bluff, I gazed at the road just traveled. I was in sync. My inward man and outward man were one.

Again, I viewed the highway below the bluff, winding into the eastern horizon. I remembered earlier in the day turning on to the soft shoulder and switching the engine off. I'd climbed an embankment and walked into an expanse. My hands touched the prairie floor as my boot heel dug at the dirt. Grabbing a handful of grain, I'd embraced everything there was to embrace. Every smell, sound, and sight was absolutely mine. All of this was completely created for me, for this moment. I tucked a bough of wheat in my leather jacket pocket and headed due west for the Missouri River.

Polkinghorne resumed, "I think God acts with open grains of nature. Just as we act within it in small ways, God acts in bigger ways, and that's sort of hidden because the open grain of nature comes from such intrinsic unpredictability. So we can never figure out who's doing what in these things."

Obviously, the appointment with Mahesh was a godsend for Fiona and me. It turned a sow's ear called 2011 into the semblance of a silk purse. My fortitude was renewed. I could now travel back to America and spend Christmas with gratitude, knowing full well I'd almost plunged over a waterfall.

"I wonder how these Managalas events turn out to be something more harmful than we ever anticipated. . . . I feel inadequate and confused."

CHAPTER 28

Welcome Back

"A Leviathan can civilize a society only when the citizens feel its laws, law enforcement, and other social arrangements are legitimate, so that they don't fall back on their worst impulses as soon as the Leviathan's back is turned."

—Steven Pinker

Rising out of the Solomon Sea, the sun broke through the morning mist that blanketed the valley of savannah with warm and inviting rays. Clouds to my left hovered over the low-lying Sibium mountain range as I sat in the screened back porch of our new home in Afore. From east to west, slivers of buoyant white clouds punctuated the background's dark-green canopy. The morning billows appeared like a school of motionless barracuda peering at the rising sun as it continued to redefine the unfolding landscape.

Indigo-blue sunbirds sat and sang on tops of the tall kunai grass, sipping droplets of moisture from the night's dew. The Anglican school's bell tolled at its appointed 7:00 a.m., prompting children to their classrooms. Streaming from bush tracks out of the same mountains, they walked hurriedly and talked excitedly in their Barai dialect. The laughter helped to put things into perspective and gave me anticipation. This morning had been renewing.

We were slowly adjusting to our home, two hours north of Tabuane. The former manager, Juda Divish, had broken bail conditions by text-messaging personal threats to Fiona. Disconcertingly, he was given refuge in the village where we married and just recently had lived. Tabuane villagers were upset that the "adopted outsiders" had left their "first garden." They requested we come back to the village, publicly apologize, and have a feast at our expense. They refused to understand by turning a blind eye to Juda's blatant actions and remained content to not confront and shame this fraud. I feared their agitation might turn on the two of us. Blood is indeed thicker than water. The tambu-wantok tribal belief system was immune to a higher moral code. It chose the convenient path of least resistance by maintaining the status quo. I grinned, realizing many of the American organizations with which I'd collaborated as an external consultant shared similar tribal values. Fortunately, the majority of my experiences were positive, and the organizations had been, for the most part, open to change.

Nevertheless, distortions neatly packaged by village sorcerers and/or chiefs paralleled the communication experts in our Western society. By shaping and molding organizational cultures for eager markets and electorates, sanctimony was deeply embedded, facilitating strategies and perhaps mutating truth.

By nature, reinforcement is fortified by frequency. Whether it is a PNG sorcerer or chief casting or supporting fear-ridden spells, or a Western corporate CEO or politician implementing marketing strategies, the results are similar. Well-constructed cultural fortresses are nearly impossible to penetrate. Leadership's defensive routines and behaviors are intransigent.

To prevail in such credibility duels or competitive quarrels, one must be fortunate enough to have the social capital of an insider in the Managalas Plateau or the money in the modern world to afford marketing and legal fees. Therefore, such duels and quarrels rarely occur.

As a change agent (shit-stirrer), I've had many spears chucked into my back. Over a twenty-five-year period, none of the inflicted wounds was professionally fatal, but, admittedly, some were emotionally painful. Now, I wondered how these Managalas events had turned out to be something more harmful than we'd ever anticipated. Could they be more than mere misgivings and ranting?

The sun had fully exposed the valley. Ritual morning prayers were heard from the classrooms. Initially, we were optimistic that 2012 would be a better year than our previous three. It had to be. At the moment, I was not convinced it would be. Somewhere intermingled in the children's prayer recitals, a Buddhist sutra, and an Old Testament psalm, a personal plea materialized. Discouraged, I needed to be empowered from a transcending source. Cause-and-effect linear thinking was not effective. I felt inadequate and confused. My prayer was a recitation from my inner-city church in Detroit, Michigan. It was taped to the inside front cover of my thirty-year-old King James Bible. It follows:

Take my weaknesses, O Lord.
Take my failures, my sins, my dishonesties, lies, pride
and desires.
You know I can't do anything with them and give me,
I pray, not so much a clean spirit, not so much a pure
heart, nor a sense of forgiveness; but give me a sense of
You, of You working in me, and me working in with You.
Then shall I be strong, balanced, and focused for and
in You.
Then shall love be focused in me, as love is focused in
You.
Amen.

231

We had arrived in Popondetta only ten days ago. On February 25, 2012, Fiona and I were welcomed by a company-wide strike, filed with the Labor Department for a host of reasons. The rats in the woodpile were the thieving transportation manager and security supervisor. They were scamming the company by removing and reselling vehicle parts, along with farm supplies and equipment.

The strike was a cover-up to assure their continued employment and to cast us, the outsiders, as the bad guys. This chicanery could possibly match my own Wall Street and Washington, DC, finger-pointing shenanigans following the 2008 world financial crisis.

One week to the day since the company-wide strike petition, on an early Monday morning, I walked into the Popondetta company yard. Over twenty-five people were in a semicircle, including Nicie, our general manager. All of them were staring at the ground. Only Dik, the chief instigator, would make eye contact. As the self-appointed spokesperson, he snarled at me, demanding I address the group.

His cap was brought low to hide his eyes. Unshaven and sweating, Dik was dressed in a pair of dirty shorts, faded red polo shirt, white socks, and worn running shoes. The charlatan nervously shifted from one foot to the other. His absent top front tooth drew my gaze to the betel nut juice accumulated and drying on both sides of his mouth. He squared off with me. It was OK Corral time! The verbal gunfight began.

Dik shouted out his demand that I speak to the group. I did not disappoint him and spoke with forcefulness, exclaiming: "You have shamed my wife and me and have hurt your own community by stealing. We will close this company down." Also, preemptively, I had showed up with two new security guards, one a policeman with an M16 and the other a senior officer of the police department, to drive home a message: If you threaten this Tau Bada, he will retaliate. This student is learning new tactics.

The Wizard of Oz was removed from the property, along with the sacked six-member security staff. Fiona terminated Steven, the computer manager, two hours later for co-orchestrating the fiasco. His sociology degree seemed incongruent with such subterfuge. It appeared there was significant role confusion for him to step into this pile of crap! The Labor Department threw out the petitioners' claims, citing them to be a waste of their time. One lone Afore security guard from the plateau somehow got wind of this uprising and filed a claim for outstanding leave payment. Okay. That had legitimacy and was settled, although he owed the company money from a previous personal loan.

The average Western-minded person would view most of their grievances as farcical, but to the average Melanesian-minded person, their grievances were serious business, fraught with ambiguity and complexity. Some of the written (and unaltered) grievance statements were:

- "John Matthew was bit cautious about what Mr. Quinlan promised him. The coordinator and farmers in the previous year's and highlighted few things he (Mr. Quinlan) mentioned to do; after six years, nothing is done. His son died since last year 2008.The company is very ignorant in helping."

- "Paulus was also concerned about the staff and salary and said there should be a staff salary increase and be taken care of the company very seriously. He also said, while working at the company since last year [Note: It was two years ago, and he did not work for the company], his wife died but the company did not try to help him."

- "Rufus (the driver) is concerned about the chilies run, and he says he needs new tires to run chilies on bad weather." [Note: As promised, he is now driving a new Toyota Land Cruiser.]
- "Tony said that there was road maintenance by local groups and therefore payments to be done by Fiona and John Quinlan." [Note: Public roads are severely neglected by the Member of Parliament and the governor.]
- "There was also a concern raised by Luke (the security guard from Afore) on the company weigh house, and he disagreed anyone sleeping in the room."
- "There was also another deadly serious accident that occurred with the Red Maroon, which overturned the driver and his passengers." [Note: The vehicle overturned into a ditch, and no one was injured.]
- "Tony (the Afore supervisor) also said that the production for this season will drop. He said ten containers estimation won't be met because of bad weather." [Note: We began purchasing coffee three weeks after he made this statement. It had rained once in six days. How could this be interpreted as a grievance?]

This list of complaints, including two formal documents, consumed two months of management time. From mid-December 2011 to our return to PNG in late February 2012, we accumulated three months of operating losses and were forced to close down the transportation and farm supplies business due to management negligence, theft, and embezzlement. It was that quick and that deliberate. The initial losses mounted to 150,000 kina ($65,000 US), pretty close to the bridge loan support that Mahesh Patel had so graciously granted.

The icing on the cake was the conclusion in the filed complaint that stated: "Upon serious discussions and conversation, the following agreements were made and petitions to the company directors to meet all demands as required. No staff or employee is to be terminated due to strike or stop work action. All casual employment is to be abolished and put on permanent employment; all staff wages are to be increased and have to be back dated to make sure that they are effective immediately without delay."

Oh my! The Leviathan was absent for nine weeks, including the holiday period when the facility was closed down for three weeks. Our backs were turned. Collectively, unfettered impulses were subjugated. Welcome back, John and Fiona. Accordingly, confession statements were collected, and one mechanic was now in a cell for theft, and another manager would soon have the same fate. Also, following the showdown, seventeen people were sacked, and two more faced criminal prosecution. Nicie inflicted the deepest wound. After four years of training, paid school fees for her son, and a nice salary, she turned her head, permitting this sham to happen. Her niece was also implicated for embezzlement. Nicie charged at Fiona at a meeting and cursed her. Fiona believed Nicie was angry because she'd been caught. We did not press charges, even though we had three witness statements. Nicie never apologized.

As employees continued to steal and middlemen to rob honest farmers of fair prices, John's anger built to a point that would soon become dangerous for him.

CHAPTER 29

OK Corrals Extraordinaire

*"Of the Seven Deadly Sins, anger is possibly the
most fun. To lick your wounds, to smack your lips
over grievances long past, to roll over your tongue
the prospect of bitter confrontations still to come, to
savor to the last toothsome morsel both the pain you
are given and the pain you are giving back--in many
ways it is a feast fit for a king. The chief drawback
is that what you are wolfing down is yourself. The
skeleton at the feast is you."*

—Frederick Buechner

The departure for Afore's serenity and fresh mountain
air was hastened by the onslaught of unsettling OK Corral
confrontations. Salutations that greeted us upon our return to
Popondetta to begin the New Year of 2012 were unforgettably
profound. Royal Papua Yacht Club dinner conversations were
consistently remindful that Popondetta was a living relic of
Papua New Guinea's early frontier days. Easy access to gold in
the shallow riverbeds of central Oro Province assured that this
town remained in a cowboy "shoot-'em-up" time warp, similar
to Tombstone, Arizona, in the 1880s. Also, fueled by quality
PNG gold marijuana, homebrewed alcohol, pokey machines
(digital slot machines), and seasoned criminals, post-colonial
lawlessness was rampant.

Young gangsters, known as rascals, roamed the streets and
housing settlements, preying on pedestrians, shopkeepers, and

the remaining few honest police officers. Shoot-to-kill orders created frequent OK Corrals, where corpses were left on the city streets following gunfights.

One recent skirmish left a young man, armed with a bush knife, shot in the chest by an M16-toting military officer. Left for dead, he lay in front of our facility late into the afternoon. Acclimated to this violence, farmers and villagers simply walked around the body to enter the open-air market to purchase vegetables and betel nut. Such was life—commerce as usual.

I likened this to the Wall Street bankers arriving for work during the Occupation Movement in New York City. The investment community largely ignored the pestering presence of protesters. Except by the police, they were hardly noticed. The things we choose to ignore may very well be the unsettling realities that will come home to be unchangeable, whether in America or Papua New Guinea. James Hollis cautions, "Our greatest sin may be choosing to remain unconscious, in spite of all the evidence that mounts through the years that the elements within us are actively making choices on our behalf, often with disastrous consequences."

The serenity afforded by Afore's refuge calmed Fiona and me. We felt more secure in our new home up in the Managalas Plateau. Someone once said, "Security is largely a superstition." I had not fully comprehended that avowal. I still yearned for its perceived comforts.

We brought up a new Afore general manager. He had obtained a four-year university technical degree in agricultural science. This young man was the fourth replacement in five years. I quietly predicted he would not last the year. He was an outsider from the Highlands—they are known for polygamy. He claimed to have one wife at the moment! (On the Plateau, they hack up a person for that practice.) Sustainable management in a third-world rural environment was a rare commodity. I recently had been informed of losing our number-one chilies village coordinator from Natanga due to adultery (he was murdered) and a chilies village coordinator manager from Kokoro, who had the top position over eight villages, to suicide. We proceeded with three days of meetings.

Predictably, the aura cast on the opening session by these untimely deaths was confusion and fear. Invariably, sorcery rose to the surface, and we were the prime suspects for the recent events. In their minds, it just had to be. Recently, a number of Mimi bush people, moving around in groups, had been preying on lone individuals. They hid and waited in the forest, surprising their victims. Encircling them, the Mimi forced these poor souls into rituals involving curses, spells, and brews. Some of the same sorcerers were assassins and would, for payment, kill to carry out acts of vengeance. Such a murder happened in our village of Tabuane a few years earlier, not far from our home. An Anglican elder, who was our Java Mama controller, dismissed it, saying, "He deserved what happened. These things are beyond our understanding and work themselves out. I do not feel it was wrong. You should accept this, and don't think about it."

It was concluded that the Mimi people put Gilcres, the chilies village coordinator, under a spell. He was directed to publicly shame his unfaithful wife, eat a poisonous vine called derris, and leave this earth. He did leave this earth as a result of derris poisoning.

I liked Peter One. He was a humble and honest man. I was spared the drama with Peter Two. This company representative was, in fact, an adulterer. He got caught with his pants down and was axed by the woman's oldest son. I did not like Peter Two. He was a con man. In both incidents, this is what I chose to believe.

I was called out in front of thirty coffee and chilies village representatives to deal with and confront these events on my second day at Afore. They wanted me to speak with the authority of a big boss. Armed with a pocket-size Gideon Bible, I recited 1 John 1:5–7, reminding them there is one Holy Spirit, and the Holy Spirit is stronger than the sorcerer's spirit that killed their friend and a coworker. I was not a missionary but a big, frightened white man. Besides committing to give kina to both families in support of their weeklong haus cries, we offered compensation for past employment. These observable actions helped the group to settle down in the following two days. The fear visibly subsided. This confrontation was with the unseen. I sensed a deeper showdown had transpired, one between good and evil and light and darkness. Graduate school was lacking in this instruction. News traveled fast. In another part of the country, a cult group fighting "unethical" sorcery killed the wrongdoers, ate their brains, and made soup from their penises. Chief trainers then created other powers with the brew. This was a far cry from the controlling vigilance of the human resource departments in corporate America. The PNG training costs were much more reasonable, though. For casting out an evil spirit or revealing the cause of a death, 1,000 kina in cash, plus a pig and a bag of rice were in order. Also, demanding sex as part of the payment for such PhD-deficient practitioners was appropriate, as long as it was not with teenagers. All of these practices, including sorcery, were illegal and pursued by the authorities. The underfunded police were spread pretty thin over the island of more than 6.5 million inhabitants.

Nevertheless, Fiona and I were cautiously optimistic since stabilizing the Afore collection center with a new general manager. With the financial support of Mahesh Patel, we projected a large collection of coffee bags. The farmers assured us we would have a double flush, which was an extended harvest, where the trees flower two times in one season. It would be satisfying to have the stars aligned to guide this vessel into the safe harbor called financial success.

Eight villages, comprising seven hundred new farmers, grew another 750,000 chilies trees down in the Popondetta area. Due to heavy rains, farmers had lost 250,000 trees the previous December. We hoped this new production would give us a consistent supply of commodities for the global market. We had another committed global buyer located in Frankfurt, Germany, who wanted to represent our company in Europe. Maybe the wheel was turning. The seventy-five daylong village field trips made last year may have paid off for this Tau Bada and his wife. The chilies farmers were gleeful. Many of them had never earned money from tilling the ground. Morobe Province would begin its coffee harvest in mid-April. Last year, we'd put in the organization structure, vehicles, and sheds and had a committed general manager. I would fly over to assist in late April. A new adventure awaited. An organizational practitioner, Fritz Roberts, said, "It is not what the vision is but what the vision does." This journey continued to define me. The adventure, in and of itself, gave me stamina to re-create daily. In Latin, *The Oxford English Dictionary* interprets stamina as "threads defined by the Fates." Forward motion on the highway fueled my inner man. The seriousness of my path would test this theory and belief.

The following day, we met with coffee and chilies representatives. It became contentious when Fiona, the new general manager, and I informed the group that the new parchment bean farm-gate price would be lowered to 3.50 kinas ($1.40) per kilo from last year's 4 kinas per kilo ($1.60). Parchment beans are dried, light-brown kernels of coffee, minus the pulped red skin. The beans were inspected, weighed, bagged, and transported four hours to Oro Bay by company vehicles. Packed into a container, they were then shipped within two days to Lae, where the bags were reloaded to vehicles, to be driven five hours to a mill in Goroka, Eastern Highlands Province. There, the bags were unloaded, reinspected, sorted, and milled to remove the parchment skin in order to get to the green bean. Trucked back to Lae, the bags were unloaded and reloaded on to a vessel bound for Australia, Europe, or the USA. It was the green bean that the global market would buy—roasted and distributed by the Starbucks of the world for your sweet lips to be acquainted with our coffee. All of these steps were costly. It was an expensive value chain. The dual Rainforest Alliance and organic certifications gave our company a reasonable premium. In fact, representatives of Allegra Coffee of Boulder, Colorado (now acquired by Whole Foods), made field visits to meet with us in Papua New Guinea and in Australia. They critically acclaimed not only the quality of our coffee but the commitment we made to the Managalas Plateau. Therefore, we could set a firm, fair, and competitive price to the farmers and purchase their coffee.

Now, with us fully and enthusiastically prepared to move into the new 2012 coffee harvest with the support of the City Pharmacy Ltd. Group, the response by our "dedicated" agents was deafening silence. I examined the building for any apparitions or signs of Mimi bushmen peering through the large open doors of the meeting shed. No such luck. The third OK Corral in one week was distilling.

The session broke down into shouting matches between the supportive representatives and nonsupportive representatives. PNG tradition usually admired the loudest and most vociferous combatants. Guess who yelled the loudest? The nonsupportive members who had been associated with past double-accounting to rob the company and the middlemen who cheated the farmer by paying below the company's official farm-gate price and pocketed the cash. The three of us became referees, separating one physical skirmish between two village coffee agents. One was the good guy and the other the bad guy. It was difficult to tell them apart—they did not wear black or white hats. We tried to control the meeting, but I was being drawn into an emotional melee. This was reminiscent of the family firms I'd consulted for in America. Albeit after six years, I realized most of these attendees not only refused to believe the facts—the world market price had dropped—but they were also prepared to boycott the company by not collecting and purchasing coffee. Hm! They publicly designated themselves as the protectors and guardians of the company and farmers. At the same time, their motivation was self-interest. I was reminded of the current Congress in America. The shylocks were playing an old song I had heard before. Slowly the words sunk in—the outsiders are the cheaters. We were the colonial plantation masters of the past, those who were considered the most vilifying. Fiona and I were to blame for the drop in the price of coffee in their plateau. It is what they chose to believe.

Prior to the meeting, while driving up to the plateau, Rufus, our Afore driver, tipped us off that, with national elections near, the Member of Parliament representing this district had distributed cash and blank checks to select villages to buy coffee at five kina per kilo. We identified the village where the MP was born. Coincidentally, the Java Mama village agent coordinator, the big boss who managed fourteen villages in the western side of the plateau, happened to be from the same village. He was now the self-proclaimed boycott leader comprising one-third of our annual production. Here at the meeting, his animated snarls pronounced by a grimaced face, stern eye contact, clenched fist, and wild arm gesticulations were the turning point for this Tau Bada. I responded with forceful and precise resolutions, instructing him to take his ass, along with the other nonsupportive village agents, out of the meeting and our company. "We don't want your support. We don't want your coffee. And good luck," I retorted. They departed, and the meeting resumed. That quickly, the third OK Corral was over, though I didn't believe that this was the last one by a long shot. Hollywood has shown me otherwise; there would be a sequel, but it would be unrehearsed.

Admittedly incensed by this event, I continued to adapt to the reality of life conditions and became more aware and wiser in my responses and decisions. I still found it excruciatingly difficult to accept the deeper cultural iceberg phenomena of the wantok-tambu system. The constant stealing, lying, and cheating that this structure propagated appears to be insurmountable. How could one begin to build and achieve anything without trust? How could one be courageous without confidence to what you were committed to?

The morning's raw beauty attempted to offset these realizations. Yet I felt I was becoming arrested and closing down. Remembrance of past endings arose . . . it ain't what it ain't . . . let it go. Many endings took place without notice or fanfare. They germinated in silence, unnoticed, as castles ultimately yield to the ground. Jim Harrison's novel *Returning to Earth* depicts this ultimate experience with a dying blackbird falling from a tree branch. I've never witnessed an expiring raven. I felt for that solitary bird as I felt my disillusionment and discouragement at the moment. This week's OK Corrals were less mercurial than previous encounters. They were more defining. The etched imprints, as I approach my sixty-sixth birthday the following month, were sonorous. Could I be realizing my own mortality, or was the stress getting to me? I wondered if the lonesome blackbird realized his mortality. These OK Corrals were far more involved and complex than the 3:00 p.m. showdown in the city of Tombstone, Cochise County, Arizona, on October 26, 1881. As expected, Hollywood made Wyatt Earp to be bigger than life. I was not feeling quite as big. The Tau Bada might very well be diminishing.

Blocked and cut off by the swollen Girua River, "I felt like I'd run into a brick wall." John's driver "estimated we would be spending the next eight hours waiting for the Girua to subside. How dare this river pose itself as a barrier to my exacting plans for the day? A surge of infantile grandiosity gripped my soul. I seethed with anger."

CHAPTER 30

The Girua River

"The great secret of power is never to will to do more than you can accomplish."

—Henrik Ibsen

Wedding bands conjure up an assortment of images and meanings. At heart, I have not been fond of finger ornaments and have little emotion attached to this marriage tradition. Now I discover a rather new affinity for this innocuous piece of jewelry. My left hand and wrist are slightly sprained, and my wedding-band finger is pierced and bruised. The ring imposes a circular indentation on my finger, slightly cutting my skin and leaving a bluish-purple discoloring. As I view this band on my finger, the swollen and raging Girua River comes to the forefront, drowning out the insignificance of such trivial wounds.

I realized a respect for this silver band on this Tuesday morning, April 3, 2012. For this ring possibly saved the Tau Bada from being swept away into the Solomon Sea the night before as I returned from the Managalas Plateau.

Reflecting on these recent events and confrontations, I seem to be morphing into a compulsive/obsessive maniac. I suspect it is largely the result of a strong Protestant work ethic, Type A personality, and insatiable high-achiever goals. Add a pinch of narcissism, and you have a wicked brew. All are markings of a disease and book uniquely labeled *Boomeritis* by author Ken Wilber.

Following World War II, I entered into the rank and file of the baby-boom generation. Rank has its privileges. I was born early on, giving me a sense of entitlement. Malcolm Gladwell amused me in his book *Outliers*. In my estimation, I also rigorously fulfilled the "10,000 hour rule" and paid my dues with significant training and conditioning. However, with my baby-boomer credentials intact, something had escaped me. There resided within me a shallowness and regret. Feelings of incompleteness, akin to a race never finished, troubled me. A quiet dissonance had been subdued and disguised. I was a competitive entrant and was afforded significant opportunity. Something had escaped me. As I looked back on forty years, I saw only faint imprints of my own generation's contributions to this planet at large. Has something escaped me?

On this day in 2012, I am still on autopilot, intensely sensitized to desperately control an uncontrollable environment. What is going on here? I was blindly determined to cross an impassible river. I had assumed I was in remission from this unswerving behavior. The cure for Boomeritis demanded a psychological detachment and amputation by a very precise surgery. This patient had to become more flexible and adaptive to diverse life conditions and various social and cultural values. In other words, my self-absorption might have to give way to a larger context in order to recognize other people's needs in a more objective and accepting way. Yes, intellectually, I understood, but it was too abstract to practice. My own psychological and cultural bents remained deeply embedded, similar to an amputee trying to comprehend the trickery of a phantom limb. Old habits are hard to break. With zeal and tenacity, I presumptuously lunged.

Rufus, the Afore driver assigned to our new vehicle, anxiously awaited our morning departure for Popondetta. In early April, the rainy season had extended itself. Torrential downpours played havoc with the roads and river crossings. This morning, clear skies gave Fiona and me false assurance that we could depart later than planned.

As we drove down the mountains to Oro Bay, the day was uneventful. Amazingly, we were on time. Rufus, pretty close to forty years old, was a keen driver mechanic. He had distinguished himself by not drinking on the job. In six years, this attribute had eluded us with every other driver we employed. Out on the Solomon Sea, the view of calm water encouraged us that we would arrive without mishap in Popondetta within thirty minutes. With such fair weather, the crossing of Girua River was an afterthought.

The bridge spanning this tributary had been washed out last November by a series of forceful plateau thunderstorms that swept away an expanse already weakened by Cyclone Guba. The only highway entering Popondetta, the capital city of Oro Province, was sliced in half. Dangling asphalt pavement and twisted, protruding guardrails were a testament to provincial government planning five months later. Where were the appropriated Cyclone Guba disaster funds? After four years, one would wonder if this province was even connected to the rest of the island nation.

Airstrip traffic, palm oil trucks, public-transportation vans, and private vehicles had to traverse forty meters (120 feet) at their own risk to get to either side. Northern plateau downpours swelling the river dictated one's schedule, including the two airlines. It was common to have air traffic stopped as passengers were stymied in trying to arrive at the airport on time to board their flights.

Carefully, Rufus turned down into a grassy ravine serving as an alternative road. Various trucks, semis, and people comingled on the gravel path descending into the riverbed. Smack! Raging rapids of brown, muddied water, swirling around rocks and swiftly and effortlessly carrying tree limbs and trunks, greeted us. We were halted dead-cold in our tracks. The Colorado River's Lava Falls at the bottom of the Grand Canyon flashed through my mind. Memories surfaced of etched crosses, dates, and names inscribed on the sandstone walls of drowned adventurers. They took little heed of the danger presented. One evening, camping above Lava Falls before descending the rapids by raft the following morning, campfire tales were shared of these less fortunate souls being swept into the Gulf of California.

I felt like I'd run into a brick wall. My plans evaporated. Rufus, unperturbed, having a good chew of betel nut, spit out a red stream of juice as he stepped out of the vehicle. He estimated we would be spending the next eight hours waiting for the Girua to subside. How dare this river pose itself as a barrier to my exacting plans for the day? A surge of infantile grandiosity gripped my soul. I seethed with anger. Where in the hell was this reaction coming from? Such invincibility! I disliked Rufus at the moment. I wanted to slay the messenger. He discharged another mouthful of betel nut juice and shrugged his drooping shoulders. My determination to change the world, even more challenged by the recent Popondetta events, would not be deterred. I fumed. Rufus spat again.

I wrestled with these horns of dilemma and realized shortly that I was out of answers and fell into sober resignation. Stepping out of the truck's cab, I went to the rear bed and unzipped my duffel bag in search of an antidote. Retrieving a bottle of Sauza tequila and a bag of Doritos, I climbed back into the cab. Fiona smiled. She knew that I knew I was having an inner reckoning. *Let it go, John.* Successfully reviving long-ago astral projection techniques, I was soon on a beach south of Puerto Vallarta, Mexico, sipping an ice-cold margarita and watching the sun sink into the Pacific Ocean. The mariachi band sounded wonderful.

This diversionary tactic moved the clock forward seven hours to 11:00 p.m. The tequila bottle was drained. Fiona suspected my restlessness, now fueled by a bag of corn chips and half a bottle of agave juice. A driving energy spiraled upward within me.

Rain started to fall. The fog, coupled with my heavy breathing, obscured the windshield. I was gagging on my own discontent. Ever so gradually, the river was subsiding. Previously submerged rocks were appearing along the riverbed. I was refuting "A watched pot never boils." My confidence rose in direct proportion to the falling water. Speaking of water, I needed to take a leak. The fresh air felt good. Standing in kunai grass, I found relief. Unknowingly, I stepped on a pile of dog shit.

While peeing, the resolve to walk across the river captured my imagination. I climbed back into the front seat. Fiona looked into my eyes and commented, "You smell like dog shit." I did not reveal my innermost secret—that I wanted to cross the river. The smell of the dog shit was so overpowering that this intention was successfully disguised.

I scraped off my right shoe at the river's edge. Staring across to the other side, I was now convinced we were going to cross the river. I was not going to wait any longer for the vehicle to safely cross. *Nobody tells me what to do*, I thought. As I walked back to the cab, Rufus informed me that rocks were shifted by the storm, making it too dangerous to drive across at night. My resolve to depart was just strengthened.

Cajoling Fiona to accompany me, a look of incomprehensibility emerged. Rufus yelled across the river, instructing three uniformed guards with M16 rifles to drive us to Popondetta. They were waiting for a stranded employee of the palm oil company to cross. The slightly built bespectacled Indian was perplexed and appeared more apprehensive than I was. Waiting for the Yankees to safely cross first, he kindly acquiesced and assured us a ride to our hotel.

Rocky cliffs appeared to my left, with a vehicle perched on top. The headlights illuminated the river and far embankment, where a large Land Cruiser was waiting. Like sharp daggers, the beams of both vehicles cut into the darkness and gave me a clearer view of the rapids. Without a doubt, the swiftness of the water looked menacing. Silhouetted granite rocks juxtaposed a concoction of dark-brown mud, uprooted kunai grass, and swirling water. The rain fell. A descending mist enshrouded the nettled rays. Clashing like swords, the shards of light simulated the inward blitzkrieg of my own anxiety and anticipation. Thoughtlessly, my soul was engaged in the moment. I was ready to cross.

Rufus and Fiona negotiated with two villagers to traverse with me. I intervened, and they were paid ten kina ($4.34) apiece. Originally, these two Wall Street traders demanded twenty kina ($8.69) apiece. Sadly, I continued to discount myself. I was surely worth more than the extra four dollars. This was fresh evidence that I was still carrying an unresolved low-self-esteem issue. I never gave much thought to how I masqueraded my intentions. Saving this enormous amount of money was indeed more prized than risking my life by crossing a potentially impassable river.

Instructions were meted out to walk up to twenty meters to the river's edge. These frail-looking yet confident young men grasped my hands and arms. The thought of not making it across the Girua did not enter my mind. We entered the cool water. Within one minute, Francis, the downstream villager, lost his footing. In midstream, he was now pulling me down as he valiantly tried to regain his traction and balance. Samuel, the upstream villager, was using all his strength to keep his grip. Slowly, the force of the current unraveled his hand on my arm. It slid down to my left hand, where his other hand had a firm grasp.

The three of us desperately inched our way upstream in order to find the sand bar, signaling the turning point where reprieve from fighting the current would come. Bingo! I glanced at the headlights. Now, we were being pushed downstream. In the ensuing seconds, I felt my wedding band cutting into my finger, realizing that was all Samuel was hanging onto.

Excruciating pain overcame my fear of being swept away. I was more galvanized by the thought of having my finger severed than of drowning. This distraction was effective. I was now stumbling downstream with the current. The grip eased, and the pain diminished as I stepped out onto the embankment.

A group of staring women, chewing betel nut and kibitzing among themselves, greeted me. *"Oro kaiva, oro kaiva"* (hello and welcome). I intuited that they felt relief for this drenched white man standing in the rain, somewhat dazed. I yelled across the river, imploring Fiona to instruct the returning Francis and Samuel to cross. It was Fiona's turn. She yelled back that she did not want to cross the river. I out-yelled her and would not be denied. I became the only voice heard.

The headlights emitted little light as I tried to get a clear view of Fiona stepping into the river. She did not hike up the shoreline as far as I did. She entered into the rapids prematurely, entering the river at the most treacherous point. Losing their balance momentarily, they gripped the rocks with their hands and stabilized themselves and stood erect. Retracing their steps, they returned to the river's edge and tried again.

My heart skipped. I saw this slightly built woman disappear like a twig whipped under water and nearly carried away. Before my eyes, self-orientation became another's orientation. This time was Fiona's orientation. In my lifetime, I wonder how I have burdened others as I strived toward my wishes and goals. Of course, undeterred, I implored her to try again. I would not give up. *Don't tell me what to do!* Thwarted, Fiona refused to make another attempt.

Francis, unperturbed by the drama, returned to me with a plastic bag atop his head containing a change of clothes, toothpaste, and toothbrush. Fiona was too much. As I was driven to the hotel, a few lessons stemming from my experience in this river crossing began to percolate. But the picture of a hot shower and clean sheets was a more appealing thought. Fiona would sleep in a village haus win on a mat with a blanket, waiting for daybreak to safely cross the river.

Sipping on a bottle of beer and nibbling cold pizza, I turned on the Al Jazeera news station. The TV, beer, and tasteless pizza gave me little comfort and distraction. As I tried to sleep, this event replayed itself throughout the morning hours. The headlights relentlessly pricked my meditations. My finger, swollen and aching, drove home a feeling of unappeasable perfectionism I found disturbing. My drive for higher achievement had turned into maladaptiveness. I knew I had to confront this attribute sooner rather than later. I did not want to lose my self-respect by presuming Fiona's love.

This zealot needed to chill out and find equilibrium to gain a more expanded perspective. I suspected this endeavor would be a nobler high-wire feat than crossing the Girua River.

Raps on the door at 7:00 a.m. awakened me to Fiona's smile, embrace, and salutation. "Hello, darling. Did you miss me as much as I missed you?" Without a misstep, Fiona showered and dressed. We breakfasted. Quickly, I was plunged into the challenges and activities of the day as we entered the Easter week and celebration. The hope of personal resurrection sustained me. It gave me the courage to cross other rivers. I pondered that I might have to develop a new theory to cross future rivers.

When John was routinely present, he could see (top photo) fully dried chilies ready for the global market. When he showed up unexpectedly: dry laundry on the company's chilies racks. This sort of thing happened over and over. "The strategic planning credentials founded on graduate school in my practicum-thesis and twenty-five years of consulting were substantial. Those qualifications became dust in the wind."

CHAPTER 31

Tattered Tunnels

"Everything simple is false. Everything which is complex is unusable."

—Paul Valéry

Papoga village was distant enough, in addition to washboard roads, steep climbs, and river crossings, to provoke me to question, "What am I trying to accomplish?" The occasional bird of paradise, eagle, and Ulysses butterfly interspersed by the waves of villagers or laughter of children eased the toil and seemed to balance things out and bring inner harmony.

The village was ninety minutes southwest of Popondetta and was bordered by commercial palm oil plantations. The area was named Asigi and was inhabited by a tribe called the Oro Kaiva people. The odious smell of discarded and uncollected palm oil fruit (ripened red cherries) was distinct and repulsive. Frequently, I spotted stagnant rainwater pools saturated with chemicals and filmed over with maggots. This also produced a unique stench.

The Malaysian-owned New Britain Palm Oil Ltd. ran this business. It purchased the mess (interest) left behind from Cargill Inc., based in Minnetonka, Minnesota. In revenue, Cargill is the largest private company in America, maybe number one or two in the world. It ranked behind AT&T in revenue and ahead of JP Morgan Chase. Cargill left deep footprints throughout Asia, becoming the largest importer (producer and trader both) to the USA of this commodity. It has been referred to as the "greasy palms" industry. General Mills was Cargill's biggest palm oil customer. The fact that Girl Scouts in America sell cookies door-to-door made with palm oil drives home the principle that we are all in this together.

One point almost escaped me—the black flies. Millions of these biting pests swarmed throughout the communities, transforming the simple act of eating to an art form. To move a spoonful of rice, let alone a cookie, to one's orifice, absent the flies, was a feat requiring deliberate practice. With a deforested landscape pockmarked by inexhaustible piles of decaying pods, the black flies felt right at home laying eggs unencumbered until their souls were content.

Refreshed by a solid night's sleep and stoked by two plungers of coffee, I was alert and anxious to arrive at Papoga. The large Toyota was fueled up. Kits was my designated driver. Elijah, the lead field manager, and Jeffery, a new hire under Eli's supervision, accompanied me. My adrenaline was pumping. I reflected on twenty months of field work beginning with chief toktoks, sorcerer confrontations, awareness training sessions, and the registration of Papoga's 120 chilies farmers. It was an alternative to the backbreaking work of palm oil and the chemicals killing their traditional land. This was the advent of a gentle cash crop.

Instituting a controlled management system, we audited and inspected 1,200 trees per farmer before we acquiesced and lent the farmers the kina to build drying tunnels, seven meters by two meters. The company (City Pharmacy Ltd. Group) paid for the clear plastic, green shade cloth, and nails. In return, the farmers would forfeit their first bag of chilies (22.5 kilos) for repayment. Each farmer and village coordinator signed a one-page contract.

Simple math works on paper. Take 700 verified farmers in eight villages and multiply that by 67.50 kina per tunnel, and you get 47,250 kina ($20,545 US). Our company purchased that amount of material to supply 700 village farmers drying tunnels. Based on 700 farmers, at 1,200 trees per farmer, you have a total of 840,000 trees, yielding approximately three kilos per tree per year, which total 2,520,000. The chilies were dried in the tunnels, reducing the weight by 50 percent. Therefore, 1,260,000 kilos of dried chilies could be ready to ship to the global market in 22.5-kilo bags, making available 56,000 bags, or 300 bags per container, or 186 containers per year, or 15.5 containers per month, or 3.8 containers per week.

The individual farmer has a minimum of 1,200 trees, at three kilos annual yield per tree, which equals 3,600 fresh kilos and 1,800 dried kilos. On a monthly basis, if the farmer optimally picked his chilies, he would end up with 150 kilos, dried. Divided into 22.5-kilo bags, he would sell 6.66 bags per month. At a farm-gate price of three kina per kilo, the farmer would receive 450 kina cash per month, or 225 kina per fortnight. This was significant money for a remote area with rampant poverty and high illiteracy. This cash infusion would assist in paying for school fees, roofing irons, lantern kerosene, clothes, and food staples like rice.

On the Managalas Plateau, approximately one thousand farmers from thirty villages planted five hundred trees each. Control management techniques were not developed back in 2009. We did not insist on a minimum of one hundred farmers per village at 1,200 trees per farmer. The average plateau plot was five hundred to six hundred trees versus the audited/inspected 1,200 trees per farmer in the Popondetta area. Optimally, the farmer could pick up to three bags per month, generating 200 kina per month or 100 kina per fortnight. In a remote area, this was significant money on a consistent basis.

Within one year in 2010, the plateau picking results were disappointing, bordering on disastrous. The farm-gate price was raised from 1.50 kina per kilo to 3 kina per kilo to motivate greater picking. No such luck. The overall picking rate hovered at 3–4 percent. Consequently, out of 500,000 trees, with one thousand farmers in thirty villages potentially yielding 1,500,000 kilos fresh and 750,000 kilos dried to produce 33,300 bags or 111 containers (300 bags per container) per year, the entire plateau averaged one container every three and a half months, or 3.5 containers per year. Based on these results, a mere 47,250 kilos of fresh chilies were picked out of an optimum 1,500,000 kilos. The picking rate was a devastating 3 percent. Bluntly, out of 1.5 million kilos of fresh chilies, 1.45 million kilos rotted and fell to the ground from not being picked.

The reasons for the low plateau results were:
1. Lazy village coordinators (management) who wanted to act like "big bosses," getting paid for doing little work, as was purported by the farmers.
2. Lazy farmers who enjoyed chewing betel nut, gambling, and bossing their wives more than working, as was purported by the village coordinators.
3. Community activities (e.g., haus cries, feasts, crusades, politics), as was purported by both farmers and village coordinators.
4. Working in their gardens in order to feed themselves.
5. Coffee season's harvest interference for three to four months, a distraction to picking chilies.
6. Birds and bad soil conditions.

Again, we scurried to the drawing boards. In 2011 and early 2012, we replaced the majority of village coordinators with new candidates who were non-tambu. Compensation was increased. We restructured the company by increasing the span of control of village coordinators to impact effectiveness. Further role training and village coordinator team building were in order. The new solar dryer (which guaranteed A-grade moisture content below 11 percent for the global market) and shed were completed. Chilies bags were provided to the farmers at no charge. Also, we supplied the farmers with drying tunnel materials, at cost, delivered by our vehicle from Popondetta. We hired a university-degree agricultural manager who had computer and bookkeeping skills and gave him a full-time office administrator. The office was furnished and powered with solar panels and a generator.

The results remained the same. We lost our Australian buyer. The German buyer was not impressed by continued shipment delays that impacted quality—the longer the product remained in storage, the greater the deterioration (e.g., mold and bacteria).

Irony seeped into my psyche, playing havoc with my self-confidence. My commitment escalated with fewer results. Insanity is defined as continually doing the same thing and expecting different results. Was I losing my mind? The acronym BHAG—for "Big Hairy Audacious Goal," coined by business author James Collins—was possibly a joint figment of the farmers' and my imagination and idealism gone awry.

The strategic-planning credentials founded in graduate school in my practicum-thesis and twenty-five years of consulting were substantial. Those qualifications became dust in the wind. I opined on noted authors such as Michael Porter of Harvard Business School and Henry Mintzberg from McGill University. I included Warren Bennis or the late Peter Drucker for a more general theory of management, but I was out of answers. Again, I turned to the studies of Clare Graves and of Don Beck's and Chris Cowan's *Spiral Dynamics* to refresh my organizational and planning theory, including a dive into cultural anthropology and ethnology. I read, numerous times, a PhD dissertation written by John Dixon on Papua New Guinea rural business. It conveyed the type of intellectual desperation and emotional frenzy that drove me to the edge. Hunter S. Thompson said, "The edge . . . there is no honest way to explain it because the only people who know where it is are the ones who have gone over."

Further to the point, Fiona compiled two laboratory results from Australia and Europe testing the pungency of our Papua New Guinea chilies. Using a Scoville scale (which measures heat units) that indicated the amount of capsaicin, which is an integral part of chilies' composition, she discovered that the plateau bird's-eye chilies had a significant part of the ingredient, giving us bragging rights in the global marketplace. We went head-to-head with the African Malawi bird's-eye chilies and successfully competed with them by obtaining new orders. We were hotter! This competing country was similar in climate, poverty, and corruption but was far more organized in enterprise development, having exported A-grade chilies since 1994.

Now, with this plateau experience under our belt, the lessons should have been positively applied to Popondetta. We needed to execute effectively. The new cash crop was not only important to the rural community but to our organization. The coffee business could not generate enough profits to fund the company. Additional revenue was required. A six-month coffee season was not sufficient. Financially, we were suffering. It was imperative to be successful in Popondetta.

Elijah was disquieted for some reason. As he turned around in the passenger seat, glare from the bright morning sun made it difficult to read his face. Jeffery, the newcomer, was characteristically silent and cautious, studying this white man. I looked to my left. Kits, chewing on betel nut, was shifting into four-wheel drive as we approached a river. Intuition prompted me to quiz Elijah. "Is Albert [the chilies village coordinator] ready for our visit?"

"Yes, John, I talked to him two days ago," he said. "The

chiefs, farmers, and the quality control supervisor are waiting."

My expectations were running high. Recent written reports from Elijah confirmed Papoga was on target. The latest drying tunnels would produce twenty-five chilies bags per week, fifty per fortnight, and one hundred per month. The start of the business—the baby was being delivered! Volume calculations raced through my mind, reminiscent of past Wall Street deal-making days. Projection scenarios flooded my thinking—120 farmers @ 120 tunnels x two bags per month equals 240 bags. This was pretty close to one container per month from one of the eight villages. I mused, *Global marketplace, here we come!*

Abruptly, my head twisted to Elijah. "What picking rate did you and Albert choose?" I asked.

He forcibly responded, "Papoga will pick 60 percent of their chilies per month. Albert is working hard with the farmers."

A 60-percent picking rate would double my initial start-up forecast of 30 percent. My heart leaped, catching these assurances. The Promised Land was beyond this last river crossing. Calculations ratcheted up akin to an initial public offering being priced for underwriting at the World Trade Center or the acquisition price offered for a client's enterprise that would exceed his wildest expectation, prompting him to giggle in private over his new fortune. The sirens of Ulysses were reverberating. The ropes binding me to the ship's mast were not unraveling. Elijah and I were now staring at one another. A turning point was in the making, or was it a counterpoint? The swooning images of past successes and accomplishments urged me to unplug my ears to listen to the melodious lure of reliving history. As we forded the river, my thoughts and feelings became disjunctive and disparate. Consolation eluded me.

The smaller river posed little challenge. Water dripping off the chassis fell into the dust of the gravel road as the tires gripped the stones. The climb up the hill was unremarkable. I glanced to the right. Three bare-breasted village women with children were drying washed pots and clothes on the rocks in the sun. The yelping of a dog blended into the background noise of the chatting mothers. A haranguing scream pierced the predictability of the moment. I looked to the driver, who appeared clueless. Instantaneously, the face of an agitated man, with a bush knife at chest level, filled my window space. Shouting in a dialect I could not comprehend, he thrust the blade into the window opening. Unfortunately, the window was jammed. Bad luck. Kits, my new interpreter, frantically explained that we had run over and killed his dog. He demanded fifty kina compensation. My pockets were empty. Bad luck. Vainly, I requested a contribution. Not one kina among the four of us could be pooled. Bad luck. I couldn't even negotiate him up by promising a future payment.

Within the twinkling of an eye, an old woman appeared. Good luck. She pulled at the villager and spun him around. He received a good talking-to. The power of his grandmother dissuaded this young man. He was not pleased with me, but he was respectful of her. She smiled and explained to me, through Kits, that she was sorry for her grandson's anger. She said we needed to pay fifty kina next week on our return. Again, she smiled and tapped my arm. I smiled back and wondered if I would ever see the Promised Land. Omens, like ravens, have double messages. I was curious why this event had transpired.

Papoga village's outskirts appeared with the first huts, haus wins, and drying tunnels. I strained to see the filled tunnels. I instructed Kits to stop the vehicle. My eyes were focused on three to four tunnels not more than fifty meters to our left.

The platforms appeared devoid of chilies. I squinted into the sunlight, remaining focused as I walked over to inspect them. Eli was looking down and away from my gaze of incomprehensibility.

Immediately, I concluded this was an aberration. Yet the absence of farmers was a disappointment. I hoped they were at the main village, waiting for me to arrive. Stepping back into the vehicle, we continued to drive to the village. Kits stopped the vehicle. As I hiked to another four to five empty tunnels, an anger rose and a feeling of betrayal gripped me with such force I began tearing off the plastic and shade cloth with rage. Running from one empty tunnel to another, I foamed with strife. Jeffery was dazed, and Eli looked as dumb as a post. I instructed them to dismantle every tunnel in sight. My aim was to retrieve my property. They'd broken an oral and written contract. The materials, now folded in neat piles, were loaded into our vehicle. We proceeded to the village to visit Albert.

Albert's home was located in the center of the village and was, to my chagrin, surrounded by empty tunnels. The wind was blowing the clear plastic off one tunnel. The flapping sound raised my irritation to a higher level. Laundry was hanging from another tunnel. I seethed with judgment as I saw Albert dozing on his doorstep, unperturbed by the black flies. The vehicle's engine stirred him enough to look at me and brush his dreadlocks to one side of his confused face. He waved Eli over, and they spoke privately. Eli walked over to me, claiming Albert was upset because we were scheduled to visit tomorrow. I ignored this retort. After six years, I knew most of the defensive antics—the lying. Glancing at his empty, soon-to-be-removed ten-meter-by-three-meter tunnel, I spotted a clear plastic bag filled with brackish water and rotten chilies. Dangling by a rope, it swayed with a slight breeze. I was ready to puke. The bile of disappointment and loss of confidence to what I was committed was coming up my throat. Retreating to the vehicle, I beckoned my crew to depart for Popondetta.

"Five hooded men . . . lunged out of the bush and pumped cartridges from rifles at our vehicle. . . . The lodged cartridge barely missed the fuel drums and was less than two feet behind our midsections."

CHAPTER 32

Bushwhacked

"The brighter the light, the darker the shadow."
—Joan Hazelton

Countrywide pandemonium, spurred by the 2012 elections, had largely subsided. Nationally, a new prime minister was elected. But locally, to our regret, the Ijivitari district of Oro Province reelected the incumbent Member of Parliament. His election was challenged amid allegations of corrupt campaigning. Allegedly, he had distributed bundles of cash to select constituents, supplied beer taped with fifty-kina notes to villages, and stuffed numerous ballot boxes—not as sophisticated as America's pork-barrel tactics but just as shrewd and equally effective.

Consequently, this MP was on the gravy train for another five years. Remember, he was the same fox who had used public funds to purchase coffee, competing with Java Mama. Such organized crime did not even raise an eyebrow in the Managalas Plateau and was considered business as usual. It was a life condition accepted for what it was. Personally, it is a chicken bone lodged in my throat to see this dog return to his vomit.

Not more than a few months earlier, I'd confronted him at the motel bar on this "business practice." With the rancor of an American tea-party zealot, he remarked, "This is a fucking free and democratic country. I have a fucking right to compete with you and Fiona, any time, everywhere." Moments before the altercation, I legitimized him by accepting four ice-cold South Pacific beers. Honestly, they tasted pretty good on that hot, humid evening. Returning to the motel room with two of the beers, I confessed my hypocrisy to Fiona, realizing this sanctified Yankee imbibed on public funds.

The geography of corruption was pervasive and seductive, even for professionals like me. I was reminded of the power of hubris and its insidious side effects. Innocent decisions such as accepting a cold beer on a hot evening, traveling on a prestigious helicopter or private jet, or voyaging in the ease of a limousine versus a cab all piled up, and before you know it, you are on the take—a legal buyout and corruption of your soul. All of the above are outwardly legitimate, but I'm referring to the inner larceny. Sucking up to power is part of the game. It is a dance to which you are invited, and you get used to the music. Ultimately, it becomes background noise, and you become part of the system that you were ordained, elected, or hired to change. Someone else largely redefines your mission, whether you want to admit it or not. You move into a stasis and start to protect your turf. This power is quite addictive, and you want more of it. Your waistline begins to expand, and before you know it, the double chin appears. These emblems indicate an implosion of your new self-serving purpose. Your original mission has dissipated.

From one pretender to another, it is effortless to blur boundaries when people of position, celebrity-media status, and power are so accommodating. Innocent and imperceptible shades of gray may unsuspectingly lead to a shadow land of obscurantism, making dark what might once, with naïveté, have appeared to be light. For instance, on a larger scale, what multinational mining, gas, and timber companies were contriving with other politicians of Papua New Guinea. I had witnessed the broad-daylight shenanigans of the alluvial gold buyers, timber thieves, animal poachers, and spice traders. The landowners were selling their futures. They did not have a clue, although the chiefs, government officials, and politicians did. The cornucopia of Australians, Chinese, Americans, New Zealanders, Brits, Filipinos, and Taiwanese, not to forget the Malaysians, were eager to supply the funds.

Oro Province did elect a new governor, which was positive news. The flip side was that our former associate Warpa Kephale, who was issued a court summons to respond to our request for a restraining order to cease threatening and interfering with our lives, came in second, losing by just 2,500 votes. He thirsted for the governorship. His "creating livelihoods" platform was centered on the business successes of both Java Mama and Chilies Mama. The campaigner's promise was to gain control of this business and retain it for the people of Managalas Plateau. Outsiders like Fiona and John were not welcome. We were an intrusion. The farmers would benefit immeasurably by his direction as the governor.

Okay! Now that he was out of a job, what did he plan to do? The undercurrent of a potential threat was a stress to Fiona and me. We suspected he would appear one day and attempt to extract money. What disturbed us was when and what tactics he might employ.

Regrettably, I viewed these events without enough seriousness. We never conceived the community where we were helping to build a sustainable business would become jealous enough to erupt into harmful actions. Unbeknownst to us, the light was dimming for these once-bright-eyed do-gooders. Popondetta was wearing me down, especially after the chilies demise and Easter-day armed robbery at the office facility. This was the third robbery in two years. I contemplated a trip back to Afore, now that the elections had concluded. On a hot and hazy Thursday afternoon, the Land Cruiser was loaded, including three 250-liter drums of petrol.

In a foul mood, I pictured myself diving into another swimming pool of daily chaos. Continued staff incompetency reinforced a feeling of hopelessness.

The vehicle would not start. Another dead battery, purchased only six months ago. How could this be? Fiona lifted up the hood and uncapped the battery cells. Dry as a bone. Lawrence, the driver-mechanic, with a sheepish look and mouthful of betel, responded: "I forgot to look." Frustration mounted. I smilingly grimaced. A favorite writer of mine, Thomas McGuane, summed up the moment: "I consider the wonder of the things that befall me, convinced that my life was the best omelet you could make with a chainsaw."

A breeze ever so lightly blew litter into stagnant water–filled ditches. An acrid haze rose over Popondetta as piles of trash from roadside merchants and shops smoldered, a daily ritual that assured this hellhole some predictability. The familiar stench was a perverse comfort to such an unpredictable petri dish of life.

Miltonian echoes of a "Paradise Lost" reverberated. Fear began its ascent from a hidden room deep within my soul. I felt disconcerted. A precise pandemonium called Popondetta entangled and began to suffocate me. A dark shadow loomed in this gathering place of demons. Without insight beyond my own human capabilities, I felt ill-prepared and exposed. Wisdom, pure and simple, eluded me as I grappled with this reality.

Tired and irritated, I barked at Fiona and Lawrence to get out of this perdition. My objective was to move on to the highway. I yearned for the coolness of the mountains and stillness of the plateau. Yet envisioning a place of refuge seemed only to aggravate me. I was on the verge of a tantrum and exhausted.

Annoyingly, they began a side conversation in Pidgin. Swiftly, they suggested we delay the departure to drive to the police headquarters and request an armed escort to follow our vehicle. Reacting in disbelief and intense incomprehensibility, I muttered, "Why do I want to spend another minute in this place to do what you want me to do?"

Without reservation, Lawrence responded with complete equanimity, "My stomach is discouraged and warns me we are in danger today. The road between Popondetta and Oro Bay makes me not feel good."

Flatly rejecting this option, I demanded we immediately leave, as we had already been delayed by three hours. They stood their ground. In seven years, this decision would be a first. It would be a capitulation to fear. I never permitted firearms before. But I had little energy left to fight this battle. I reluctantly acquiesced. There would not be a Girua River crossing today.

Within forty-five minutes, an M16-armed police escort followed us out of Popondetta. I focused on the unfolding road as the roadside litter gave way to lush green kunai grass on both sides of the highway. Drifting into an almost forgotten *terza rima*, my immediate objections diminished enough to let me glance at the Owen Stanley mountains to my right.

Brusquely, the vehicle veered to the center as an object loudly and forcibly hit the Land Cruiser. Fiona screeched. To our left, five hooded men, three of them armed with what looked like spears, lunged out of the bush and pumped cartridges from rifles at our vehicle. Most shots missed, but the first one thudded into the truck's side. Hollywood sound effects would be hard-pressed to replicate the effect. The lodged cartridge barely missed the fuel drums and was less than two feet behind our midsections.

Lawrence swerved to the roadside, stopping the vehicle. I stepped out of the cab, doing a 360-degree turn, frantically scanning the immediate landscape for other rascals and fearing their emergence at any moment. Climbing back into the truck, I shouted at Fiona and Lawrence to proceed back down the road, where the police escort was straddling the pavement, returning gunfire. I estimated the distance at one hundred meters. It was the longest three hundred feet I have ever encountered. Later, on reflection, I thought, *This was longer than the three hundred feet down the right-field line at Detroit's Tiger Stadium on Trumbull Avenue, where home runs would once glide over the lower deck wire-mesh fence.*

But now my driver sat motionless. Fiona was in a trance, incapacitated by the initial shock. I yelled, "Turn around and get to our escort!"

The rifle shots brought out numerous villagers to the highway. In front and back of us, we could not distinguish friend from foe. Suddenly, a lone man farther up the road started to run toward us. I could not make out if he was part of the ambush. My heart throbbed. Again, I bellowed out to turn the damn vehicle around. Lawrence regained his composure. I felt overwhelmed and vulnerable as we cautiously drove back to the other vehicle. We were sitting ducks.

Confusion reigned as my judgment foundered. My mind would not shift fast enough to fully come to terms with this onslaught. I anticipated another round of shots and was alerted to move forward versus staying put. Obviously, they were terrible marksmen. A moving target was harder to hit. What an extraordinary deduction for this once-well-paid consultant. Memories of duck-hunting days with a Potawatomi Indian guide named Jasper John popped up. On Walpole Island, east of Detroit, Michigan, he instructed me to carefully lead the ducks and shoot forward. Following his instruction, I began to accurately shoot more mallards. I yelled at Lawrence, "Step on it!"

Suspended animation sensitized my senses. In a deafening silence, we quickly headed back to the safety of our police escort. I viewed the two policemen and the M16 rifle leaning against the leg of one of the officers. Blood pooled on the roadside near the pavement. They had wounded one of the shooters, and I noted a satisfaction with this. My anger surged, and I felt a perfect hatred. I wish they would have maimed— or, better yet, killed—him. My moral compass went haywire. I did not feel forgiving or reconciling. What had I adapted to? Vengeance or the PNG payback code was not that different from America's gunboat diplomacy or free-market capitalism. My mother's Sicilian forefathers were smiling with approval. But a foreboding realization gripped me as I concluded that someone had deliberately tried to kill Fiona and me. At my age, such epiphanies are rare; the phrase "never say never" took on a new meaning.

We limped back to the police station. A crowd of gawkers surrounded the vehicle and beheld a .30-caliber cartridge hole produced by a World War II vintage M1 rifle. The chrysanthemum gunmetal cavity reminded me of the deadly force of the semiautomatic weapon so prized by US infantry and feared by the Japanese and German forces. M1s proved to be stalwart companions of our soldiers in the battle of Guadalcanal.

Once upon a time, while enrolled at Howe Military School in Howe, Indiana, I mistakenly called my issued M1 rifle a gun. I was ordered to sleep with it for one week to learn to respect the prowess of this weapon. Such pedagogy was ineffective. Now, fifty years later, through a new application, I did indeed venerate this killing instrument. Our US armament industry tries harder. As the leader of the arms pack, it keeps on ticking, making obsolete what was once considered the best that money can buy.

Lawrence and his three boss crew boys jumped off the truck, feverishly biting and peeling the shells off their betel nuts to obtain immediate relief with this handy tranquilizer. I preferred a bottle of Jack Daniel's whiskey. No such luck. Witness statements were written.

Less than three hours after we had departed for Afore, we were back where we began. Now, we were sequestered in a guarded motel room. Hollywood sequels ran through my mind. I pondered panicked foreigners desperately calling their embassy for sanctuary. Naturally, I followed suit. I retrieved a business card from a previous consulate cocktail party and called the American embassy in Port Moresby. Finally reaching the correct department, I received a cordial standard operating policy. "Go back to the police station with armed protection. We will call the provisional administration to afford you and your wife an armed escort to the airport. You should leave Popondetta immediately."

Merry Christmas and Happy New Year
2012

"Like most others, I was a seeker, a mover, a malcontent, and at times a stupid hell-raiser. I was never idle long enough to do much thinking, but I felt somehow that some of us were making real progress, that we had taken an honest road, and that the best of us would inevitably make it over the top. At the same time, I shared a dark suspicion that the life we were leading was a lost cause, that we were all actors, kidding ourselves along on a senseless odyssey. It was the tension between these two poles - a restless idealism on one hand and a sense of impending doom on the other - that kept me going."

Hunter S. Thompson, *The Rum Diary*

This Christmas card, with the last photo taken of John in Papua New Guinea, was to go to everyone on his annual card list. The Hunter Thompson quote expressed exactly what John was feeling. The card was never sent.

CHAPTER 33

Diminishment

"Men get taller because testosterone makes them competitive. It's all about power issues. Anyone over 6 feet is passive-aggressive: You can count on it. And counseling can help? Yes. It can lead to a height loss of 2, 3, and even 6 to 8 inches. Now I'm comfortable on airplanes and people don't yell at me when I sit in front of them at movies. So if you suffer from excess height, send 'em to us. We'll take 'em down a few notches. . . . The American Diminishment Clinic."

—Garrison Keillor

The reality of a bureaucratic process afflicted us with an overpowering inertia. I was jolted to recall that a third-world country contained me.

On the second day, the Popondetta police commander and tactical response unit officer visited, offering reassurance. Yet I expected few results. We paid for our own security to guard us at the motel room. Still, Fiona and I were haunted by the police commander's opening comment: "The mastermind to kill you is still at large." He frightfully confirmed our own suspicions when he named individuals who had menaced us in the past.

Feeling exposed, I pondered whether it was time to get out of Dodge City. Was it time to head back to America? Gaining speed, my mind began to spin like a carousel. Reflections from the carousel's centered mirrors transfixed me. A kaleidoscope of PNG experiences flooded this Tau Bada. I felt weak and defeated. There was little rhyme or reason to why I should remain in Papua New Guinea. The Montana Zen cowboy leaning down from his horse whispered, "Let it go, John."

Being cooped up in a cinder-block motel room was physically draining. The inaction made my body ache. Stretched out on a bed, with pillows to prop myself up, I glowered through dingy windows fortified by a lattice of doubled-wired mesh. A clip-lock ten-foot fence topped by razor wire protected us in the motel from rascals and the outside world. We were imprisoned. Emotionally shattered, we crouched with every door knock. Food tasted like ashes. Through a window, I looked up into the sky. A solitary raven circled over the palm trees. With derision, this familiar trickster beckoned me to take a deeper walk into the woods. William Shakespeare, in *Twelfth Night*, lamented, "No prisons are more confining than those we know not we are in."

Simil, our administrative manager, offered little relief or sympathy as we visited her at our office, escorted by a guard with a shotgun. She did not make eye contact with Fiona. Fortified behind a desk, her computer screen serving as a convenient shield, the crackling of her chewing gum amplified her nervousness. The woman, whom we'd embraced along with her family, became a nonperson. The absence of intimacy, inquiry, and positive regard felt like a concussion grenade had exploded. We were not collateral damage caused by friendly fire. We were the enemy. Presto! Just like that. There was absolutely no empathy. I stared at Simil, seeing beads of sweat accumulate on her brow. She brushed a fly over her face and shifted the gum between her cheeks. Without further provocation, she was silent. My heart moved into a vacuum of disbelief. I was numb. Fiona recoiled with an iciness I have rarely witnessed.

Late in the afternoon, following the previous discouraging encounter, Millie, the company's administrative manager from the Managalas Plateau, visited. Speaking for the members of Java Mama and the Managalas community, Millie was on a mission of encouragement and gratitude. For this downcast couple, the simple word *thanks* was a powerful tonic. I needed this social currency. I observed the plateau delegation with satisfaction. The three employees displayed attributes of confidence and self-management. Hmm . . . was I the eyewitness to personal and team commitment and a concern for our safety? Admittedly, I was professionally and personally heartened.

A small crack of light appeared. Recognition for our hard work felt damn good following the chilies fiasco and now after being bushwhacked and almost killed. Ever so slightly, courage and purpose were rekindled, and I was reminded not to underestimate the power of external conditioning. All of us need a rebound through affirmation every so often. Nevertheless, I was striving to learn the power of my own internal conditioning, the shaping and morphing of my own inner man. Within the contextual reality of Papua New Guinea, life circumstances and conditions were harsh and could be demoralizing and invalidating. Would the glass remain half full, or would I succumb and spiral downward chronically to a half-empty status? This was a question of faith. It was a conscious choice. I feared that without this essential ingredient, I would be lost, much like a hiker depending on a dysfunctional compass.

Unexpectedly, there was a knock on our door at 8:00 a.m. on day twelve. Staff detective Prudence Koru, who had been assigned to the case after one and a half weeks, appeared in the doorway. We were dumbfounded yet elated, as we had been constricted in self-imposed solitary confinement for so long. The opening of the "cell door" let in daylight as she ambled into the room. We studied this plump middle-aged woman with squinted eyes. Her navy blue uniform snugly draped her body. Perspiration collected on her forehead and nose from the morning's humidity. Her police cap barely contained a shimmering head of fuzzy black hair. Fascinated, I wondered if the cap would pop off instantaneously without provocation.

Prudence's manner was deliberate. The officer spoke, slowly repeating, "I cannot guarantee this will be done by tomorrow." Mercifully, we extracted a nugget of information— the wounded assailant had fled the province. How nice! It appeared, again, maladroitness had triumphed. What a ruse for already-cynical Fiona and me. We never saw or heard from Officer Prudence again.

Nonetheless, in the previous week, we had instructed our own security manager to access a trusted police officer to obtain two witness statements from helpful villagers. We had assumed that such an initiative from the victims would prod the investigation along, and we were again proven wrong. Inaction prevailed. The villagers across from the shooting site were frustrated as well. As they waited for the culprits to be picked up, they wondered, with fondness, why, for the love of Fiona, we'd received such little help from the police.

Our creativity to outsmart the rascals and manage a slack and corrupt police force flourished. We tried desperately to instill a sense of urgency. On two occasions, to assist the police, we provided the vehicle, petrol, and customary witness fees. Fearful of reprisal, the witnesses waited for darkness, walked into the bush, and appeared on the highway over a kilometer away, to be picked up by our company vehicle. They refused to go to the police station for fear of retaliation from a corrupt department.

The miasma of duplicity made me recall the movie *Serpico*, in which an NYC cop, played by Al Pacino, valiantly battled police corruption. Despite his bravery, he ended up being shot in the face. Fiona and I were in unchartered waters.

Yet there were interviews, held in a secluded conference room, well hidden from the motel guests. The witnesses supplied written statements. Separate statements in Pidgin were translated into English, dated, and signed over three days. The corroborating evidence not only named the wounded culprit and four others, but it also implicated our office manager, Simil, along with her husband. He was one of the shooters. Besides, it was discovered within the tambu labyrinth that our former associate Warpa Kephale was Simil's uncle. The plot thickened. Warpa's mother was from the same village as Simil's father. Until this event, I was generally not enamored by conspiracy theories.

One early morning, as we fitfully tried to sleep, Fiona remarked how grateful she felt to be alive. She yearned for her daughters. I shared the same pang for family and friends in America. A brush with death can reorient one's perceptions. Things suddenly seemed different.

My wife's foot brushed against my leg. Ouch! Her toenails were in need of cutting and her legs begged for a shave. Fiona was a bush woman at heart. Besides confounding the village populace by being a man in a woman's body, Fiona was now known as "the woman who would not be shot." They were at a loss to explain how she could be as powerful and invincible as a man. Resiliency and composure were attributes ascribed to that rarefied bird called a man. Again, this third-world country mirrored the glass-ceiling phenomenon of corporate America. Gawd, her métier was shrinking this Harley-Davidson highway biker of past as he struggled with his own heroic descent.

Spooning together, I quietly chuckled. Undetected, a private musing surfaced. The image of Thomas McGuane's dead and rotting wahoo on a pier down in the Florida Keys appeared. The long-ago *Ninety-Two in the Shade* novel gave me a dosage of well-deserved levity. Like McGuane's character, I felt completely stupid and ill-equipped to even walk across a well-marked and lit street to get to the other side. The sheer cognitive act of stepping across the paved avenue and being killed was akin to an unfortunate hooked wahoo, rotting away on a dock in the early afternoon sun. Broken visions were miserable to handle. They engulfed me in futility and shredded my sense of purpose. Smiling, I was reluctant to inquire of Fiona if I stank like a dead wahoo, even though I convinced myself with her embrace that I did not appear like one.

Sheepishly, I began to call for help from God. As of late, I had become estranged from the Giver of my life source. I was in a dry patch. The "Father of Lights" is constant, never changing, never diminishing. The bushwhacking encounter, so adversarial in nature, injured my heart.

I ended up in a chamber of darkness and fear. Consciously, I moved back again into the chamber of lightness and hope. This subliminal act was inexplicable and irreducible. It is what it is. It ain't what it ain't. The reassuring words of the Master of Hearts began to soothe me: "Do not let your hearts be troubled" (John 14:1 NIV). Yet I persisted in moving to my head. My heart was indeed troubled. I would transcend my feelings. Besides faith, I became willful.

I desired a deep healing from emotional, physical, and mental wounds accumulated from a series of swampland events beyond my imagination. The River Girua, which I'd crossed a few months ago, challenged my own concept of invincibility. My stubbornness distorted reality. It was neither working nor efficacious.

Admittedly, as a slow learner, I began to comprehend the evolutionary quality of personal development. As of late, the path had been a solitary journey. I yearned for a support community. I was on my own. Collective sympathy was in short supply. The succession of ball-busting events squeezed the living crap out of me. The rapidity and frequency of these trials was insanely unreasonable. Without sufficient time to examine my own "a priori," I was sinking fast, over my head and gulping for air. The challenging of my own cultural and historical systems had shaken me with such torment that I concluded I was devolving into a nitwit. Presto—I had bushwhacked myself! I had looped the loop. Such inner pandemonium became a haywire calamity. To end up with a mess that was "fucked up beyond all recognition," compared to the original vision, was hard to swallow. This crow would be difficult to digest. It is time for a revision. I was stepping off this carousel. The escalation of my commitment had run its course. As Hunter S. Thompson proclaimed—and I concur—I did buy the ticket, and I did take the ride.

The conventional definition of bushwhack is "to assault someone unexpectedly." In contrast, the Urban Dictionary said it is "to completely undermine or destroy anything (up to and including a nation) through untiring dedication to your goal, your friends or your mistaken belief you are something better than inept." I can identify with this perspective.

Yes, Fiona and I were obviously bushwhacked by five rascals waiting in kunai grass. They did, in fact, assault and attempt to kill us. Hitherto, the frontal free-will assault I propagated against myself had been just as devastating and mortifying. The bushwhacked condition of my inner man would require a willingness and openness for didactic exchanges within me. Honest conversation would be essential for me to reconfigure my reality, as well as to remove Fiona and me from this knee-deep muddy water. It was time to let it go. The feelings of resignation for this ending were difficult for me to confront. I preferred the hope of new beginnings.

"Newly fallen snow blanketed the front lawn and bare gardens of the Grosse Pointe Club. . . . Nature was powerful and encouraged me to comprehend that I counted and fit into a scheme of things." Yet: "The feelings of failure wouldn't go away and continued to dog this Tau Bada who no longer exists."

CHAPTER 34

Spiraling

"We shall not cease from exploration and the end of all our exploring will be to arrive where we started and know that place for the first time."

—T. S. Eliot

Newly fallen snow blanketed the front lawn and bare gardens of the Grosse Pointe Club. The entrance drive's NO TRESPASSING sign failed with its prosecutorial warning to deter me from paying homage to an old friend. Out of all the places to return to, I mused, after innumerable rainforest bush tracks trekked and rivers traversed. I felt safe. The snow squeaked under my feet, reminding me I was in a cultural conundrum. The past year's encounters and present transition had weathered me. I was tentative as defeatist thoughts ensnarled me. The River Girua crossing seemed remote and now unfathomable.

I stepped down the embankment and was halted by a locked gate. The pier and marina obtruded into the lake, outside of my reach. Nevertheless, this January day afforded me privacy as I viewed exposed rocks made visible by the low level of Lake Saint Clair. Caught without a wool cap, I cupped gloveless hands over my ears as a westerly wind, blowing up from the Detroit River, numbed my face and drew tears from squinting eyes.

A flock of geese, unperturbed by the cold wind, appeared to be decoys, uniformly facing the waning afternoon sun. Silhouetted by churning pale-brown water, a pair of swans served as a reminder that beauty is innately revealed in the most unlikely places. Nature is powerful and encourages me to comprehend that I count and fit into a scheme of things. Its luminosity reminds me of my beauty, with all of its manifestations. Lately, I had lost the image of my beauty within the backdrop of Papua New Guinea. The feelings of failure continued to dog this Tau Bada who no longer exists.

Ice chips intermingled with dead seaweed, pebbles, and mud droned in the wind. "Within life's muddle is a sun dance," claimed writer James Joyce. I was reaching for that sweet spot. It eluded me at the moment.

Unexpectedly, the splendor of verdant mountains moved into the periphery of my memories. Managalas Plateau images flooded me with such vividness that I became disoriented. These oxymorons jolted me to realize that I was entering into a stasis. I no longer was drawn forward or pulled backward. The tension to do anything subsided. I was surprised and relieved. The glass was perfectly full and empty at the same time. The polarization was exacting. The emergence of this equilibrium gave me a reason to smile. I felt buoyant and free from the inclinations to advance or retreat. Are arrested states or possibly emotional dead zones essential to emptiness? This was unfamiliar territory for a man who thought he was the author of unerring maps and crosser of daunting rivers. Lewis Carroll describes such maps: "They had the scale of a mile to a mile." Now this does impose logistical problems. He further states: "We now use the country as itself, as its own map, and I assure you it does nearly as well." Okay, so much for my map prowess and river crossings, even though they are inexorably tied to my upbringing, academic training, and personal development theories. I thought I heard the raging River Girua as the wind gusted. The deserted club served as a reminder of my own barrenness on this Monday, as I remembered that not so long ago I was stuck in the town of Popondetta, Papua New Guinea, feeling disparaged as in *Paradise Lost*. Milton cautions, "And fear of death deliver to the winds."

Instinctively, I turned my back to the wind gust. Peering up to the club's dining room, I searched for the ghost of Bob Valk. This elder-mentor had died seven years ago. Without a doubt, my friend's unseen presence was my companion. He clasped my hand with reassurance. Sentiments filled my soul. The din spiraling upward from an undisclosed room deep within me brought a whimsical smile to my face. I wept. The wind was not beckoning to fear death but to embrace life.

I murmured, "Bob, I am not the man I used to be. I lost my way, but I seem to have found my way. I am not sure who I am at the moment." Silence was the response. The stillness was quietly interrupted. *"That really isn't important, is it?"* he whispered. *"You have been burned by the wind, John. Forward motion abrades and winnows. It comes with the ride. You know what riding is all about."*

I unexpectedly sniggered, recalling the transfiguration of Bob Valk into Bob Dylan. The luncheon seemed out of reach—too long ago. Undaunted by a lapse in memory, time and space vaporized. I recalled the lyrics from an old Dylan song, "Death Is Not the End":

Oh, the tree of life is growing
where the spirit never dies
and the bright light of salvation shines
in dark and empty skies.

I concluded the conversation as the eastern sky darkened. Emptiness engulfed me. I felt okay. This past December and now January had been taxing. To strain myself to action as opposed to inaction had been a task. Fiona was recuperating in distant Australia, yet we were in the same bubble, protectively closing down and mending as the spectacle of the ambush faded. Gawd, did I miss her, though. I had a hole within me. We both desired gentle abreactions as we sought relief and healing.

The expanse of Lake Saint Clair to the east eased my pensiveness as the skyline vanished into the firmament. The dense bush of Papua New Guinea offered few vantage points like the one I was savoring at the moment. This wind was sweeping. I smelled and tasted its inimitable dignity.

Exposed rocks jutting above the waterline reminded me how unfathomable I was. I never suspected these impediments were present. I wondered what other hidden rooms within me were to be discovered and entered. The journey of self-exploration is unceasing and infinite if one chooses to view one's life that way. What is the way? Could it be that the way is not the way?

During the past year, I was introduced to a Maori missionary from the Anglican Church. He had just arrived from New Zealand and was a guest at the Comfort Inn. Recently, he'd spent months in Africa, working in a famine-stricken area. It was a hot and humid morning in Popondetta. To eat breakfast was an effort, as the dining room's air conditioner had broken down. Without distraction, while breakfasting over scrambled eggs, toast, and coffee, he inquired if I understood *the Way* that Christ espoused.

I replied, "No. Do you?"

The middle-aged handsome man grinned and said, "No, but I have endeavored to figure it out most of my life."

Previous to this afternoon's walk in Grosse Pointe, I had been ill. Soon after I arrived from Australia, the ferocity of acute bronchitis and intestinal flu hit me like a tractor-trailer. Bedridden, I was a prime candidate for an uninvited grand catharsis and a grand enema. With deliberation, I reached for medicine. My doctor obliged with antibiotics, steroid injection, and a vitamin B12 shot. Ex-monk Thomas Moore prescribed a soul antidote for the spiritual flu. Also a doctor in his own right, he unabashedly shared his mistakes and foolish acts of life (pies in the face) in the book *Dark Nights of the Soul.*

Reflecting on the Papua New Guinea episode, I had my fair share of "pies in the face." The financial and logistical mess in which I found myself was a testament to my inner proclivities to view my existence as a continuous motorcycle ride to make heroic sense of my life. I was understanding my addictions to idealism and lust for curiosity. But what a ride this has been! Yet my impulsiveness reoccurred in one event after another. Admittedly, I liked and felt accustomed to these habits. Did I have an endgame? Was I capable again of transcending my present circumstances in order to proceed forward?

It was a conscious-choice point. Yet these events created a pattern, after many years, akin to the still-visible Oregon Trail wheel ruts made in the 1830s. I marveled at those tracks as I stooped over and felt the ruts once, on a motorcycle trip in Wyoming. How firm and intractable they still were!

Thomas Moore empathizes and admits to his own blocks against his foolishness. My symptoms were abating already. I only hoped this was not a placebo effect. He shares: "My insanities define me. Without them, I would be wondering who I am and when my life will begin. My healing requires I honor the foolishness of all the moments."

Foolishness indeed became a mantra as I stepped off the plane weeks ago. The Detroit ground under my soles reminded me that I was back—and back for a long time. The initial reentry into Grosse Pointe was laden with irony and contradictions. Unprepared for the minefield of events to come, I endured as best as I could.

Writhing in another dark room, I intuited, reimaged, and prayed to get to the other side. These events were episodic and served as a harbinger to my illness.

Moore contends that levity can help those overwhelmed by life to extricate themselves from their muddle by making the ordeal interesting and enjoyable. Egad! I was repelled by such a suggestion and preferred to cling to cynicism. The murder attempt and separation from Fiona were deep wounds and harsh realities. Being judgmental appealed to me. I felt in control by such a posture.

Nevertheless, I vowed to loosen up and at least try to understand Papua New Guinea from an alternate perspective, including this pond called Grosse Pointe. Could knowledge be obtained in the opposing view? Was it accessible if I was willing to seek it? As a "proclaimed" expert of change, I felt inadequate. The courage to be open, self-forgiving, and forgiving of others was not present. Yet I intuited and realized my inner space was necessary to reignite a raison d'être and would be possible only if I transcended both Papua New Guinea and Grosse Pointe simultaneously. The alchemy required was too demanding as I condescended. Presumptions so dearly held have to ignobly die. To laugh my way out of an abyss was an unusual regimen. Paraphrasing Camus, an acquaintance of mine shared: "When you look into the pit, the pit looks into you. Don't give up. There is no shame in visiting the pit, but don't move in."

Though back home in orderly Grosse Pointe and newly refitted in a business suit, just like in old times, John felt himself in a swirl of juxtapositions.

CHAPTER 35

Reaching Home

*"In this ancient house, paved with a hundred stones,
ferns grow in the eaves; but numerous as they are, my
old memories are more."*

—anonymous Japanese poem

A series of out-of-body experiences (OBE) unfolded in
the span of two weeks after I landed in Detroit, confirming my
insanities.

Without shame, I confessed to my social-cultural deviance
disorder (SCDD). I was also convinced everyone around
me knew I was possessed with this affliction of recondite
awkwardness. Ask the bartender at Jack Kerouac's onetime
haunt. The owner of the tavern also affirmed my condition
and homespun SCDD diagnosis by buying me a shot of Jack
Daniel's. The Rustic Cabins offered me refuge. On the border
of Detroit, this bar seemed closer to Papua New Guinea. When
would I release my urge to individuate? The more upscale
restaurant and bar known as The Hill, located deeper into the
Pointes, offered little consolation and less anonymity. Besides,
the wealthy proprietor did not provide a jukebox. He made his
millions passionately and with excellence collecting garbage.
Have I not differentiated myself from my fellow weirdos? I was
tiring from this lifelong endeavor. Fittingly, in the "Spirit of the
Schlemiel," poet Delmore Schwartz and musician Lou Reed
characterized this self-perception in their poems and songs as
indelible misfits. This gave me further consolation for feeling
like an odd-one-out. Yes, I had to accept my present existence,

but the lonely possibility that my transcendence, perchance, be found in an unending downward spiral troubled me. Mercifully, electric currents were not administered for this OBE disorder. But I did zap my brain with an occasional vodka martini, Manhattan, and shot of tequila. I tried vainly to recover my composure as I dealt with a sequence of reentry distortions. This condition of distortions has been labeled as the Alice in Wonderland syndrome (AIWS). My God, experts have acronyms for everything that needs to appear to be serious. Profundity has been diluted. Leave Alice in Wonderland alone. Keep your dirty hands off her. A word is a word is a word. No need to further mutate meaning. A word is meant to be what it is meant to be. Reflecting on Papua New Guinea's Oro Province, I deduced, with less gravity and more humor, to mutate the following words by utilizing abbreviations to describe my PNG experience and to make a point (thank you, Thomas Moore):

HB = home brew

BN = betel nut

WB = wife beater

Driven by the seriousness to appear to be exhaustively serious, the label for this Papua New Guinea social-psychological-cultural phenomenon is the HBBNWB disorder. Now that that is established, Big Pharma will come up with a pill to support another FUBAR acronym.

Where am I going? My aggression, anger, and disappointment are seeping out and becoming diffused. I am no longer in control. My emotions are close to becoming unregulated—I was not prepared for such an admission. My right hand has finally grabbed my throat and is choking the living crap out of me. Am I laughing at the moment I am penning this episode? You betcha.

On a cold Tuesday afternoon, jet-lag surrealism entranced this returning Tau Bada. The genesis of his PNG deconstruction was the severing of his ponytail and removal of his earring. The salon proprietor, with cupped hands, presented the braid with jewelry attached. My ponytail is now a relic of the past. She briskly commented, "You look better this way." Her salon associates and an elderly woman patron solemnly nodded and gently smiled. This scene was a finale to the movie *The Stepford Wives*, with a tinge of reverse stereotyping. Yes, change is the only constant.

Conveniently, the Rustic Cabins was down the street. Sipping on a Molson's Canadian ale, my body squirmed on the bar stool. A mirror at the end of the counter blocked by a peanut rack made it difficult to view my reentry. The blow-dried gel gently spiked my hair, giving me a "get with it" look. I felt disjointed and suspected the patrons knew that I knew I was a misfit or an intellectual hobo. In Kerouac's book *The Dharma Bums*, character Ray Smith is the "homeless brother who dreamt of freedom and the hills of holy silence and holy privacy." Thank you, Rustic Cabins, for the refuge granting this holy fool this prerogative.

Procrastination worked its magic. What a wonderful defensive routine it is. I sighed as I sipped from the long-neck bottle. Another rite of passage would have to wait one more day. After a ten-year hiatus absolving me from the purchase of sport coats, suits, and ties, I pondered the reprieve.

Quelling the anxiety with ale, I munched on a bag of pretzels and soon headed to the digital jukebox for a dose of lamentations. John Prine and Leonard Cohen, along with Lou Reed, crooned and twanged away, immersing me into the moment. Oh, I was struggling with this reentry. I recognized a familiar wardrobe was being discarded. Ouch! My self-concept was being tinkered with. The vulnerability demanded was too great to handle. Reminiscing, I seemed to have a deeper empathy and less righteousness toward the executives I coached and tried to help in the past.

I pined for a companion/mentor/shaman with whom I could share these disclosures. There appeared to be few takers as I peered down the bar. No such luck. Loneliness became an uninvited guest as it sat down next to my stool. The image of Jonah suffocating in the Leviathan's belly caught me off guard. Determined to wallow in the womb, I wrestled with my internal dichotomies. I was twisted like the pretzel I was biting into. Spiritual and psychological cords were attempting to cocoon this vagabond. I got hold of that debilitating emotion called self-pity; nevertheless, I felt a remarkable loss of self-confidence. My self-worth was dust. I thought I'd eaten an illusion as I munched on the pretzel. It was possible to fall off a mountain. Yes, wounds are inevitable, but I felt somewhat softer and pliable. I have been smoothed. My God, I seem to be moving forward. I was on the road again . . . possibly a higher road. The highway marker labeled individuation faded as I glanced into the rearview mirror. But I thought I'd passed that marker long ago. Also, I knew I had little time to wallow in the belly of a whale. It was time to practice locomotion and change position to view things from a different perspective. The patrons at the end of the counter knew it. The secret is, there are no secrets. Leonard Cohen reminded me of this koan in a song on the jukebox, "Everybody Knows."

Inconspicuously, I lifted myself off the stool and walked out of the saloon. Wet snowflakes dropping from darkened skies cooled my countenance. I felt relief. The struggle subsided. Redemption has a price. Yet this saloon skirmish did not demand much effort. Practice makes perfect. Acts of self-denial, refusing to be defined by circumstances and emotions, again may be stepping stones to a new beginning. The emptiness of the moment displaced the loneliness I felt in the saloon. My tongue slipped out of my mouth to catch and taste the falling flakes. What a wonderful appendage. The mystical identity of opposites continued to draw me into an inscrutable and hopefully authentic person. Such fusion, I anticipated, would move me forward into the future. Kerouac echoes, "But let the mind beware the flesh be bugged, the circumstances of existence are pretty glorious."

The following afternoon, I gazed out through a store's windows on the corner of Kercheval and Saint Clair. Vehicles and Christmas shoppers passed by. I stood erect as the tailor fitted me for my new wardrobe. A haze overcame my eyesight as the seamstress took measurements. Papua New Guinea village food had increased my waistline. Was it time to rejoin the Detroit Athletic Club (DAC) and pick up a squash racquet? *Too much change too soon*, I thought, yet the DAC business-networking epicenter would appreciate these new threads. Not more than six months ago, an open market with betel-nut chewers looking for a place to spit would serve the same function. Business networking had focused on yams, bananas, and coconuts. Betel nut was always available and used as a social currency to affiliate and gain kudos for being generous. The town criers, politicians, and elders would congregate. The ones who shouted the loudest usually got the most attention. They had one distinct advantage. Most community members had only one set of clothes. Their budget for apparel was substantially lower. Brooks Brothers and JoS. A. Bank would suffer.

In the name of the American Protestant work ethic, commerce, and the need to generate greenbacks, my determination had to be pronounced. I had little social capital in Grosse Pointe, and I had to display self-confidence and look professional. The transmutation into WEIRD—Western, educated, industrialized, rich, and democratic—society demanded nothing less.

The seamstress fitted two sport jackets and three pairs of trousers. The dark-blue suit was my last hurdle. Upright in front of the mirrors, I began to perspire profusely. The reflection triggered a carousel of images. Standing bare-chested and barefoot in a tapa cloth sarong, I noticed a necklace of beads, wrist bands, and a feathered headdress. My face had painted stripes on both cheeks. I remembered once feeling prideful and confident. I looked deeper into the mirrors and saw a pool of blood along a highway. What was going on here? How could Papua New Guinea have turned out the way it did? It went from being embraced on my wedding day to a murder attempt on my life.

The tailor inquired if I was all right, and I reacted with enough self-control to respond that I was just fine. She commented that I looked pale as I stared into a thousand-foot looking glass. The fitting excursion was surreal but not tantamount to ingesting magic mushrooms and drinking cold beer while hanging out with a good friend and a Native American on a Zuni reservation close to Show Low, Arizona, in the early 1990s. It was one of my favorite motorcycle escapades. I'd felt like I belonged. Unfortunately, today was a bad trip. I was out of sync with myself as I tried to make heads or tails out of my life. Like a runaway train, my life was moving too fast. I did not belong.

In dire need of a cup of joe, I quickly slipped back into a faded and hole-ridden pair of jeans and flannel shirt. I paid the bill and departed. These ordinary and calculated tasks were an enormous drain of energy. I felt like I was walking on thin ice and, at any moment, would plunge into deep water. A blast of arctic air hit me in the face, reorienting me enough to turn left and amble one block down to a Starbucks café.

After the fitting, I became strangely detached and adrift. I focused on the display racks of roasted coffee beans. The price per pound was twelve dollars, on average. Old picture negatives on my mental projector replayed. I viewed coffee farmers lugging forty-kilo bags to our Afore warehouse. These poor souls received about fifty cents per pound the past year and at today's prices even less. It was a mere pittance compared to the Starbucks markup. I'm sure corporate communications has an explanation. Someone has to be right, or someone has to be proven wrong.

My idealism soon gave way to the aroma of freshly brewed coffee and the sight of cinnamon cake. Another choice point presented itself. Did I participate or withdraw from Western economics and consumerism? I inched closer to the counter. The crowd of earnest aficionados torqued up my now over-alert state. Hyper-vigilance kicked in, almost persuading me to exit the café—though these intrusions were muffled by the scent of the java.

An African American woman was the only obstacle to my gratification. Another film negative appeared on the projector as I saw Tabuane village elders and farmers gathered around Fiona and me. We were spilling their roasted coffee beans onto tin plates for the members to see, touch, and smell. In all the time since the first 1963 plantings, they had never seen a roasted bean. Outside the haus win, the women stood and handed the men salt and pepper. The husbands assumed the beans were to be eaten, and they certainly were. It never dawned on them that the beans would be ground and used to make a beverage.

The well-attired African American woman politely ordered one "skinny vanilla latte with sugar in the raw, soymilk at 170 degrees." A "Neapolitan Frappuccino with extra vanilla-bean powder and two pumps of mocha" was tagged on. She pulled out her iPhone, extended it to the clerk, and made a mobile payment.

Reality slammed this techno laggard. I was still mulling over the coffee beans on the tin plates as I listened and marveled at her technological fluency. I had much to catch up on. I would visit Radio Shack tomorrow. Feeling inadequate in the face of the technological savvy just displayed, I made the decision to get another instructional lesson on my new iPhone 5.

The barista glared at me, wondering what planet I was from

as I ordered one large plain coffee in a mug. Simplicity driven by necessity had been a concept I adapted in Papua New Guinea. It was a tribal way of life that was pretty well lost in Western society. For all of the ugliness I recently had experienced, many qualities and values of Papua New Guinea would help resolve numerous social ills that plague us today in America. Opining on Jared Diamond's book *The World Until Yesterday: What Can We Learn from Traditional Societies?*, learning to live with less is a good starting point. Slowing down in order to speed up may be another primer. Talking with one another without distraction is another worthwhile building block. Turning off the TV and limiting Internet time are other ideas worth contemplating. Young people toning down competiveness and self-interest are other worthy discussion points. A grandniece remarked last week that I was out of touch, and only old people used Facebook. I needed to get with it and use Instagram. Breathlessly, she remarked, "It is quicker, Uncle Johnny." Fully engaged, she returned messages with both thumbs on her smartphone, barely able to concentrate long enough to eat one lone hot dog. Her brain was on fire. The remoteness of the Managalas Plateau pre-mobile phones was not forgotten. Also not forgotten was the privilege to have no-nonsense bluntness in real conversations without tethered distractions. Collectively, we are on a self-centeredness binge, thinking, *My attention span is solely devoted to me and me only.* The seductiveness of this self-absorption will catch up. But it is so damn slick.

My generation had to work a lot harder to achieve such sustainable levels of narcissism. Now I am starting to sound like my own parents, uncles, and aunts. They also claimed to have worked harder. I wonder if I will be an anomaly.

I settled down into a corner couch and had an epiphany or a brain fart. Somehow, some way, some day this year, I would be functional. This hybrid immigrant would have his landline, AT&T, Comcast, iPhone, Macbook Air, mini iPad. The technology would support a social marketing strategy that would incorporate a company website, blog, and Facebook, with LinkedIn. How would I get all of this on one business card? I felt relieved as I fetched a refill, realizing I knew what I did not know. There was liberty in knowing my limitations or realizing I was just plain stupid. Possibly, there would be an easing of self-imposed expectations as I recognized my foibles and felt comfortable enough to admit I wanted help in addition to asking for help. Could this be the path to humility?

Winter's solitude began to draw me out and open me up. Through self-inquiry, I began to appreciate my worthiness and capability to resume the act of consciously breathing and engaging life. Snow cresting on the pines continued to accumulate in my front yard. An inward purging blanched my inner man. The Old Testament psalmist pleads, "Create in me a clean heart, O God; and renew [change] a right spirit within me."

The horrible aftermath of the past year started to find a resting place somewhere between my head and my heart. Musician Van Morrison aches and sings: "If my heart could do the thinking, and my head begin to feel, then I'd look upon the world anew. And know what's truly real." Practice makes perfect for such transfigurations to take place.

Nullifying past images in order for new images to gestate requires effort and courage, especially in the early morning hours. I lay awake, seeing shadows dance on my bedroom walls as the limbs of trees sway in the wind, creating silhouettes from the emitting streetlight. I think of meeting Fiona and the subsequent adventure to Papua New Guinea and now returning home. What am I to do with myself? Where do I go with this experience? How can I expand others from this odyssey as I move forward with my life? Is a rekindling possible after a mere five months since the ambush? Fretting over the future is a disclaimer to faith. The faith to claim that I am in this present moment must be evidenced. It would be difficult to create a clearer reality.

A Canadian cold front dropped down on Detroit, plummeting temperatures to a two-year low. Coincidentally, Papua New Guinea's Oro Province was battered by near-cyclonic rains. The new governor petitioned the new prime minister for food, water, medical supplies, and new bridges. This sounded mighty familiar. Was the wheel turning?

The flames in my living room's fireplace radiated warmth as birch logs burned. My new iPhone chimed (to the sound of a revved-up motorcycle). Obediently, I answered its command and impulsively accepted an all-men's steak dinner invitation. My intuition chimed in and pricked me for acting so quickly.

Unaccustomed to the abundance of appetizers, liquor, and wine, I also marveled at the treats so elegantly displayed on the kitchen's marble island. The men gathered in a circle around the island. The tribe imbibed and nibbled. Initial salutations gave way to jokes, wife sarcasm, laughter, and backslapping. All in all, they were nice guys, having a good time. My host was one of the most consistent friends I had and was bone honest. I suspected the guests gathered this evening were a reflection of him and were trustworthy.

The TV built into a ceiling corner was perched to peer down on this social-cultural milieu. President Obama and his wife were standing behind a podium, waving. Members of the party glanced up and instinctively jeered, "See the nigger couple—four more years of this crap." The group nodded and joined in. A chorus of vilifications filled the kitchen. My host ignored the clamor.

Vestiges of concentric circles moving counterclockwise on a hot, humid afternoon as the curse was lifted at Tabuane crowded my mind and churned my belly. Shame and confusion repelled me at the moment. I thought, *I'm in a familiar place. I am back in a circle.* I removed myself by stepping into the den.

Transfixed by the fireplace, I was surrounded by ancient cliff ruins on a moonlit night. Embers were swirling into the sky. A forgotten voice emanated from the fire pit, embracing me with the words "Ese, John, ese."

I pulled myself out of the secluded Colorado canyon and immediately found myself with Fiona in another circle, surrounded by Managalas village elders and farmers shouting and vilifying us for being white outsiders and colonial slave drivers. Oh, did that sting as we tried to deal with the misperceptions and misunderstandings. Dichotomies are troublesome. How does one consciously make sense of contradictions, rather than moving into the autopilot reactions of stereotypes and labels? It made little difference whether I was in the village of Tabuane or a kitchen setting in Grosse Pointe, Michigan. There you are. Only now was I beginning to realize I was becoming more in tune to what I was feeling and why I felt the way I did. Again, this was very distinct to the experience itself at any given moment.

My host appeared and beckoned me to join the group. The meal was being served, and I reveled in my steak. I departed soon after dinner. The men were most gracious. We viewed a homemade DVD on the construction of a cabin owned by one of the guests. I enjoyed the conversation and music that accompanied the video.

Hurriedly, I retired to bed, stoked for the following morning. A new client would arrive for an introductory session. I wanted to be sharp and on my toes. I had not felt this anticipation in a long time. I was moving back into a familiar competency, giving me a self-confidence that had escaped me for some time. The more significant challenge would be for me to gain confidence in people in general. Did they sincerely want help?

Just last week, I acquiesced to have this meeting on a pro-bono basis. I wanted to help a Hispanic friend and her husband. They were members of my church. A third individual, Patrick, would join. He was to be the CEO of this new start-up business. In preparation, I reviewed their résumés and responses to a questionnaire I'd developed. Reality gripped me as I realized this was my first gig in America since 2009. The practitioner was back on stage in front of a new audience.

The husband and wife, Michael and Jessica, arrived late. Invariably, outsiders get lost in the crossroads and village streets of Grosse Pointe. Patrick was tardy. Waiting, we sipped coffee and tea in my kitchen. The entrance bell rang. I opened the door to be greeted by a very dark African in his middle thirties. My friend never mentioned his race. The immediacy of this surprise lifted my countenance. Shifting his feet, he nervously smiled. His teeth gleamed and right shoulder dropped. Looking down, I saw a cradled baby. The snuggled child looked up and gurgled. I thought of the previous evening and gurgled back.

With instructions, the guests settled down on the third floor where my office was located. The meeting lasted for three hours. I found myself immersed in their strategy and obstacles. Time flew by quickly. I was back into a zone. The baby cried and was fed. The baby cried, and diapers were changed. The absence of exposed breasts, barking dogs, squealing pigs, betel-nut spitting, and village odors was noted. I admired Jessica as she clicked off pictures of flipchart notes with a smartphone. Blackboards, chalk, and writing pads were scarce in the Managalas Plateau. Individual coffee and chilies agents transcribed meeting notes in their own dialect.

After concluding the meeting, the guests stepped down slippery stairs onto a snow-powdered sidewalk. I chuckled. There weren't any palm trees. They did not have to contend with falling coconuts but only losing their balance and slipping on the ice. They seemed much more tentative than the sure-footed yet barefoot villagers who were fully loaded with cargo while hiking through muddy bush tracks that led to our home in Tabuane.

Effortlessly, the departing guests reached into their jackets to pull out and press their vehicle keys. The doors unlocked, and they drove off. Most of the Managalas Plateau participants had at least three hours of bush tracking before arriving home. Richard from Natanga had eight hours before arriving in his village. He was my strongest and most criticizing supporter. He never complained. I missed his friendship. Unfortunately, Fiona informed me that he had died of a common cold. He did not have the strength to walk to the Afore station to get transportation to a clinic.

I built a late-afternoon fire as awareness examen lulled me into reflection. Lying on the couch, I stared into the flames. My inner man was expanding. I did not feel as diminished. The stones reflected the fire's heat. They appeared to be ancient. Within their crevices were innumerable conversations over the eighty-six years since they were laid. My, these same stones had been viewing me since I was thirty-two years old. They had seen my outward and inner man change. I find comfort and reassurance in my past. It is really the only map I trust. The highway behind gives me courage to move into the future. I desired to see the first light of tomorrow. I seek newness. Within the grottoes of glowing embers, a tender green branch extends. I am home.

"The road is the sinew of soul, undisclosed rooms, and obscure crevices."

EPILOGUE:

Minturn Crows

Beyond the guardrails, whitecaps peppered the Straits of Mackinac as the great deep-blue waters of Lake Michigan and Lake Huron clashed. Within ten minutes, Fiona and I will finish crossing the Mackinac Bridge, with a final glimpse of the awesomeness of this expansion in my motorcycle's rearview mirror as we turn due west on Highway 2 and drive to the sun. Already feeling invigorated, I am reminded of Eugene Peterson's text, *The Message*, where in Psalm 19:4–5, King David exclaims:

> *God makes a huge dome*
> *for the sun—a superdome!*
> *The morning sun's a new husband*
> *leaping from his honeymoon bed.*
> *The day breaking sun an athlete*
> *racing to the tape.*

My 1997 Road King Harley-Davidson odometer clocked at 72,885.4 miles at the time we departed Grosse Pointe, Michigan, the morning of July 26, 2014. The fluids, fork, clutch, brake pads, and tire pressure were checked and maintenance performed. Fiona's additional weight, plus our three leather cargo bags, necessitated the rear air shocks to be reset to 25 psi. The dealership service assistant assured me I had 80 percent tread on my tires, sufficient for the contemplated 4,000-mile journey. This adventure will take us through Michigan's Upper Peninsula and Wisconsin's forest into the prairies of Minnesota and North Dakota, across the Great Plains of Montana into Idaho's Hells Canyon near White Bird, and southeast, back into Wyoming's

Teton Mountains, then entering Utah to view the Flaming Gorge, and ending up in the lush mountain meadows of Colorado. All in all, less than one hundred miles of freeways would be necessary. Two-laners and, if possible, rural county roads were mapped out. I assumed we would stumble across hidden and more obscure pavement, either by getting lost or being enlightened by helpful café owners, bartenders, or farmers, again realizing there is an alternative way to get to where I want to go that is far more beautiful than the road I was planning on traveling.

Since the assassination attempt nearly two years ago— August 16, 2012—we have spent four weeks together. The longest separation was thirteen months, which ended when I flew back to Cairns, Australia, for a Christmas holiday in 2013. Both of us have been stretched as we tried to grapple with the trauma of the shooting. The emotional healing has been an evolvement, where we are feeling almost whole. The financial ruin is still a challenge. The company has yet to be sold. Low self-esteem played havoc with me, leading me to question if Fiona still loved me. Even more disconcerting was to conjecture that equal love for the most part is a figment of my imagination, and I wouldn't find it in this world. Frequently, I was not myself, as I attempted to rebuild my self-confidence and regain trust in people.

My attempt to gentrify and assimilate back into the Grosse Pointe society and Detroit business community has been largely successful, yet lonely. I felt like a misfit and bumbler on frequent occasions, preferring solitude and my own company. This made life much less complicated. Besides, in the digital world's fast pace, it seemed to make little difference whether I was present and/or acknowledged. Joseph Campbell comforts me by saying, "The whole point of this journey is the reintroduction of this potential into the world . . . to you living in this world." He advocates I am "to bring this treasure back and integrate it into a rational life." Then he cautions, "Bringing the boon back can be even more difficult than going down into your own depths in the first place." I agree. Confounded by a flood tide of alienation, estrangement, and impersonality, I yearned for plain human interaction. I was reminded of the severity of the change that impacted Papua New Guinea's Managalas Plateau once the first satellite tower was built on top of Kweno Mountain, introducing cell phone technology. Tabuane's once-quiet village is now chiming away, and its simple huts are lit up by the glow of these ingenious devices and toys. The village crier is doomed to obsolescence? Betel-nut chewing is challenged as the preferred addiction? After rotting gums and decayed teeth, the residents now have a chronic "brains on fire" mania that can be regulated only once batteries are drained and the villager is compelled to walk to a source of power and pay kina to the owner of a power generator.

The motorcycle trip will be an effective antidote for this busy and tethered existence. As of late, this pace and a new office environment have clogged my pipes. Angst, accompanied by tightness, was beginning to choke me. Running on fumes, my day job has drained my tank and emotional commitment. I need to get to the high country with Fiona and vision quest together to gain inner clarity and an accurate bearing from my interior compass. Her arms around my waist, with no real schedule outside of arriving, elate me. I could not find myself any happier and contented.

Moreover, I fully anticipate the journey will be the reward. Together, on a motorcycle with Fiona, we are riding the highway to the source of abundance. Whether the highway ahead is asphalt, concrete, gravel, or dirt, the road is the sinew of soul, undisclosed rooms, and obscure crevices. The spirit of life, if invited through inquiry, will roam and winnow to find the opening to dwell in one's most secret places. Reacquiring the *terza rima* or iambic pentameter, this flow brings unmistakable peace, a peace like a river that will surely hasten the advent.

Nearly four hundred miles after crossing the bridge, we spent the night in Ashland, Wisconsin. Chilled to the bone by a cold front and exasperated by a strong northwesterly crosswind, we checked into the Ashland Motel for seventy-five dollars, spitting distance from a genuine Mexican restaurant called the El Dorado, where I once dined on Veracruz shrimp and pork carnitas. We ordered the same dishes. Sipping Silver Patrón margaritas, we sat on the front deck. The setting sun pinked the horizon. Fiona, in motorcycle attire, looked drop-dead beautiful. I licked the salt from my lips as I viewed the still Lake Superior inlet. I was encouraged by the sky colors, knowing tomorrow would be a fair and warm day to bike and meander around countless inland lakes and rolling farm country. I giggled as we embraced this evening together.

Glacial ponds on both sides of North Dakota's Highway 200 mirrored cumulus clouds against a soft blue sky after the russet flat prairie of Minnesota. The day was warming up but leather jackets and gloves were still required to insulate us from a lingering chill. We reached the city of Killdeer, close to the Montana state line, around 4:00 p.m. A twenty-five-mile stretch once famed for extraordinary natural majesty was being bulldozed over for a four-laner to accommodate the movement of oil, equipment, and other materials from the fracking bonanza. This serene valley and surrounding hills were now being desecrated by earthmoving machines, trailer parks, subdivisions, congestion, and filth. Bilious and depressed, we crossed over into Montana and spent the night in Sydney, which, disappointingly, was also overtaken by the same economic windfall. Oil independence and jobs, yes, but at what price?

The following day we biked close to five hundred miles straight across Montana in 103-degree heat. T-shirt biking is the finest, and we savored the opportunity all the way to the hamlet of East Glacier, which is south of the main entranceway to the national park. We secured a motel room and ate a hearty meal across the street at Luna's café, which specializes in huckleberry pie.

The looming Mount Henry attracted us to hike the Scenic Point Mountain trail the next afternoon. Medicine Lake, used as a reference point as we ascended switchbacks for the first three miles and a vertical of 2,350 feet, became diminutive, appearing like an encrusted sapphire resting on a velvet green hassock of soft pine needles. As we arrived at the summit, monsoon clouds darkened the southern horizon and encroached on the afternoon sun. Viewing the Great Plains from this vantage point fused my thoughts, as the terrain we had just traveled was clearly visible. A collage of images including mile markers, service stations, motels, restaurants, and towns surfaced within me. Poignant conversations with Fiona, friendly salutations with farmers, and roadside chatter with café and tavern owners and their customers all came to consciousness. I thought of one bartender's sad tale of cancer consuming his wife, told as he lit up a cigarette, clearly following her fate. I felt all of these experiences were in touching distance. Straining my eyes, I searched the distant horizon in a futile attempt to recapture the entire past vista. I realized I could spend the rest of the day lost in my thoughts and decided we should begin our descent. The rain started to fall. Slippery stones and mud hindered the return. My concentration shifted to the meticulousness of each footstep placed upon the trail as we realized we were in for a hazardous three-mile descent. Temperatures dropped, and the daylight was fleeting. Fiona became ill from the altitude and exertion and requested the privacy to heave. I was determined to get to our destination.

Images of the grand western vista quickly gave way to roots, rocks, and crevices. The exterior territory took on a different meaning. What was once hospitable became threatening within the blink of an eye.

At last. The motorcycle awaited our return near the trailhead. After wiping down the rain-covered seats with a bandanna, I hit the starter. The bike sputtered and would not easily turn over as it had done for 2,500 miles. Quickly, I throttled the bike and mounted the motorcycle, fearing the engine would die. The rain fell hard as we biked ten miles in shorts and T-shirts until arriving safely at the room. Sipping a shot of Jack Daniel's, I listened to the warm shower comforting Fiona. Served on a bed, Luna's chicken soup was the extent of our meal. We slept soundly and looked forward to biking Glacier National Park's Road to the Sun early the next morning.

Rain fell as the leather bags were tied down securely on the bike. Rain gear over our jackets made us feel clumsy as we mounted the motorcycle. The bike failed to start. Two Canadian bikers assisted in push-starting me out of the parking lot. Between the rain and chill and bike sputtering, I had a foreboding feeling this was going to be a difficult day. Within ten minutes on the highway, the engine cut out completely. It would not restart. The battery was charged and my fuel tank was full. I felt betrayed by my computerized whiz machine and momentarily overwhelmed by the fact I couldn't do a damn thing to extract myself from this distress. The remoteness of the area afforded no cell phone service. I hiked to a closed restaurant down the highway, ultimately pulling the owner out of bed to assist me. Lying along the roadside ditch with a cap over my eyes to keep out the now-bright morning sunlight, we waited for a tow truck to come one hundred miles out of Kalispell, Montana. Estimated time of arrival was three hours. The swiftness of this mishap jolted me to reflect and free-associate on other unpleasant events. The assassination attempt in particular came to mind as I lay in the grass. Fiona had recently received word that the fired Popondetta office manager was seeking compensation for duress and defamation. Sadly, she lost a young child to sickness and felt Fiona was to blame. Also, all of the named shooters who were released on twenty-five dollars bail continue to pose a threat to the company. The police file was lost, giving them a reprieve to exact vengeance at will in the future. Our former associate Warpa continues to threaten our Java Mama employees who are the caretakers of our property. He trespasses with impunity. This bad dream, with all of its surrealism, still hooks me. I cannot extract it from my being, as hard as I try to let go of it.

The tow truck arrives and one and a half days later, we are back on the road, on the way to see my friend Max in White Bird, Idaho. The Harley-Davidson mechanic, through a computer diagnostic, found a $14.40 grounding wire detached from the fuel pump, which is connected to the ignition. Therefore, electricity could not flow to the fuel pump to get gas to the engine. How did this happen? The service manger could not put a name on it. Some things are unexplainable.

Turning back east on Highway 12 between Grangeville, Idaho, and Missoula, Montana, the Lochsa River paralleled the road, a route that Lewis and Clark followed in mid-September 1805. This was the end of our race to the sun as gauged by a compass. A tinge of sadness struck my heart as I realized we were now retreating, which seemed counterintuitive to the purpose of the trip. I find little delight and meaning in recrossing rivers. Wyoming's Yellowstone National Park and the Grand Tetons were engulfed in rain and fog as we traveled southeast to the Utah state line to view the Flaming Gorge, just northwest of Vernal. The weather warmed up and skies became sunny while traversing into Rangely and Grand Junction, Colorado. An afternoon monsoon shower, accompanied by lightning bolts, hit with such ferocity that we were forced to seek shelter under a railroad overpass. With my arms around Fiona to keep her warm, the concrete piling protected us from the gale-force wind. Passing truck drivers saluted this romantic gesture with long honks from their horns. We waved and laughed together. Spending the night in a motel room above a feed store in Crawford, Colorado, gave us solitude. Famed rocker Joe Cocker lives outside this hamlet on a ranch. We did not see him as we sat on a picnic table, viewing a reservoir surrounded by mountains, sipping tequila washed down by cold beer, watching the sunset. A sense of accomplishment touched us as the odometer clocked close to four thousand miles. Harmel's Ranch was our destination tomorrow, timed fifteen years by the full moon to the day that I first saw Fiona. Admittedly, for this compasser, recrossing this river gave me great satisfaction. I felt rightness in this pace, as if everything was coming together. The destiny was obvious—to return to the cabin where we first embraced. My anticipation to complete the circle increased, even though I was not traveling due west but southeast. We were in a celebrative disposition. My pipes were becoming unclogged. The purpose of this vision quest became clearer. Feeling more centered, I hungered to get on the highway early the next morning. Curiosity is a powerful stimulant. I tried to recall a time in my life that it was absent.

The Harmel's Ranch resort manager remembered Fiona and her entourage of girls and the lone biker who had acquiesced to give a number of them a motorcycle ride. Soon after checking in to the same cabin where the mocktail girls left the "John loves Fiona" pillow, we biked back to the Taylor reservoir. The impermanence of the wildflowers was absent. As we horsebacked the mountain overlooking the valley the following day, I spotted the gravel road where I had made the left turn leading back to Fiona. She has indeed been found. My heart was forever opened up to the universe by making that chance turn on the road.

The three days vaporized. The Valley View Hot Springs in the San Luis Valley, not more than three hours of biking from Harmel's Ranch, was our next revisitation. We rented the same cabin we had occupied back in 2001. The natural hot springs soothed our bike-wearied bodies. Also, the dinner at the Bliss Café in the village of Crestone, where numerous Zen centers are located, was a throwback to the early 1970s. We felt safe and welcome. The children were polite. They were without cell phones and they engaged in conversation. Returning, we visited the High Valley Healing medical cannabis store to purchase pot-infused cherry pie for dessert. Snugly back in the cabin, we lit votive candles and listened to Neil Young's album *After the Gold Rush* on my smartphone. The pie was delicious.

Two days later brought us to the small and undisturbed mining town of Minturn, a little west of the well-known ski resort and tourist mecca Vail. Checking into a bed-and-breakfast, we soon strolled down the main street, hoping to spot my nephew and his family, who were also visiting the town, as we were planning on dinner together and then biking into Denver the next day, the final hundred miles of our journey.

Afternoon sunlight touched the mountaintops overlooking the town. A pink haze settled on the backdrop, highlighting five squawking crows on an upper branch of a pine tree. One crow deliberately fanned its tail to blow a current of air in our faces as it continued to loudly squawk. Annoyed, I snickered at this trickster. How dare he disturb such a mood and peace! A vestige of the Anasazi ruins flashed across my mind. My intuition spiked. Immediately, both Fiona and I knew we were in for a surprise. But what, where, and when? The puzzle faded as we found my family and headed for dinner to celebrate our reunion and Fiona's return to America, thankful to see her and me recover from the assassination attempt.

Saturday's ride into Denver felt like a funeral procession. The highways leading into this mass of humanity were akin to arteries pulsating with plasma, feeding a cornucopia of insatiable locusts. The contrast to the stillness of the last three weeks could not be starker. I felt panicked and gripped my handles. My right foot was in a prone position to step on the brake immediately if needed. Confounded, I wondered why I was becoming uptight, knowing that I had driven through worse congestion than this.

A family dinner was scheduled that evening at my nephew's home. The next day, we biked up to the town of Evergreen, lunching at the iconic Little Bear tavern and then visiting the concert venue Red Rocks. I took several photos of famous 1970s rockers displayed on the planked walls for my longtime associate and friend back in Grosse Pointe. He was also an active musician. Leon Russell's picture kindled in me the memorable lyrics of his "A Song for You." This was it. We hit a crescendo switchbacking down the mountain as the afternoon sun set. It all came together.

Upon my return, I was intent on moving in a different direction with my current career choice and future plans with Fiona. I would ultimately resume independent executive coaching, and she would begin the spouse visa process and join me in Grosse Pointe. The trip was complete. Monday morning, we would drop off the bike (with its back tire worn slick) at the Mile High Harley-Davidson dealership, to be trucked back to Detroit, and hop a ride to the airport to return home.

Before the farewell dinner on Sunday, I perused my e-mail for the first time in three or four days. I spotted one from my business partner, the first communication I'd had from him since leaving. The previous month, we had conversed on speakerphone minutes after I picked up Fiona from the airport, newly arrived from Papua New Guinea. With affection, he warmly welcomed my wife to Detroit and invited us for a boat ride and dinner, once we returned from the planned bike trip. As president of a ten-person firm, I had spent sixteen months restructuring and positioning the company for future growth. The opportunity to take a unique product to the market in an entrepreneurial setting was appealing. I was contracted as an executive coach for the first six months, and then I accepted a full-time position as president. My partner was given access to my University of Michigan and Detroit business community network. It was not always pleasant work, particularly in a tough change-resistant culture prone to conflict-avoidance and ingenious defensive routines. I had my successes and made mistakes as I habituated back to America. Nevertheless, I was happy to see that he had e-mailed me. I was recharged to return home to have an essential conversation with my partner. A "window of vulnerability" had presented itself, permitting me to risk emotional exposure within a safe harbor. I trusted him and therefore was capable of being susceptible to being wounded.

The e-mail formally denounced me: I was terminated as an "at-will employee." Where did my partnership status evaporate? My belief as well as trust in a "psychological contract" was thrown on a trash heap. I was not to attempt to set foot on the office premises. My files were confiscated, and no severance package was to be awarded. All intellectual property developed during my tenure was his exclusive property. Compensation, including my health insurance, would end by August 31, 2014. It was now August 17. The parent spoke, and the child got spanked. Where was the adult in this equation?

315

Feeling like a leper, I called out to Fiona to come into the bedroom. This assassination was as deliberate as the Papua New Guinea episode, but my partner efficiently pulled this one off. I did not have a policeman and an M16 to return fire. Shocked, we both thought, *Could this be a prank?* No, after rereading the text, we knew it was dead serious and irrevocable. I was denuded. An unmistakable fear gripped me, so resembling the one in Papua New Guinea that I began to take deep breaths to calm myself.

At the family farewell dinner, drinking Perrier water, I nibbled on a dinner salad and dabbled with a cup of chowder. Distracted, I almost ordered a double shot of tequila. The dinner table swirled before me as power issues emerged—greed, manipulation, and nontransparency thoughts. The "should have and could have" self-talk tapped my head and emotional musical chairs unmercifully tugged my heart. Maybe it was a wise decision not to drink and maybe not. So be it for a celebration. The Minturn crows squawking in my memory reminded me that the ignorance of the elenchus was plentiful. The fallaciousness of his charges made me realize I would pay a price for my incautious gullibility. But who was fooling and outdueling whom? The last thing I aspired to do was go to the OK Corral to figure out I was fighting a straw man. More disturbing, though, was my own complicity and culpability that permitted this dance to transpire. I wanted to bury my face in my lap as I smiled with the rest of the family at the dinner table. The smartphone picture-taking was incessant. I recalled being stung by a hornet that cleverly maneuvered past my glove and under my leather jacket sleeve while I was traveling at fifty miles per hour, west of the Minnesota state line on Highway 2, just two weeks ago. I had pulled off the road to discard my jacket, vest, and T-shirt. Too late! Three stings, and with a soon-to-be-swollen forearm, wrist, and thumb, I was hurting. The wound inflicted by my associate was throbbing far more than the hornet's sting.

Intellectually intrigued by this highly choreographed business exploit, two lawyers are willing to counsel me on a contingency-fee basis if I decide to file a legal complaint. They were aghast at this "high-tech lynching" and the cowardice evidenced by this partner, not even waiting until the vacation was over to have a "mano a mano" discussion. Also, my twenty-five-year friend and business associate, whom I had brought into the company, did not warn me, nor has he made any attempt to contact me upon my return. He lives two miles down the road. Examining my motives and intentions, I am bewildered by the lack of candor and transparency on both their parts. But what pricked me upmost was the thoughtlessness or unwillingness to have a conversation. Heck, I would have retrieved my 1990s Santa Fe talking stick and invited them to join me in a "talking circle."

During twenty-eight years of consulting, I found that very few C-Suites trusted themselves, beginning with the CEO, to take the risk to allow dialogue that accented a cleaner language fortifying straight-talk. But the suspension of one's assumptions emboldens truth to manifest itself. The twenty-five-inch stick that was gifted to me is seared at both ends to contain a "life force" and is painted and carved with indigenous symbols. The stick symbolizes an object of transcendence. It permits one's individual needs to be subordinated to a higher purpose, a collective empathy resulting in greater group trust and integrity. It is an amazing experience, okaying us to be emotionally clumsy without feeling embarrassed. Our own empathy deficits are displaced by the willingness to be vulnerable. Such emotional commitment takes courage. But in the present circumstances, I suspect fear and possibly self-deceit had the upper hand. Are these values and norms

John's talking stick. In a group, only the person holding the stick is allowed to talk. The talking stick can be a tool of transcendence—to vulnerability. (Photo by Michelle Andonian)

becoming embedded in our unrelenting narcissistic and fragmented culture, so much so that such behavior doesn't even raise an eyebrow? As in a bad marriage finally running its course, who wants or has the time to listen to or understand the issues? Delmore Schwartz avows in his short story "America! America!": "No one exists in the real world because no one knows all that he is to other human beings, all they say behind his back and all the foolishness the future will bring."

It is now business as usual. I boxed up a company sweater with attached company logo and posted it to my former partner without a note. After the *Bent Sound* fishing escapade, I returned a gifted rugby cap to one of the crew members who also had befriended me and my family, yet was caught up in the larceny and betrayal. It was left on his doorstep. Within six months, he hung himself.

Am I simple-minded to believe in universal truth and justice as well as an immutable life-sustaining force that does keep count? Are there true and lasting consequences for our choices, whether it is the destruction of our physical planet or the deprivation of our interior soul and broader "mother culture"? Is our salvation really the opportunity to evolve to a higher transcendent level, enabling us to subordinate our individual needs to a higher, integral universal good? Are the silver cords of empathy and compassion unraveling, leaving our planet to unfettered self-interest and self-centeredness? Could a skulking collective shadow ultimately blot out the light? Again, firmly engaged in a rational, manifested, and "real" world, I am determined to learn from the past, calling on all of my will and what's left of my testosterone to hit back by proceeding on the highway that lies before me.

I will attempt not to betray myself to a downward negative and invulnerable spiral. The latest mishap—or should I say, mismatch—and emanated feelings will not define me. August's vision quest has given me the clarity I sought. My own filters have been named and blind spots examined. They are as highway markers now seen in my rearview mirror as I venture into the unknown. I trust my past. It is prologue and the essence of my character. I will remain "transparent to the transcendent." Without hope in the unseen I would inwardly perish, falling into a gray, purposeless twilight. I relish chasing the sun. This forms the bedrock of my integrity and is the source of my courage to move forward. I have found no other reliable way to find myself. Unfortunately, it is not expeditious; making "good time" rarely is.

On a better, less Socratic note, Fiona just this week received an e-mail from the governor of Oro Province, Papua New Guinea, stating the economic development department was now prepared to proceed and purchase Java Mama. He also informed Fiona that he was instituting legal action for cash compensation against our former associate for election shenanigans. I have been offered, orally, a principal position with another Michigan firm, permitting me to resume my executive coaching, if I choose this path. Maybe Fiona and I can finally find a way to be continually together. Who knows? I may be ready to revisit the Managalas Plateau. We have been told that the farmers want to see the Tau Bada and the "woman who would not be shot."

ACKNOWLEDGEMENTS

The cover says I'm the author of this book and its pages are about what happened where I was involved. But who persists on this earth without being shaped by others? In this space, I thank people who, here and there, co-wrote my life.

I was powerful. I was big and bright, quick and observant, open-minded, on my way up, on top of the world, invulnerable. Later, when humbled and empty, when asking myself why it was so difficult to be genuine and trusting, when coming to know what I didn't know and what I had blindly denied, when peeling away layers of presumption and digging to mine my own ore, I found with it the wisdom of my life's coauthors—people whose values and insights had attached to what in me was genuinely worthy. Now I let their wisdom wash through me.

Unbeknownst to them, their affirmations have inspired me as well as confirmed that we are connected and are in this life together. Our planet is not invulnerable. We need to be more vulnerable, beginning with ourselves and with one another. My hope is that this book will contribute to this effort.

So this book is for:
Professor John Hart.

Bruce Gibb, PhD.

Robert Valk.

Jim Rooks.

Rita.

Stafford.

Radford and Kate MacCready of Destiny Bay.

Richard and Michele Martinez of Santa Fe.

Paul Freeman, who gave me my first job mowing his lawn, painting, and chauffeuring and had me paint (gratis) the house of his neighbor (a widow stricken with cancer) while she was on vacation. He taught me neighborly love.

Palmer Heenan, a former board member and mayor of Grosse Pointe Park, who tried to humbly teach me to "get rich slowly." Foolishly, I did not listen.

Joe Alam, who has been a consistent friend to my family and me as a professional in the Detroit financial community. He stood by me unwaveringly. Also, being Lebanese, Joe taught me how to eat and appreciate kibbeh and fattoush.

Walter Swyers, the "Masked Marvel" (professional wrestler), sports trainer, and bar brawler. He was the town Santa Claus for decades in Albion, Michigan, and worked with underprivileged children. His beard was real.

Phil Matthews, a friend, investment banker, and my first executive coaching client, who taught me how to select and wear a good tie as a centerpiece as well as to drink fine wine. He escorted me to both the New York Stock Exchange and Chicago Commodities Board. Over luncheons there, he imprinted on me the art of doing a deal but with elegance.

Jim Todd, commercial fisherman and skipper (thirty-meter vessel) and damn good friend in Cairns, Australia, who taught me how to gently listen.

Pastor Peter Smith, who helped me try to understand the mystery of "the way."

Detroit police officer Avery Jackson, who was the first African American I encountered. He lovingly escorted my brother Patrick and me (ages thirteen and fourteen) home after we shoplifted at the J. L. Hudson's department store. At our house in very white Grosse Pointe, he counseled my parents. Officer Jackson taught me dignity and honesty.

John Hribjlan (Dr. Crow), my former therapist and shaman, who taught me how to mindfully observe blackbirds, ravens, and crows. As a Vietnam veteran he practiced humanism and peace. His PTSD skills were very helpful after Papua New Guinea. He thoroughly co-reviewed my book. It was effective therapy at no charge. John drove to Grosse Pointe twice a month from Ann Arbor with fresh Zingerman pastries for six months. His compassion helped me to belong again.

Richard Beadle, my first motorcycle companion and constant encourager, and founder of the global executive development organization Vistage Michigan.

Tom Osborn, my roommate and close friend at the American University, who taught me how to thank and forgive my parents. He also instructed me how to be more empathetic.

Jean Fitzsimmons, my former bioenergetics therapist and shaman, who supported me in the toughest and most intimate personal development work I ever did. She taught me how to lovingly comprehend and embrace, without shame, the vulnerable lover within me. She also taught me how to breathe.

Gabriel Thallon, hell-raiser from Ireland, good husband and father, and my best man at the Wangetti Beach wedding in northern Queensland, Australia. His generosity toward my family and me, as a newly arrived Yankee, was impeccable.

Tom Soper, teacher and track coach at Howe Military School, who trained me to run and to know and appreciate the difference between one's first and second wind.

Joe and Rip Coughlin, my first "big client" for fifteen years after I lost my company. They hired me based on the fact I failed as a CEO and possibly had something to teach them.

Eeva (Tellu) Perttu, Helsinki, Finland. We met in 1968 in Saginaw, Michigan, while I was selling life insurance door-to-door. We have had a long-distance friendship since. Time and space do not exist in friendships (*Anam Cara*).

Fred Sherman (Philadelphia radio host), who taught me how to smoke a good cigar. My first lesson was in the Oak Bar at the Plaza Hotel in New York City. His ash won out.

Gordon Areen, founder of Chrysler Financial Corp. and a board member of my company. He tried to teach me how to set difficult boundaries by not avoiding conflict. He was tough as nails.

John Pagin, teacher and phrenologist at Howe Military Academy, Howe, Indiana, who taught me how to feel ridiculous by laughing at myself. We were together, along with fellow student Todd Sprague, in his empty and humorless classroom when President John F. Kennedy was assassinated.

Bob Poole, Stewart Dykstra, David Orr Williams, Ned Ranger, Cheryl Harrington, Larry Vandermark, Warren Long, and John Gleason, who died too young but gave me the opportunity to learn to cherish who and what I have.

Joe McMillan, an ex-CEO, former client, and cancer survivor, who taught me "never to give up hope." When I returned from Papua New Guinea, he bought me my first lunch at a Grosse Pointe restaurant. I still had a ponytail and earring. He encouraged me to publish my book and get a haircut.

Yale Levin, ex-partner and role model (warrior) at Price Waterhouse Co., who loved to spar with the SEC and rarely lost. He modeled a quiet and authentic bravado.

Jerome, doorman and valet at the Detroit Athletic Club, who always made me feel welcome.

Hugh Makens, former director of the Michigan Financial Institutions Bureau, who wrote me a personal condolence letter esteeming my father's character after he passed away. It takes one to know one. He taught me the toughness of thoroughness (deep integrity) as opposed to superficiality.

Jasper John of the Potawatomi tribe (Walpole Island) and his family, who taught me how to shoot, clean, and cook ducks and geese and how to prepare smoked sturgeon.

Robert Evans, former chairman of American Motors (circa Jeep) and a mentor to me. He encouraged me with refinement not to feel shame when my first failure-ridden nervous breakdown (NBD) comes. Rental-car magnate Warren Avis was a role model for Robert and a good friend. Avis shared and concealed his own NBD with Robert. Also as an oddball, Avis gave me invaluable insights about personal visioning. Without it, one will perish.

Jim Siudara, who taught me how to throw horseshoes. I already knew how to ride a horse. We met at the Kentucky Derby.

The honorable Detroit mayor Dennis Archer, who gave it his best. As a third-party change agent, he was a nice guy to work with as he desperately tried to lead change in Detroit. I have avoided government work since.

Dave Rundquist, past owner of Dave's Stag Bar in Albion, Michigan, who gave me the initial student bartending job. He was a magician and trickster and taught me how to never grow up.

Bruce Coleman, Howe Military School, who became my first Jewish friend and always shared his bagels and hard salami with me. He helped me feel welcome in the abject machismo of a military culture by practicing shalom.

Bob Seger and the Silver Bullet Band. Going all the way back to Dave's Hideout, his music, like Motown, made me feel culturally proud of my city, Detroit. Thank you, Punch Andrews, as well. I admired their grit and unpretentiousness.

Jim Brophy, James Houhlihan, and Ben Tower, former board members and gray-hairs who coached me as a young CEO over lunches at the Roma Café, Sindbad's, and Jacoby's in how to be courageous and now, thirty-five years later, to fill their shoes.

My close friends Rodney Luzi (fifth grade), Vincent Vehar, Max Cawley, Pam Evans, Albert Berres, Gordon Smith, and Bill (Skitchy) Skitch.

Henry Ford II, who, with enormous laughter, lectured me on having fun by not taking myself too seriously. He practiced what he preached and "never complained, never explained."

Tom Jordan, who taught me how to play squash and be gracious.

Former client, wood craftsman, rabid fisherman, and "spiritual brother" Michael Mancinelli, who taught me much about the perils of perfectionism. He made homemade pasta, meatballs, and sauce for his plant employees' Saturday lunch in Hamtramck, Michigan.

Jerome, the iconic Bayview Yacht Club bartender, creator of the Hummer, who charmingly served my mother her last dry gin martini (up) in front of the fireplace before she died. He taught me class.

Professor Morley Segal, cofounder of the American University/ National Training Laboratory joint master's degree program. He demonstrated and lectured me in how to dance with my shadow.

Alvenia Hull, who held my hand as I tried to understand racism, sexism, and upper mobility in Detroit from a black woman's perspective, while we were students in the Leadership Detroit program. I unashamedly wept in front of her on numerous occasions.

Dr. Jack Macintyre, founder of the "barn" therapy center in Auburn Heights, Michigan. He counseled me to understand and practice the koan "Who cares?" He tried to convince me I was too tough on myself.

My cousin Pamlynn Hansen of Calumet, in Michigan's Upper Peninsula, who lovingly loves her cousin and makes superb biscotti. We motorcycled together along with her significant other, Tim Pratt. She had her own bike, a 1990 Yamaha FZR400.

Mark Gregory, who was an extraordinary "made in Detroit" in-your-face commercial banker and set a professional standard to know your shit or shut up. His zeal did, in fact, intimidate a lot of people, including me.

Russ Bowen, who entranced this city slicker into fly-fishing in the Seney wilderness in Michigan's Upper Peninsula in my early twenties. Russ was a mixed-blood Cherokee orphan. In Grosse Pointe during the early '60s this was a unique and wonderful social differentiator.

Joe Muer, restaurateur and friend, who taught me a lot about seafood and how not to lower customer standards. He fired employees who believed the customer was not always right. His restaurant rivaled Philadelphia's Bookbinders and Boston's Tony's Fish Market and gave Joe's Stone Crab of Miami Beach a run for its money.

David and Karen DiChiera, tireless visionaries and founders of the Michigan Opera Theatre. As friends and community supporters, they taught me servitude and envisaged the way in which a king and a queen should behave.

Karl Payne, who became my first and best black friend. As a Vietnam veteran, he asked me to accompany him to "the Wall." We cried together over his lost friends. He demonstrated unabashed grieving. I stood in for him at his grandmother's funeral in Detroit.

Forest Strand, former director of the Leadership Detroit program. He taught me politeness and kindness.

John DeLorean, former General Motors executive and creative designer (gull-wing sports car). He gave me his courtroom notes and caricatures one afternoon in Detroit's Caucus Club restaurant as an encouragement to fight the good battle ahead of me after I was booted out of my company. I learned there is a price to pay "if you choose to go against the grain." Around the same time, Steve Jobs was betrayed and kicked out of Apple.

The emotional parallels were unmistakable. Both DeLorean and Jobs modeled resiliency, imaged warriorship, and, like wizards, positively distorted vision in their attempt to achieve ambitions.

Robert Marshak, professor at the American University, who emphasized that "the experience is the test and the lessons will follow."

Max and Lanie Pincus of the London Chop House restaurant, who practiced cordiality, along with the bartender, Farouk, and hostess, Angie. I preferred the Chop House (superior cuisine) to NYC's 21 Club. Max and Lanie were lovers of people and walked their talk. Farouk, my friend Max, and I would serve Thanksgiving dinners at the Salvation Army.

All my closeted and not closeted gay friends who have elegantly loved my family and me.

Armando, owner of Detroit's Acapulco restaurant, who gave my father a bottle of Chivas whiskey for his last birthday. One month after dad died, my brothers and I drank it at his wake. Armando was also a class act. He taught me how to make people feel better about themselves.

My first transgendered friend, who has honored me with vulnerability and courage by sharing this journey with me.

Joseph LePla, former public relations director for my company and cofounder of his own firm in Seattle. Joe co-drafted my final public speech to the Detroit Chamber of Commerce's entrepreneurship forum. The title of the speech was "Failure: Friend or Foe?" It was delivered shortly after I lost my company and set off the only standing ovation I ever received. Joe practiced tireless loyalty, in addition to being a sweet man.

Chuck Otto and Karen Marshall, for their editorial assistance and hand-holding in the development of the initial manuscript.

Alex Cruden and Eric Hohauser, who helped renew my faith that "all things are possible." I have acquired two new friends since returning from Papua New Guinea. While there, sitting in my screened porch one evening near a remote village, I wondered if that would ever again be possible. My prayers were answered.

To the unnamed people who are still teaching me lessons in how to forgive. I am a slow learner.

Katen.

My brothers, Patrick, James, and Jack.

My sisters-in-law and friends, Cheryl and Margaret.

My goddaughter, Holly Kubek.

My sister, Diane Williams.

My father, John E. Quinlan Sr.

My mother, Bonnie B. Quinlan.

The unexpected gifts of Fiona, Jasmine, Kaia, and Mahealani, who taught me how to love, without strings attached.

ABOUT THE AUTHOR

An organization development specialist, including advising family-founded and closely held businesses, John E. Quinlan has been a founder and chief executive officer of a publicly traded company, a management consultant, a leadership coach, and a traveling student of life. He was born in Detroit, Michigan, and lives just east of the city, in Grosse Pointe. He graduated from Albion College in Michigan with a BA in economics and earned a master's of science in organizational development (MSOD) from the American University in Washington, DC. Not surprisingly, given his recent experience in Papua New Guinea, he makes great coffee. This is his first book.

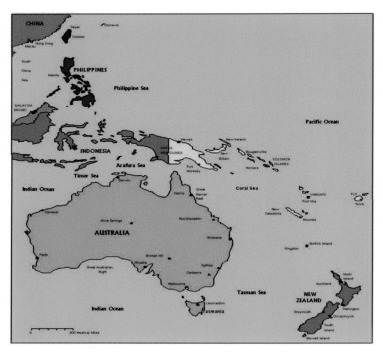

Papua New Guinea is north of Australia and not far from the Equator.